BRIAN JOINES • BACHAN

IMAGINE
AGENTS ™

BOOM!
STUDIOS

CASE FILE REFERENCE IMAGE: 8971-845-15-B

NAME: FURDLEGURR ASSIGNED CHILD: ELLIOT

NAME: BLOUNDER ASSIGNED CHILD: MOLLY

IMAGINE AGENTS, December 2014. Published by BOOM! Studios, a division of Boom Entertainment, Inc. Imagine Agents is ™ & © 2014 Boom Entertainment, Inc. Originally published in single magazine form as IMAGINE AGENTS No. 1-4. ™ & © 2013, 2014 Boom Entertainment, Inc. All rights reserved. BOOM! Studios™ and the BOOM! Studios logo are trademarks of Boom Entertainment, Inc., registered in various countries and categories. All characters, events, and institutions depicted herein are fictional. Any similarity between any of the names, characters, persons, events, and/or institutions in this publication to actual names, characters, and persons, whether living or dead, events, and/or institutions is unintended and purely coincidental. BOOM! Studios does not read or accept unsolicited submissions of ideas, stories, or artwork.

BOOM! Studios, 5670 Wilshire Boulevard, Suite 450, Los Angeles, CA 90036-5679. Printed in China. First Printing.

ISBN: 978-1-60886-428-7, eISBN: 978-1-61398-282-2

CASE FILE REFERENCE IMAGE: 6781-436-18-K

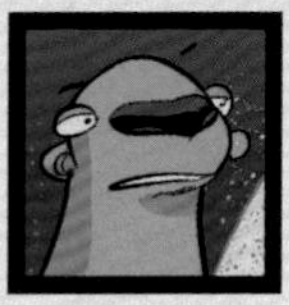

Created & Written by
BRIAN JOINES

CLASSIFICATION: AR-576843032-24 : 456-O

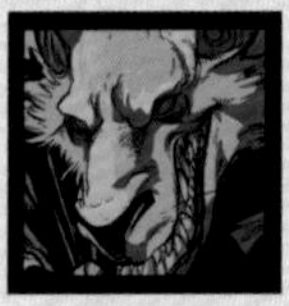

Illustrated by
BACHAN

CLASSIFICATION: ES-849300472-03 : 334-M

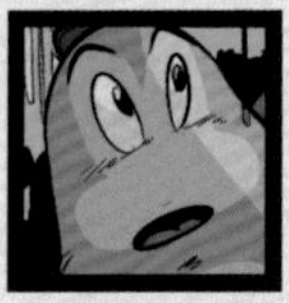

Colors by
RUTH REDMOND

CLASSIFICATION: DV-094611823-56 : 707-L

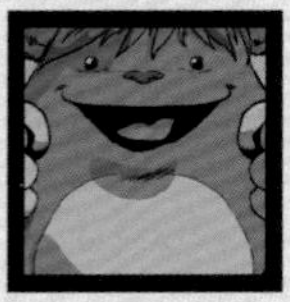

Letters by
DERON BENNETT

CLASSIFICATION: GG-948026212-18 : 480-D

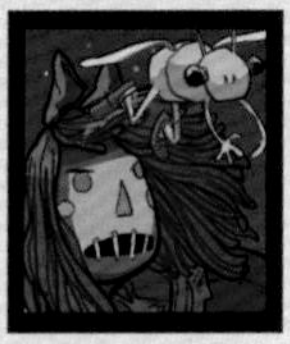

Cover by
KHARY RANDOLPH
With colors by
MATTHEW WILSON

CLASSIFICATION: AR-576843032-24 : 456-K

IMAGINE AGENTS CHARACTER DESIGNS BY
KHARY RANDOLPH & BACHAN

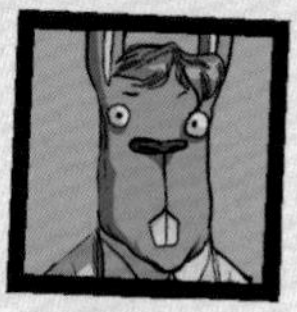

Designer
KELSEY DIETERICH

CLASSIFICATION: LA-049593878-03 : 322-J

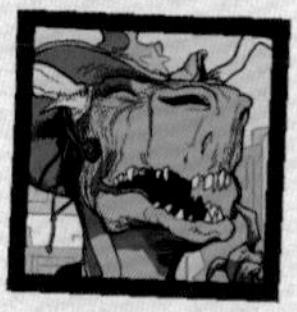

Assistant Editor
ALEX GALER

CLASSIFICATION: TR-039284823-56 : 948-T

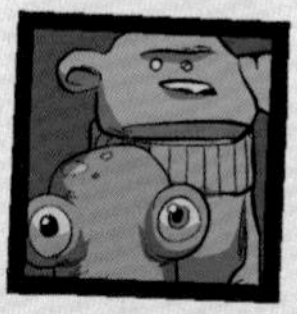

Editors
DAFNA PLEBAN
& BRYCE CARLSON

CLASSIFICATION: MD-480292503-80 : 439-U

CIAL AGENT
LD MANUAL

REVISED EDITION NO. 12-D

PROPERTY OF: SNOWGOOSE, TERRY
AGENT NO.: ST-3645784-091

NAME: BLOUNDER   ASSIGNED CHILD: MOLLY
CURRENT STATUS: RELOCATION REQUIRED

CASE FILE REFERENCE IMAGE: 0234-5

CHAPTER
ONE

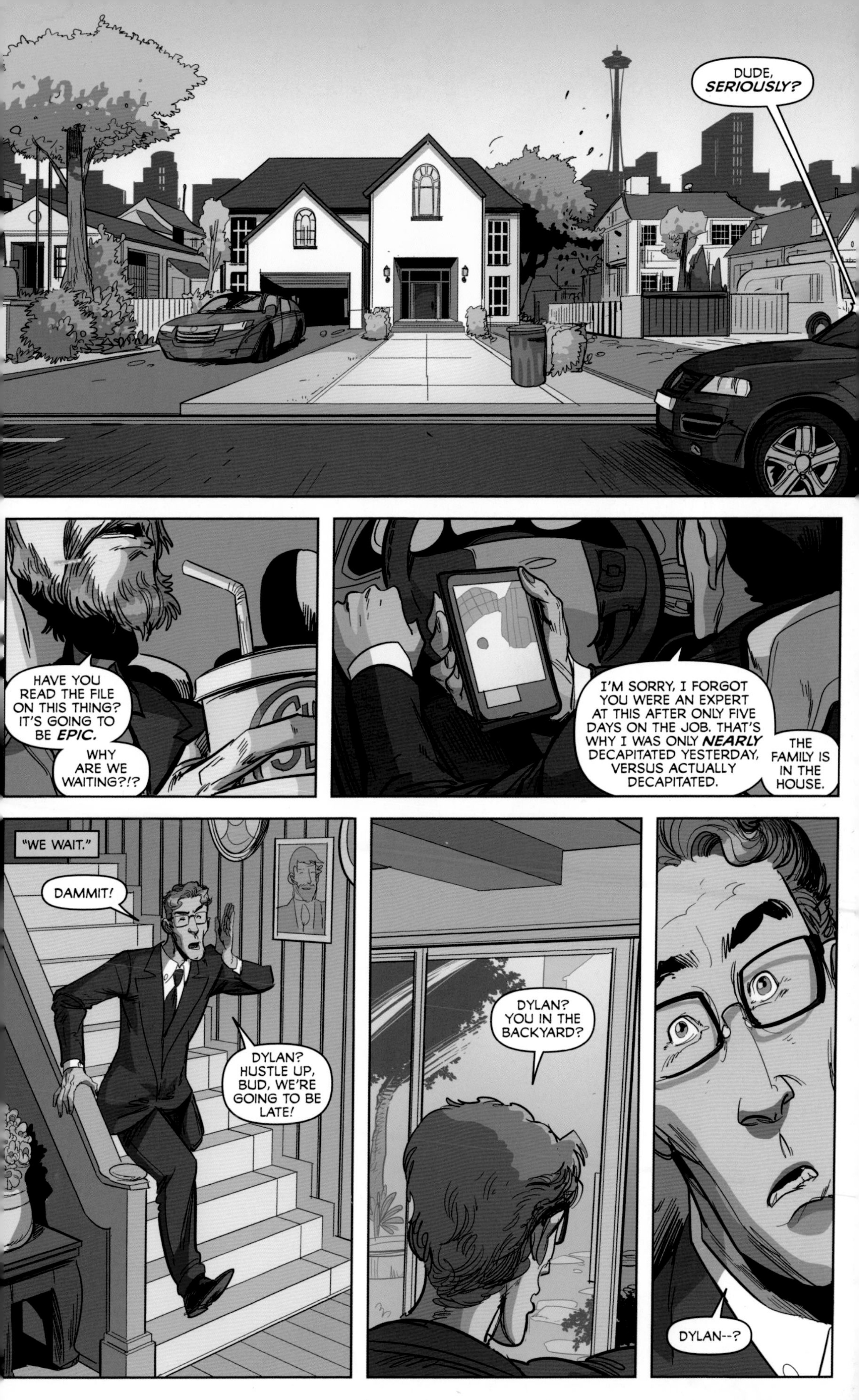
DUDE, *SERIOUSLY?*
HAVE YOU READ THE FILE ON THIS THING? IT'S GOING TO BE *EPIC.*
WHY ARE WE WAITING?!?
I'M SORRY, I FORGOT YOU WERE AN EXPERT AT THIS AFTER ONLY FIVE DAYS ON THE JOB. THAT'S WHY I WAS ONLY *NEARLY* DECAPITATED YESTERDAY, VERSUS ACTUALLY DECAPITATED.
THE FAMILY IS IN THE HOUSE.
"WE WAIT."
DAMMIT!
DYLAN? HUSTLE UP, BUD, WE'RE GOING TO BE LATE!
DYLAN? YOU IN THE BACKYARD?
DYLAN--?

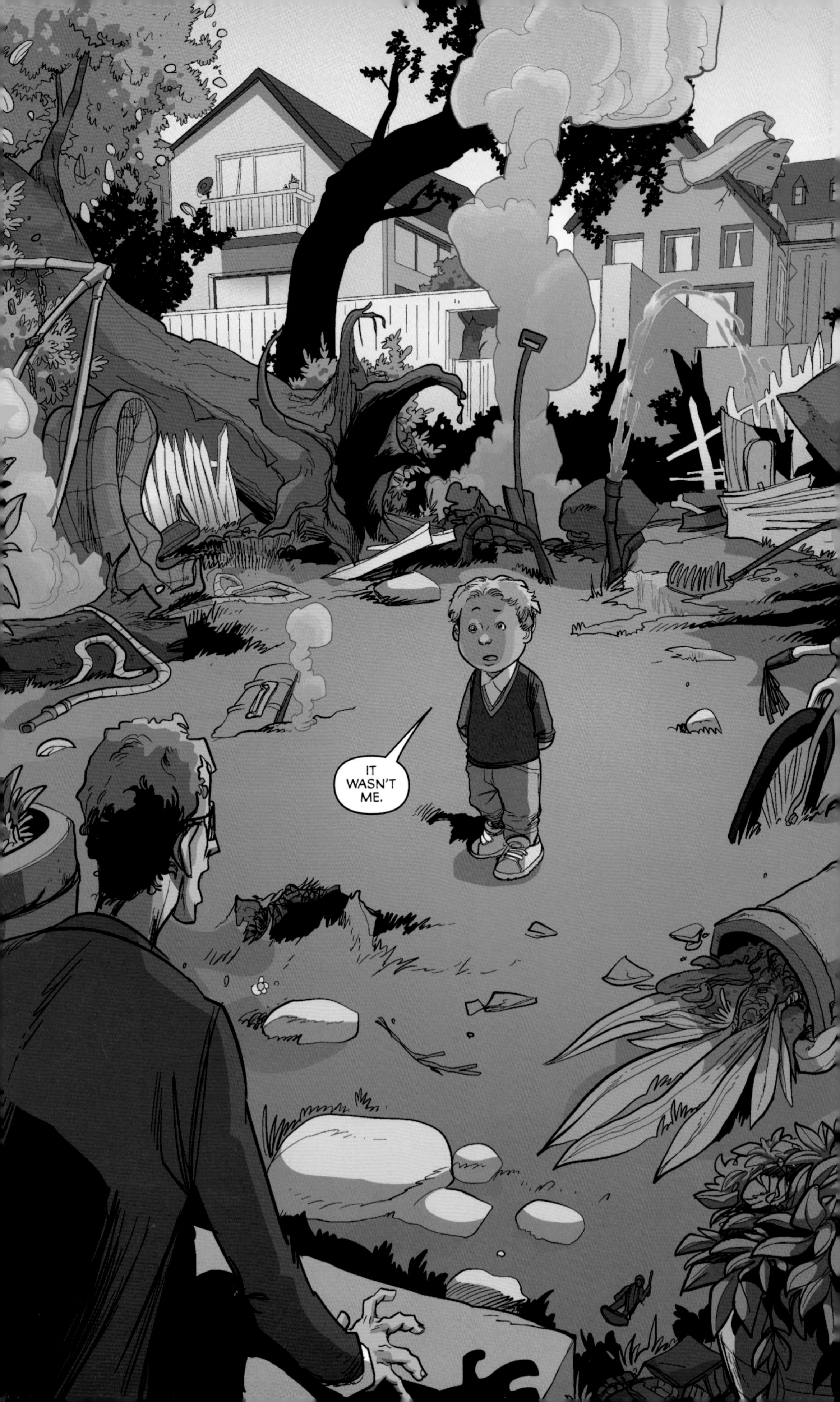
IT WASN'T ME.

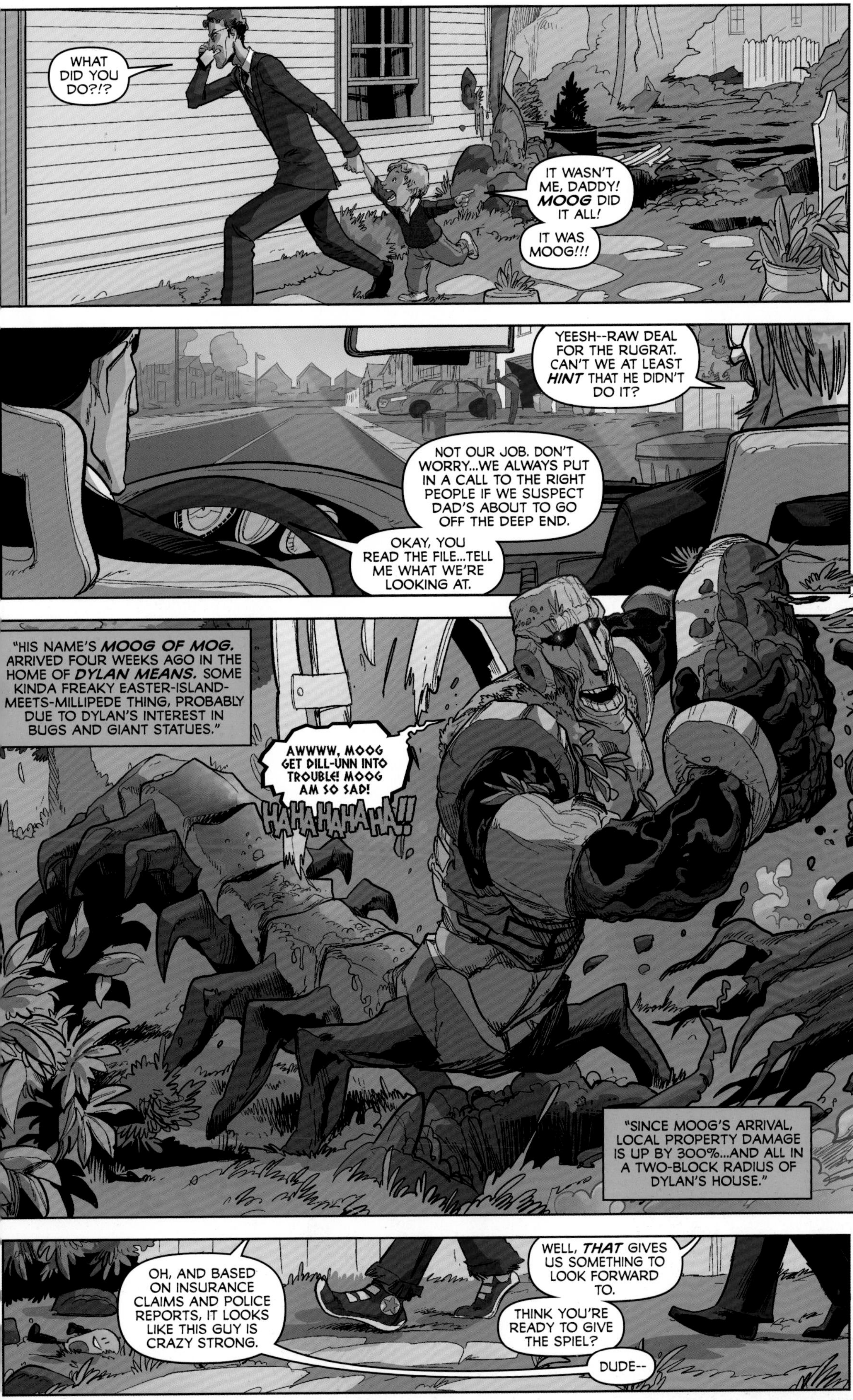

WHAT DID YOU DO?!?
IT WASN'T ME, DADDY! MOOG DID IT ALL!
IT WAS MOOG!!!
YEESH--RAW DEAL FOR THE RUGRAT. CAN'T WE AT LEAST HINT THAT HE DIDN'T DO IT?
NOT OUR JOB. DON'T WORRY...WE ALWAYS PUT IN A CALL TO THE RIGHT PEOPLE IF WE SUSPECT DAD'S ABOUT TO GO OFF THE DEEP END.
OKAY, YOU READ THE FILE...TELL ME WHAT WE'RE LOOKING AT.
"HIS NAME'S MOOG OF MOG. ARRIVED FOUR WEEKS AGO IN THE HOME OF DYLAN MEANS. SOME KINDA FREAKY EASTER-ISLAND-MEETS-MILLIPEDE THING, PROBABLY DUE TO DYLAN'S INTEREST IN BUGS AND GIANT STATUES."
AWWWW, MOOG GET DILL-UNN INTO TROUBLE! MOOG AM SO SAD!
HAHAHAHAHA!!
"SINCE MOOG'S ARRIVAL, LOCAL PROPERTY DAMAGE IS UP BY 300%...AND ALL IN A TWO-BLOCK RADIUS OF DYLAN'S HOUSE."
OH, AND BASED ON INSURANCE CLAIMS AND POLICE REPORTS, IT LOOKS LIKE THIS GUY IS CRAZY STRONG.
WELL, THAT GIVES US SOMETHING TO LOOK FORWARD TO.
THINK YOU'RE READY TO GIVE THE SPIEL?
DUDE--

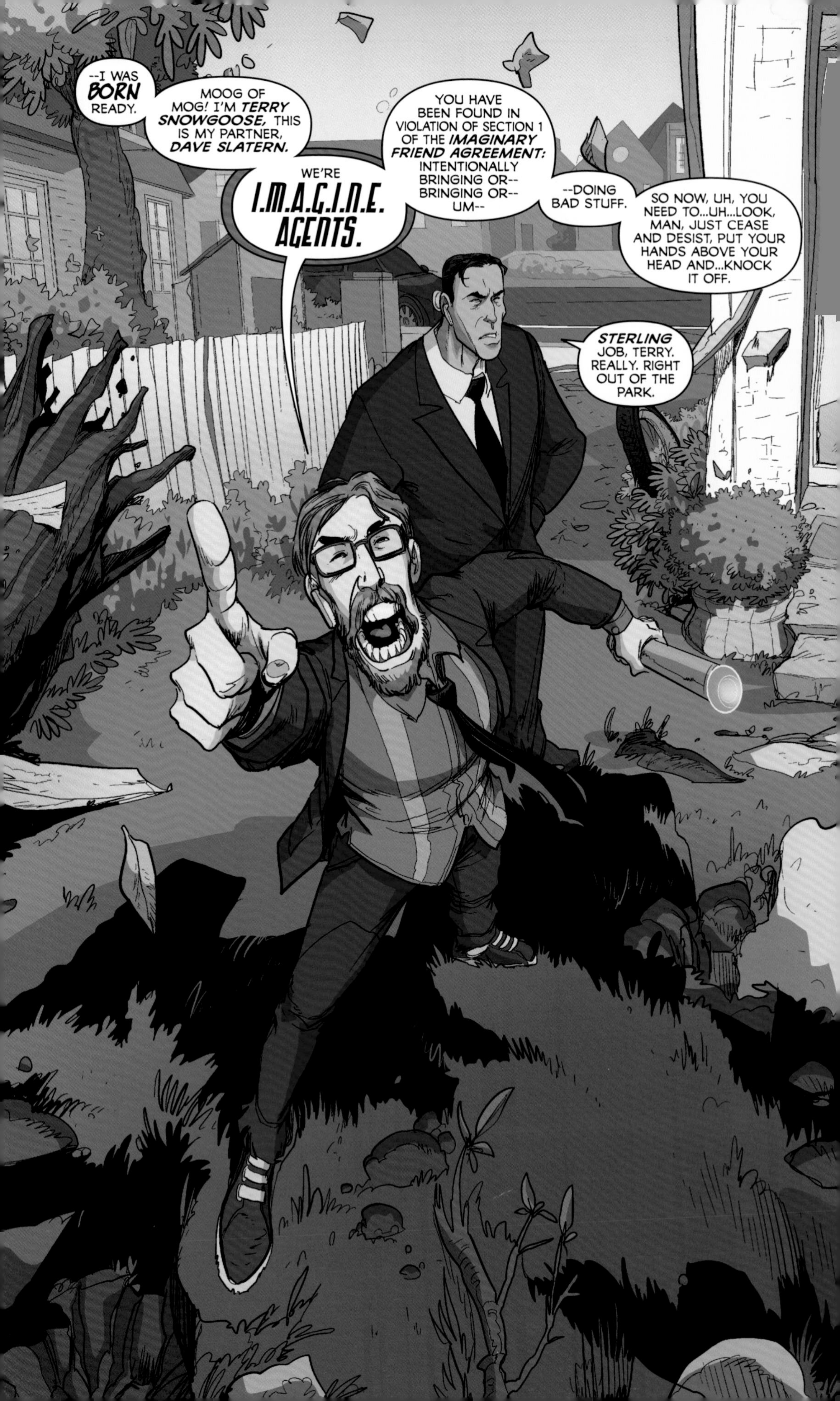
--I WAS *BORN* READY.
MOOG OF MOG! I'M *TERRY SNOWGOOSE,* THIS IS MY PARTNER, *DAVE SLATERN.*
WE'RE I.M.A.G.I.N.E. AGENTS.
YOU HAVE BEEN FOUND IN VIOLATION OF SECTION 1 OF THE *IMAGINARY FRIEND AGREEMENT:* INTENTIONALLY BRINGING OR-- BRINGING OR-- UM--
--DOING BAD STUFF.
SO NOW, UH, YOU NEED TO...UH...LOOK, MAN, JUST CEASE AND DESIST, PUT YOUR HANDS ABOVE YOUR HEAD AND...KNOCK IT OFF.
STERLING JOB, TERRY. REALLY. RIGHT OUT OF THE PARK.

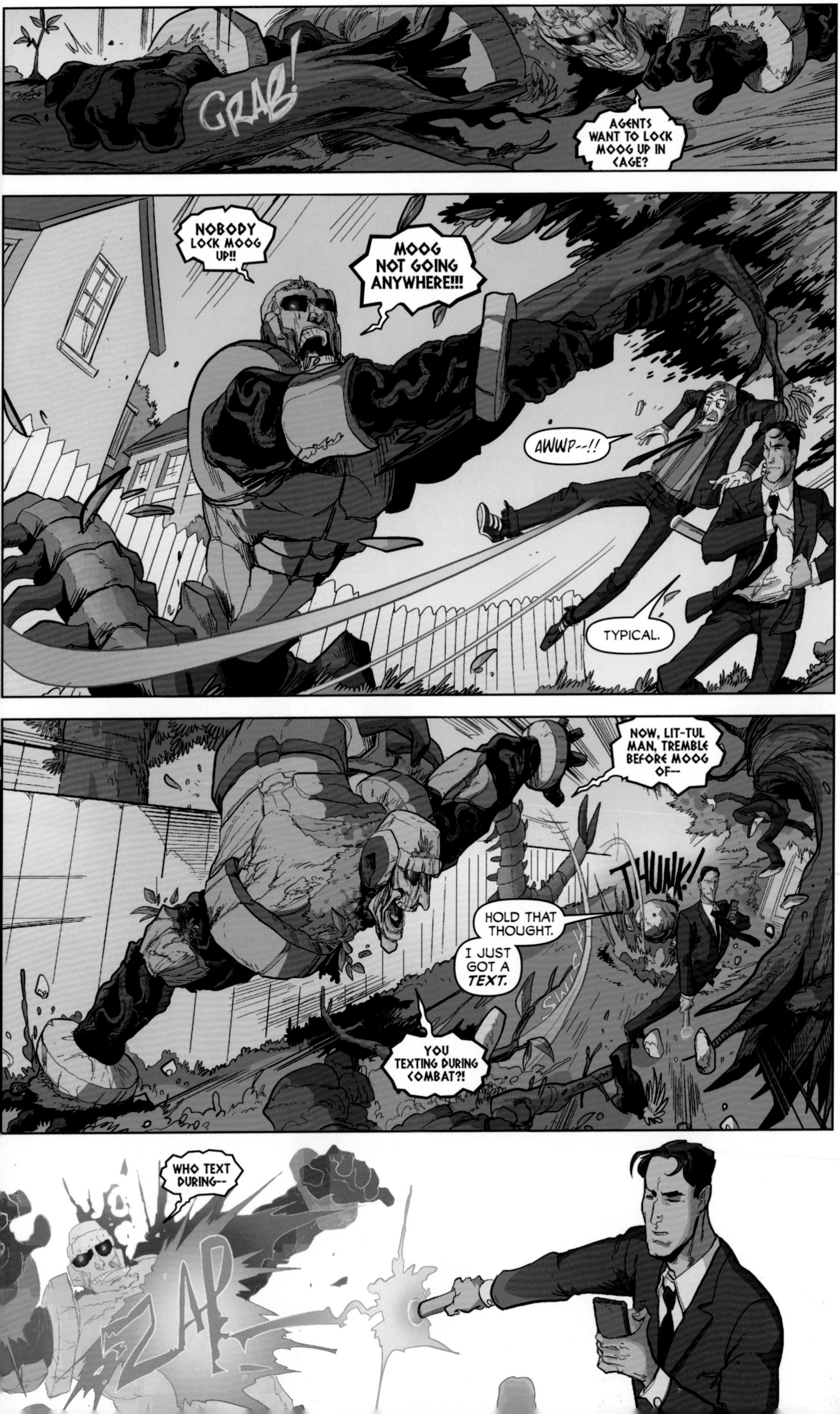
GRAB!
AGENTS WANT TO LOCK MOOG UP IN CAGE?
NOBODY LOCK MOOG UP!!
MOOG NOT GOING ANYWHERE!!!
AWWP--!!
TYPICAL.
NOW, LIT-TUL MAN, TREMBLE BEFORE MOOG OF--
THUNK!
HOLD THAT THOUGHT.
I JUST GOT A *TEXT.*
YOU TEXTING DURING COMBAT?!
WHO TEXT DURING--
ZAP

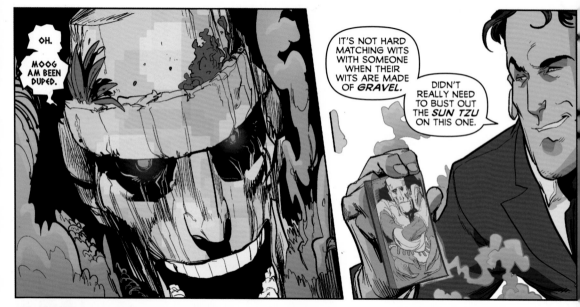

OH. MOOG AM BEEN DUPED.

IT'S NOT HARD MATCHING WITS WITH SOMEONE WHEN THEIR WITS ARE MADE OF *GRAVEL.*

DIDN'T REALLY NEED TO BUST OUT THE *SUN TZU* ON THIS ONE.

BING

SWISHHH

NOW, AS SOON AS I GATHER UP *BOY WONDER* WE CAN RUN YOU--

I'M GOOD! I'M GOOD! I'M BACK IN!

OKAY, MOOG, YOU'RE GOING--

SMAK!

THAT SEEMS ABOUT RIGHT.

DID WE FORGET TO PUT OUR EARPIECE BACK IN?

YES.

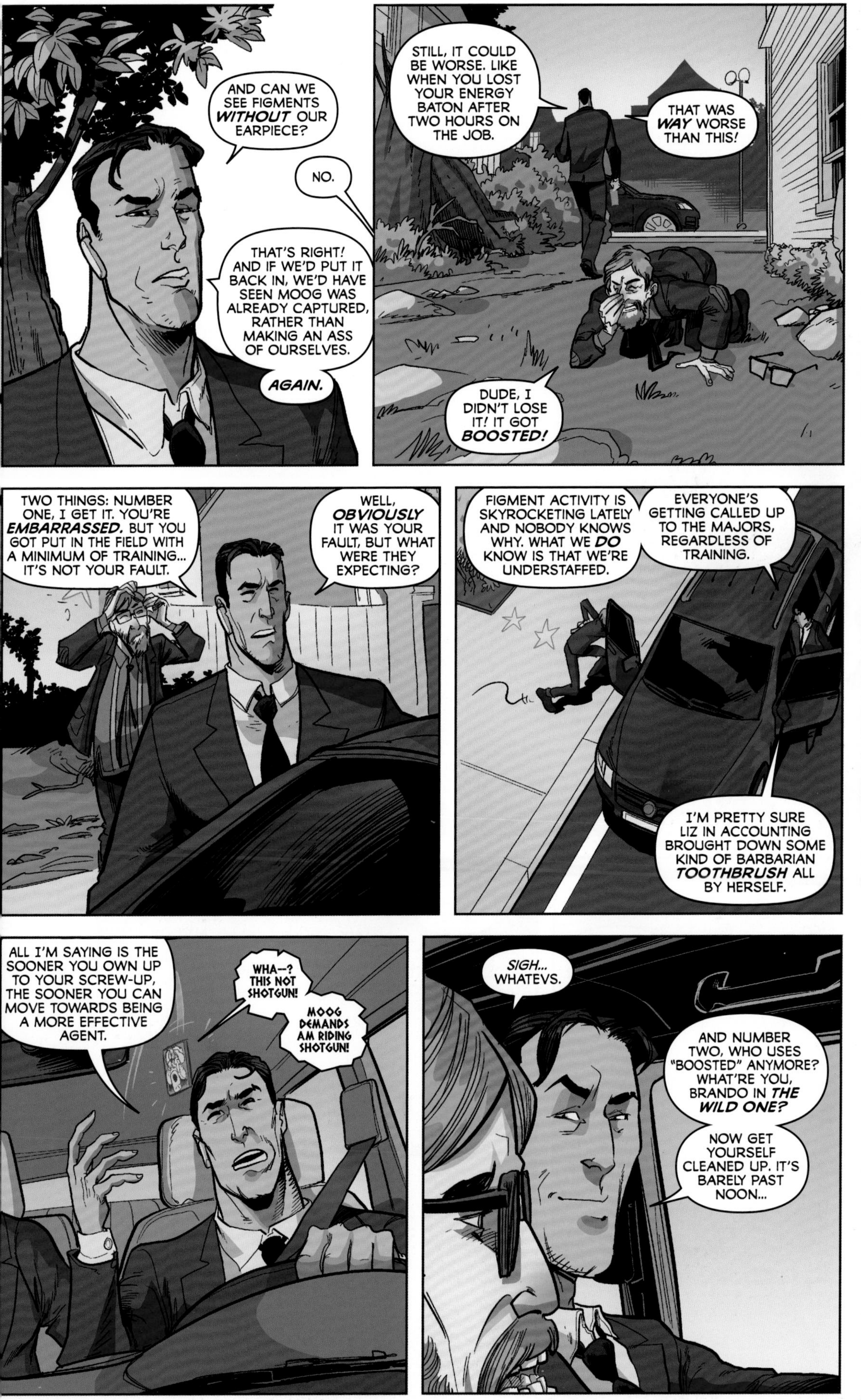
AND CAN WE SEE FIGMENTS *WITHOUT* OUR EARPIECE?
NO.
THAT'S RIGHT! AND IF WE'D PUT IT BACK IN, WE'D HAVE SEEN MOOG WAS ALREADY CAPTURED, RATHER THAN MAKING AN ASS OF OURSELVES.
AGAIN.
STILL, IT COULD BE WORSE. LIKE WHEN YOU LOST YOUR ENERGY BATON AFTER TWO HOURS ON THE JOB.
THAT WAS *WAY* WORSE THAN THIS!
DUDE, I DIDN'T LOSE IT! IT GOT *BOOSTED!*
TWO THINGS: NUMBER ONE, I GET IT. YOU'RE *EMBARRASSED.* BUT YOU GOT PUT IN THE FIELD WITH A MINIMUM OF TRAINING... IT'S NOT YOUR FAULT.
WELL, *OBVIOUSLY* IT WAS YOUR FAULT, BUT WHAT WERE THEY EXPECTING?
FIGMENT ACTIVITY IS SKYROCKETING LATELY AND NOBODY KNOWS WHY. WHAT WE *DO* KNOW IS THAT WE'RE UNDERSTAFFED.
EVERYONE'S GETTING CALLED UP TO THE MAJORS, REGARDLESS OF TRAINING.
I'M PRETTY SURE LIZ IN ACCOUNTING BROUGHT DOWN SOME KIND OF BARBARIAN *TOOTHBRUSH* ALL BY HERSELF.
ALL I'M SAYING IS THE SOONER YOU OWN UP TO YOUR SCREW-UP, THE SOONER YOU CAN MOVE TOWARDS BEING A MORE EFFECTIVE AGENT.
WHA--? THIS NOT SHOTGUN!
MOOG DEMANDS AM RIDING SHOTGUN!
SIGH... WHATEVS.
AND NUMBER TWO, WHO USES "BOOSTED" ANYMORE? WHAT'RE YOU, BRANDO IN *THE WILD ONE?*
NOW GET YOURSELF CLEANED UP. IT'S BARELY PAST NOON...

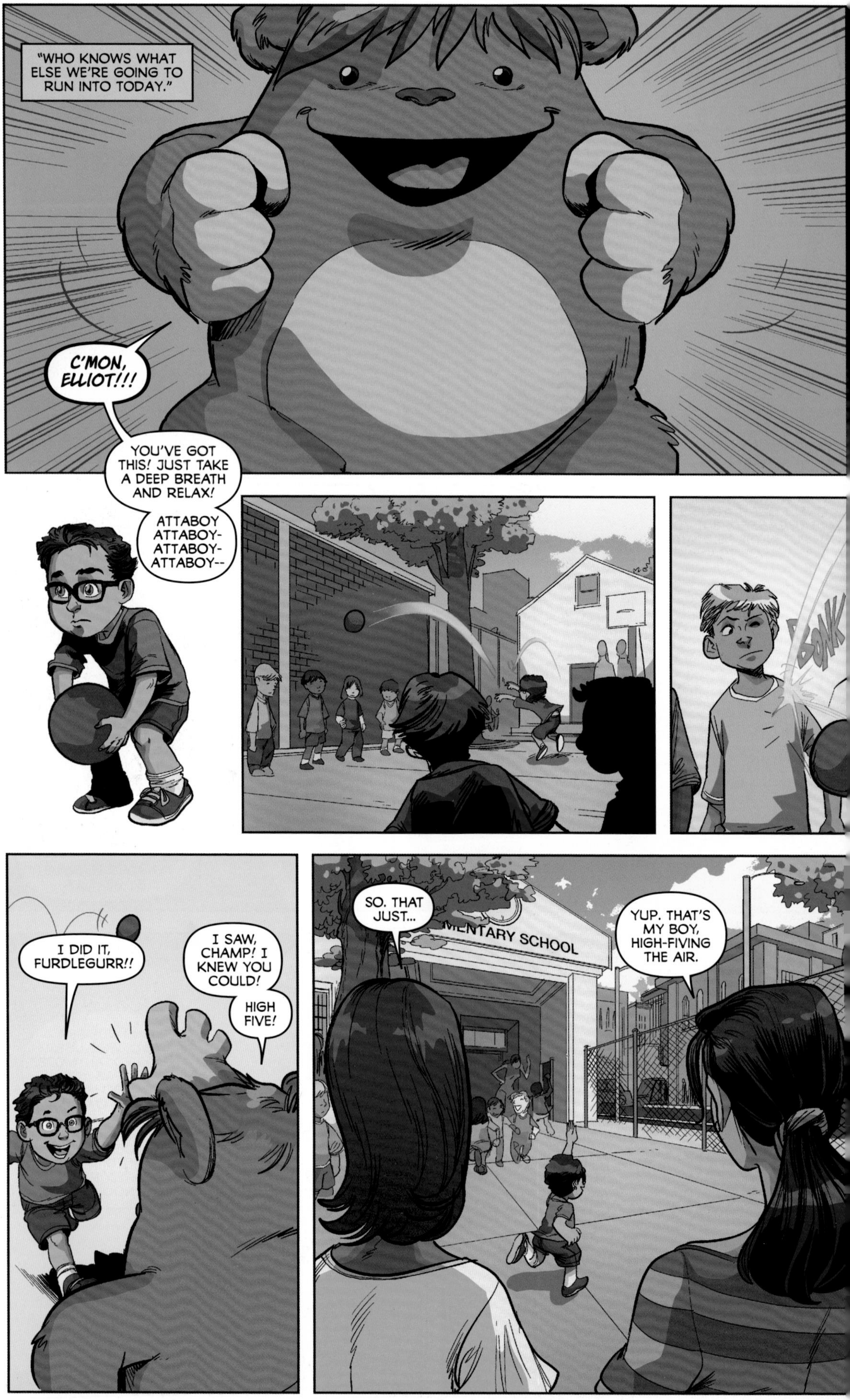
"WHO KNOWS WHAT ELSE WE'RE GOING TO RUN INTO TODAY."
C'MON, ELLIOT!!!
YOU'VE GOT THIS! JUST TAKE A DEEP BREATH AND RELAX!
ATTABOY ATTABOY-ATTABOY-ATTABOY--
BONK
I DID IT, FURDLEGURR!!
I SAW, CHAMP! I KNEW YOU COULD!
HIGH FIVE!
SO. THAT JUST...
MENTARY SCHOOL
YUP. THAT'S MY BOY, HIGH-FIVING THE AIR.

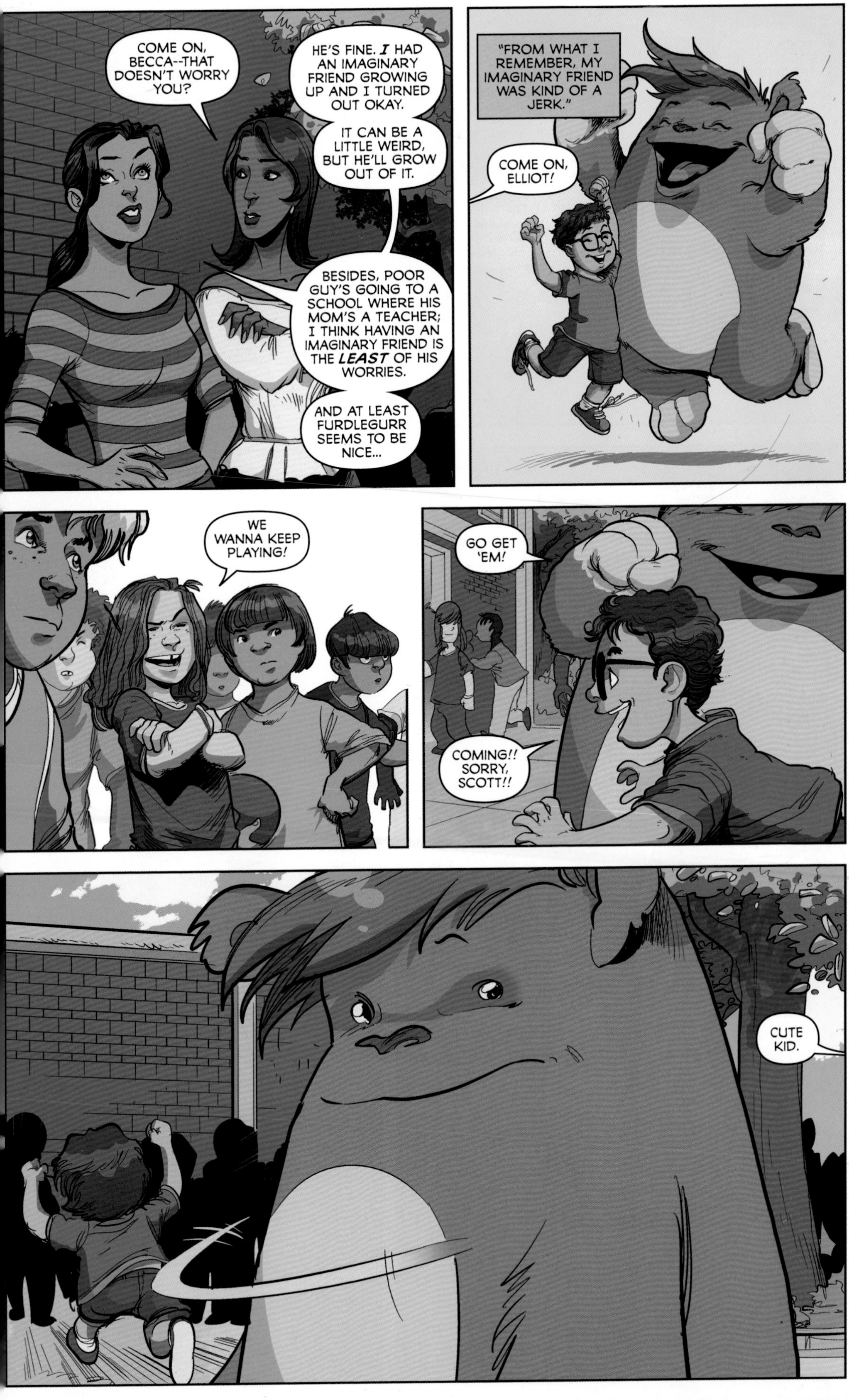
COME ON, BECCA--THAT DOESN'T WORRY YOU?
HE'S FINE. *I* HAD AN IMAGINARY FRIEND GROWING UP AND I TURNED OUT OKAY.
IT CAN BE A LITTLE WEIRD, BUT HE'LL GROW OUT OF IT.
BESIDES, POOR GUY'S GOING TO A SCHOOL WHERE HIS MOM'S A TEACHER; I THINK HAVING AN IMAGINARY FRIEND IS THE *LEAST* OF HIS WORRIES.
AND AT LEAST FURDLEGURR SEEMS TO BE NICE...
"FROM WHAT I REMEMBER, MY IMAGINARY FRIEND WAS KIND OF A JERK."
COME ON, ELLIOT!
WE WANNA KEEP PLAYING!
GO GET 'EM!
COMING!! SORRY, SCOTT!!
CUTE KID.

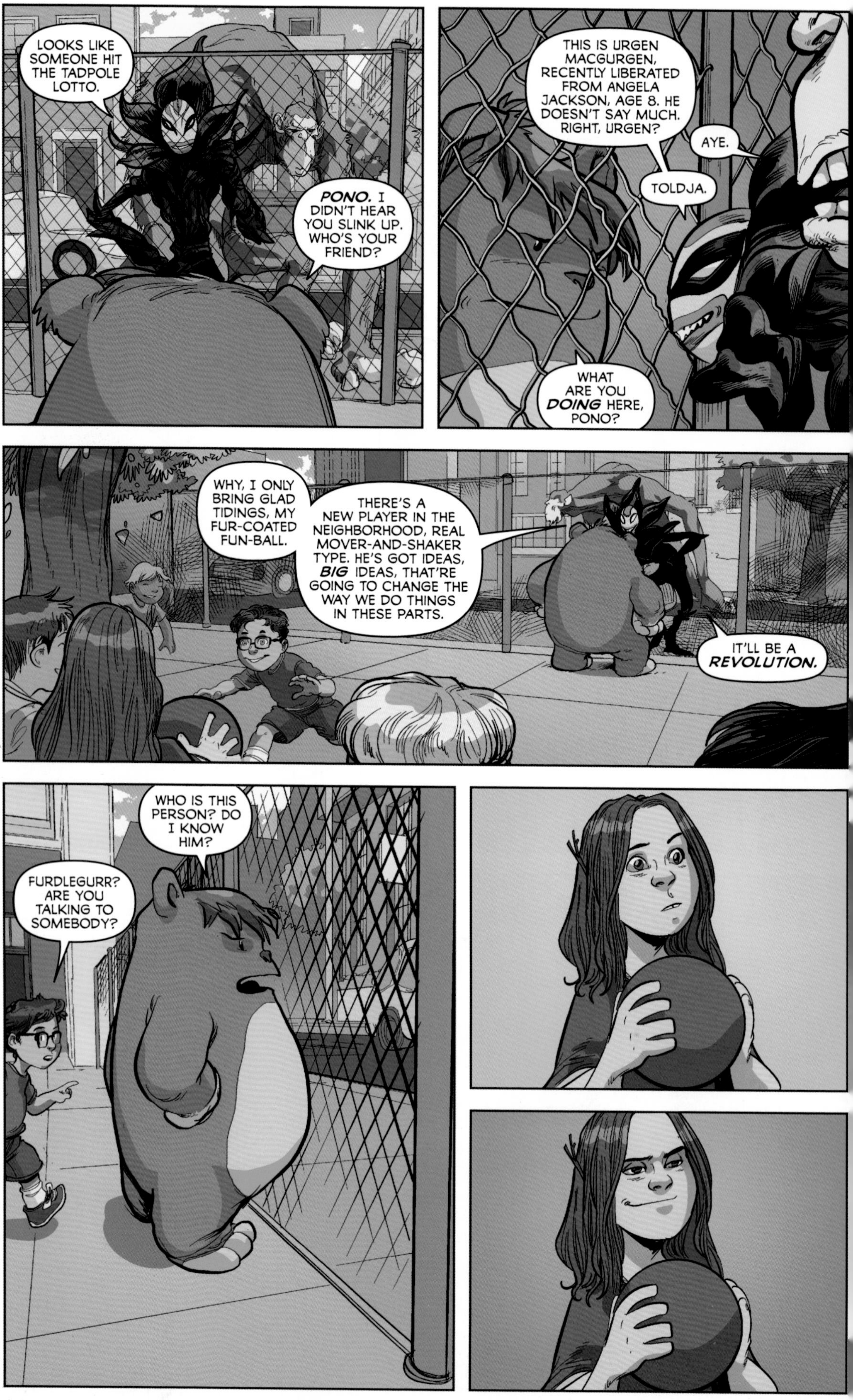
LOOKS LIKE SOMEONE HIT THE TADPOLE LOTTO.
PONO. I DIDN'T HEAR YOU SLINK UP. WHO'S YOUR FRIEND?
THIS IS URGEN MACGURGEN, RECENTLY LIBERATED FROM ANGELA JACKSON, AGE 8. HE DOESN'T SAY MUCH. RIGHT, URGEN?
AYE.
TOLDJA.
WHAT ARE YOU ***DOING*** HERE, PONO?
WHY, I ONLY BRING GLAD TIDINGS, MY FUR-COATED FUN-BALL.
THERE'S A NEW PLAYER IN THE NEIGHBORHOOD, REAL MOVER-AND-SHAKER TYPE. HE'S GOT IDEAS, ***BIG*** IDEAS, THAT'RE GOING TO CHANGE THE WAY WE DO THINGS IN THESE PARTS.
IT'LL BE A ***REVOLUTION.***
WHO IS THIS PERSON? DO I KNOW HIM?
FURDLEGURR? ARE YOU TALKING TO SOMEBODY?

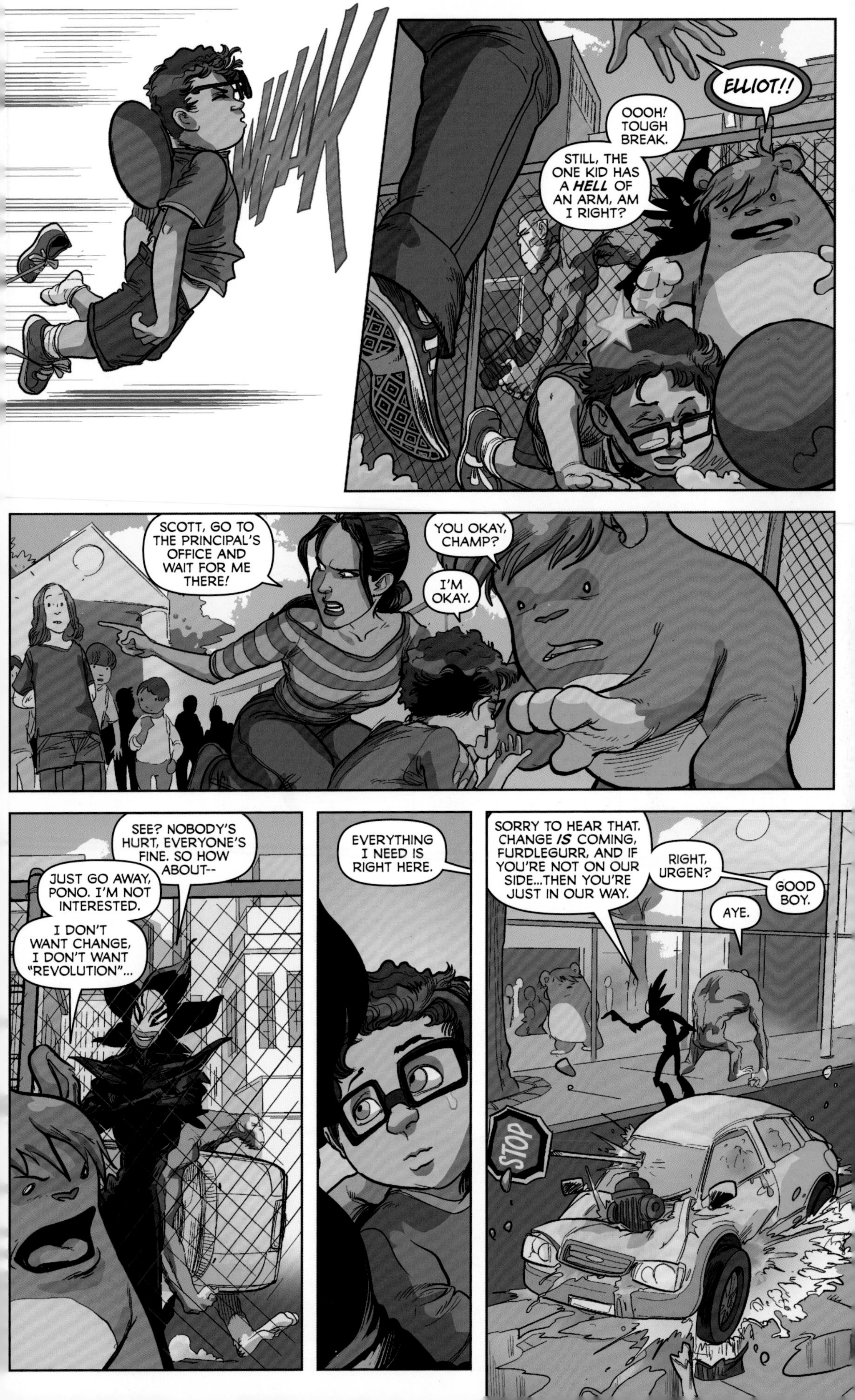
WHAK
ELLIOT!!
OOOH! TOUGH BREAK.
STILL, THE ONE KID HAS A *HELL* OF AN ARM, AM I RIGHT?
SCOTT, GO TO THE PRINCIPAL'S OFFICE AND WAIT FOR ME THERE!
YOU OKAY, CHAMP?
I'M OKAY.
SEE? NOBODY'S HURT, EVERYONE'S FINE. SO HOW ABOUT--
JUST GO AWAY, PONO. I'M NOT INTERESTED.
I DON'T WANT CHANGE, I DON'T WANT "REVOLUTION"...
EVERYTHING I NEED IS RIGHT HERE.
SORRY TO HEAR THAT. CHANGE *IS* COMING, FURDLEGURR, AND IF YOU'RE NOT ON OUR SIDE...THEN YOU'RE JUST IN OUR WAY.
RIGHT, URGEN?
AYE.
GOOD BOY.
STOP

I HATE CHANGE.

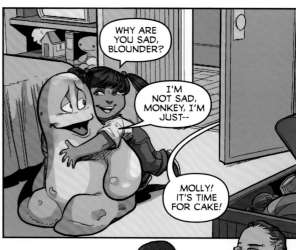

WHY ARE YOU SAD, BLOUNDER?

I'M NOT SAD, MONKEY, I'M JUST--

MOLLY! IT'S TIME FOR CAKE!

WE CAN'T START WITHOUT BLOUNDER!

GOD, I CAN'T BELIEVE SHE STILL BELIEVES IN THAT STUPID THING.

YOU BELIEVED IN HIM UNTIL *YOU* WERE EIGHT.

OKAY, SWEETIE, HAVE A SEAT!

♫ HAPPY BIRTHDAY TO YOU, HAPPY BIRTHDAY TO YOU! HAPPY BIRTHDAY, DEAR MOLLY... ♫

BYE-BYE, MONKEY. I LOVE YOU.

♫ ...HAPPY BIRTHDAY TO YOU! ♫

BLOUNDER?

HUH.

OKAY, BIRTHDAY GIRL! READY FOR PRESENTS?

YAY! PRESENTS!!

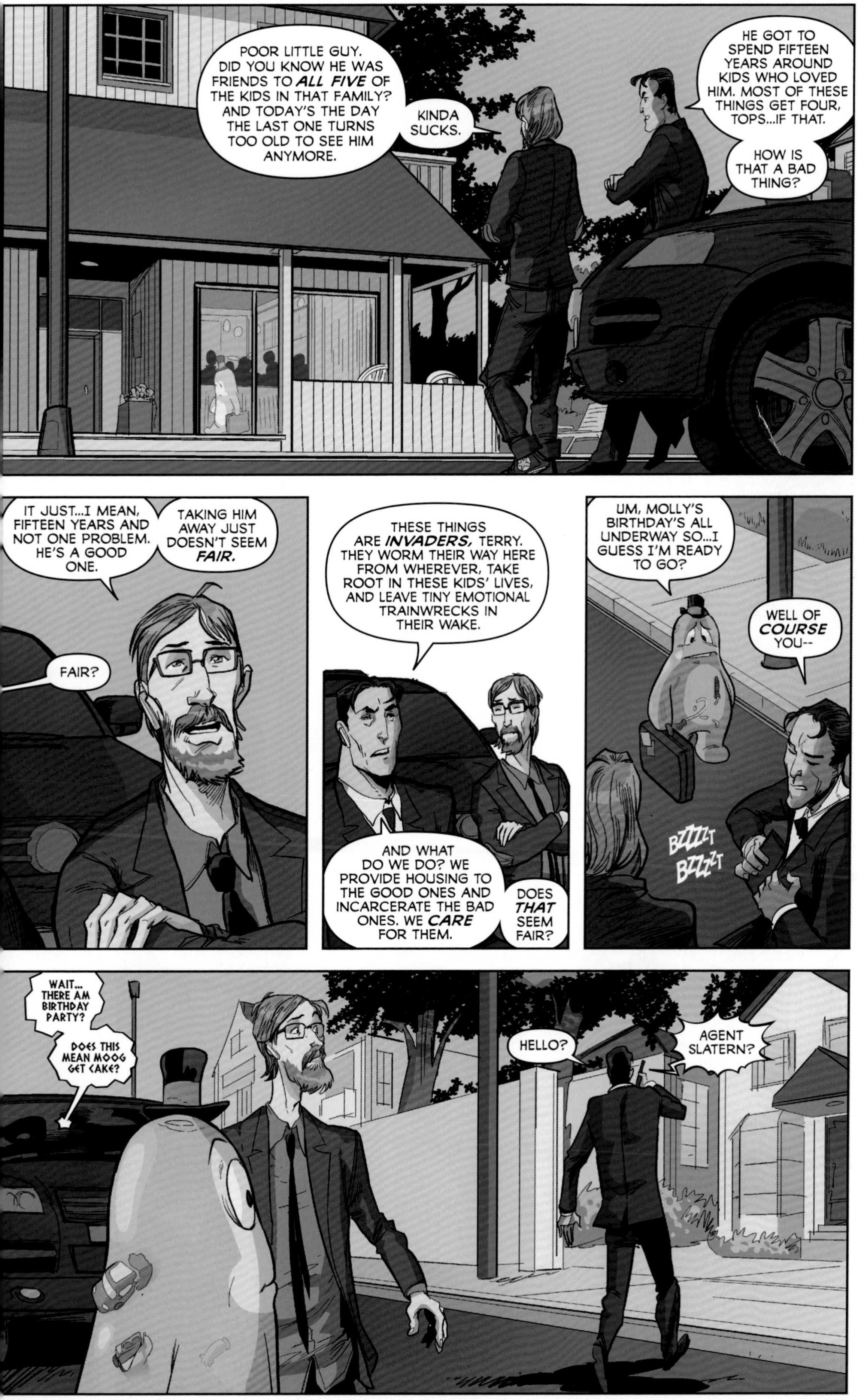
POOR LITTLE GUY. DID YOU KNOW HE WAS FRIENDS TO ALL FIVE OF THE KIDS IN THAT FAMILY? AND TODAY'S THE DAY THE LAST ONE TURNS TOO OLD TO SEE HIM ANYMORE.
KINDA SUCKS.
HE GOT TO SPEND FIFTEEN YEARS AROUND KIDS WHO LOVED HIM. MOST OF THESE THINGS GET FOUR, TOPS...IF THAT.
HOW IS THAT A BAD THING?
IT JUST...I MEAN, FIFTEEN YEARS AND NOT ONE PROBLEM. HE'S A GOOD ONE.
TAKING HIM AWAY JUST DOESN'T SEEM FAIR.
FAIR?
THESE THINGS ARE INVADERS, TERRY. THEY WORM THEIR WAY HERE FROM WHEREVER, TAKE ROOT IN THESE KIDS' LIVES, AND LEAVE TINY EMOTIONAL TRAINWRECKS IN THEIR WAKE.
AND WHAT DO WE DO? WE PROVIDE HOUSING TO THE GOOD ONES AND INCARCERATE THE BAD ONES. WE CARE FOR THEM.
DOES THAT SEEM FAIR?
UM, MOLLY'S BIRTHDAY'S ALL UNDERWAY SO...I GUESS I'M READY TO GO?
WELL OF COURSE YOU--
BZZZZT BZZZZT
WAIT... THERE AM BIRTHDAY PARTY?
DOES THIS MEAN MOOG GET CAKE?
HELLO?
AGENT SLATERN?

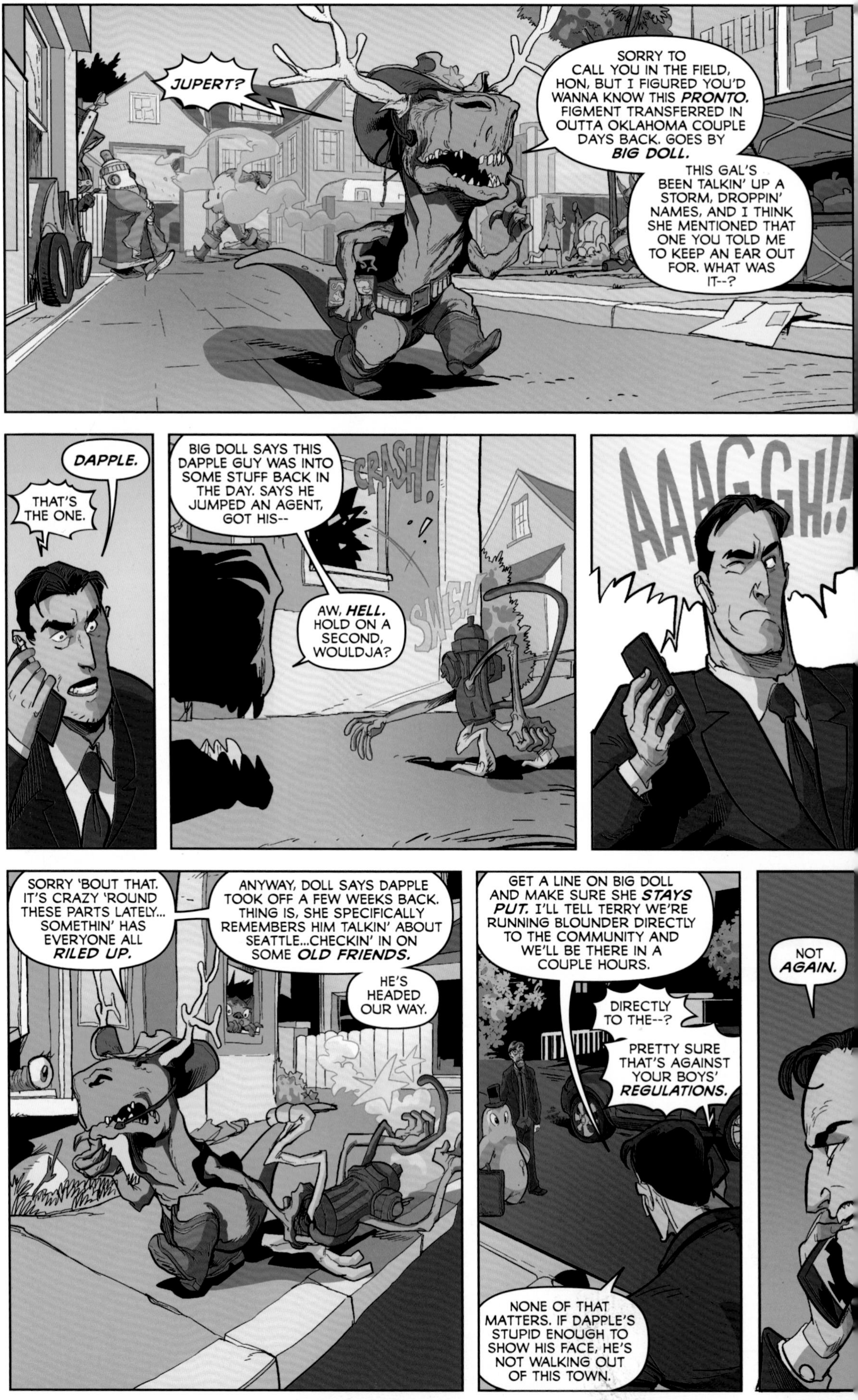

JUPERT?
SORRY TO CALL YOU IN THE FIELD, HON, BUT I FIGURED YOU'D WANNA KNOW THIS PRONTO. FIGMENT TRANSFERRED IN OUTTA OKLAHOMA COUPLE DAYS BACK. GOES BY BIG DOLL.
THIS GAL'S BEEN TALKIN' UP A STORM, DROPPIN' NAMES, AND I THINK SHE MENTIONED THAT ONE YOU TOLD ME TO KEEP AN EAR OUT FOR. WHAT WAS IT--?
DAPPLE.
THAT'S THE ONE.
BIG DOLL SAYS THIS DAPPLE GUY WAS INTO SOME STUFF BACK IN THE DAY. SAYS HE JUMPED AN AGENT, GOT HIS--
CRASH!
SWISH
AW, HELL. HOLD ON A SECOND, WOULDJA?
AAAGGH!!
SORRY 'BOUT THAT. IT'S CRAZY 'ROUND THESE PARTS LATELY... SOMETHIN' HAS EVERYONE ALL RILED UP.
ANYWAY, DOLL SAYS DAPPLE TOOK OFF A FEW WEEKS BACK. THING IS, SHE SPECIFICALLY REMEMBERS HIM TALKIN' ABOUT SEATTLE...CHECKIN' IN ON SOME OLD FRIENDS.
HE'S HEADED OUR WAY.
GET A LINE ON BIG DOLL AND MAKE SURE SHE STAYS PUT. I'LL TELL TERRY WE'RE RUNNING BLOUNDER DIRECTLY TO THE COMMUNITY AND WE'LL BE THERE IN A COUPLE HOURS.
DIRECTLY TO THE--?
PRETTY SURE THAT'S AGAINST YOUR BOYS' REGULATIONS.
NONE OF THAT MATTERS. IF DAPPLE'S STUPID ENOUGH TO SHOW HIS FACE, HE'S NOT WALKING OUT OF THIS TOWN.
NOT AGAIN.

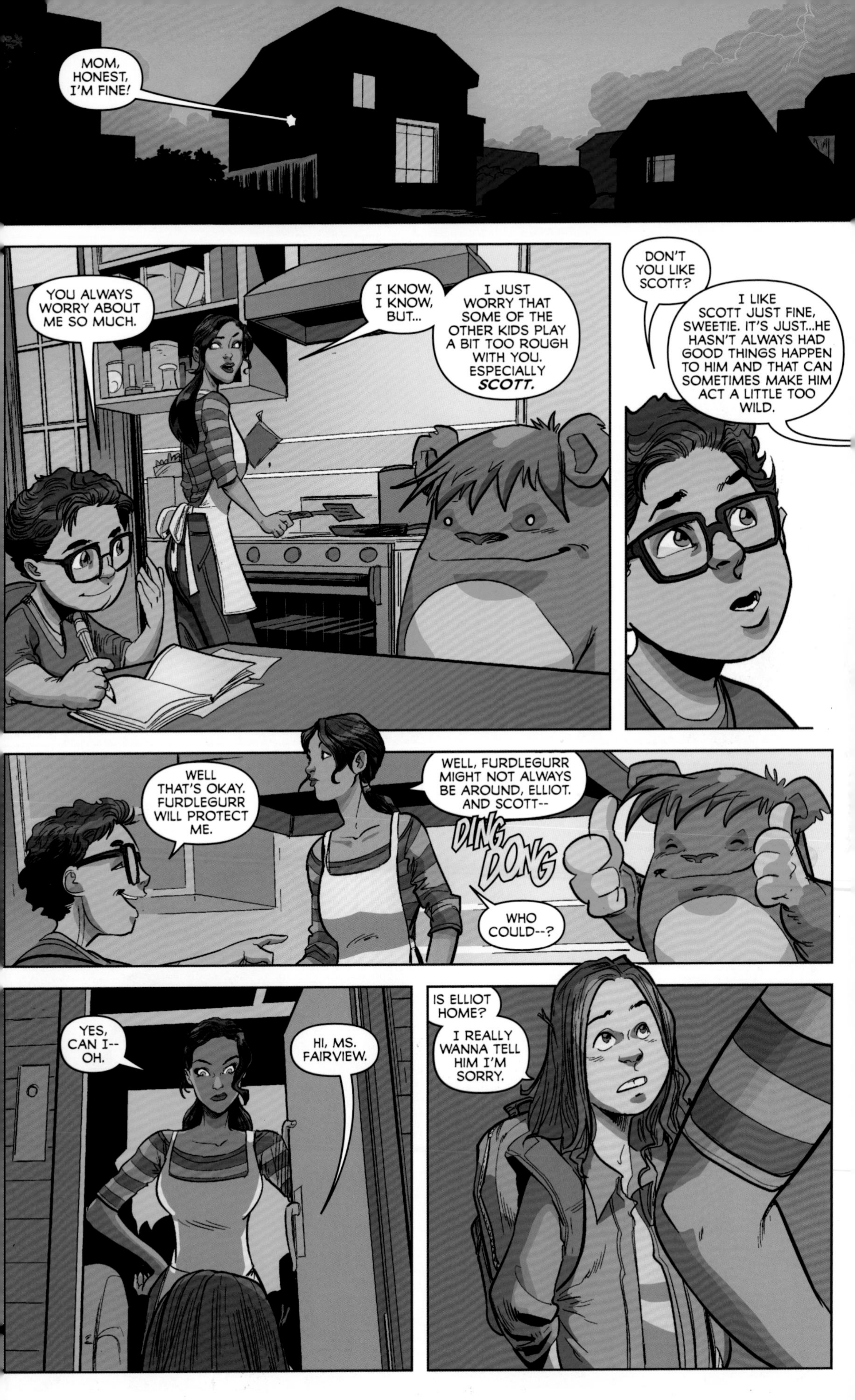

MOM, HONEST, I'M FINE!
YOU ALWAYS WORRY ABOUT ME SO MUCH.
I KNOW, I KNOW, BUT...
I JUST WORRY THAT SOME OF THE OTHER KIDS PLAY A BIT TOO ROUGH WITH YOU. ESPECIALLY SCOTT.
DON'T YOU LIKE SCOTT?
I LIKE SCOTT JUST FINE, SWEETIE. IT'S JUST...HE HASN'T ALWAYS HAD GOOD THINGS HAPPEN TO HIM AND THAT CAN SOMETIMES MAKE HIM ACT A LITTLE TOO WILD.
WELL THAT'S OKAY. FURDLEGURR WILL PROTECT ME.
WELL, FURDLEGURR MIGHT NOT ALWAYS BE AROUND, ELLIOT. AND SCOTT--
DING DONG
WHO COULD--?
YES, CAN I-- OH.
HI, MS. FAIRVIEW.
IS ELLIOT HOME?
I REALLY WANNA TELL HIM I'M SORRY.

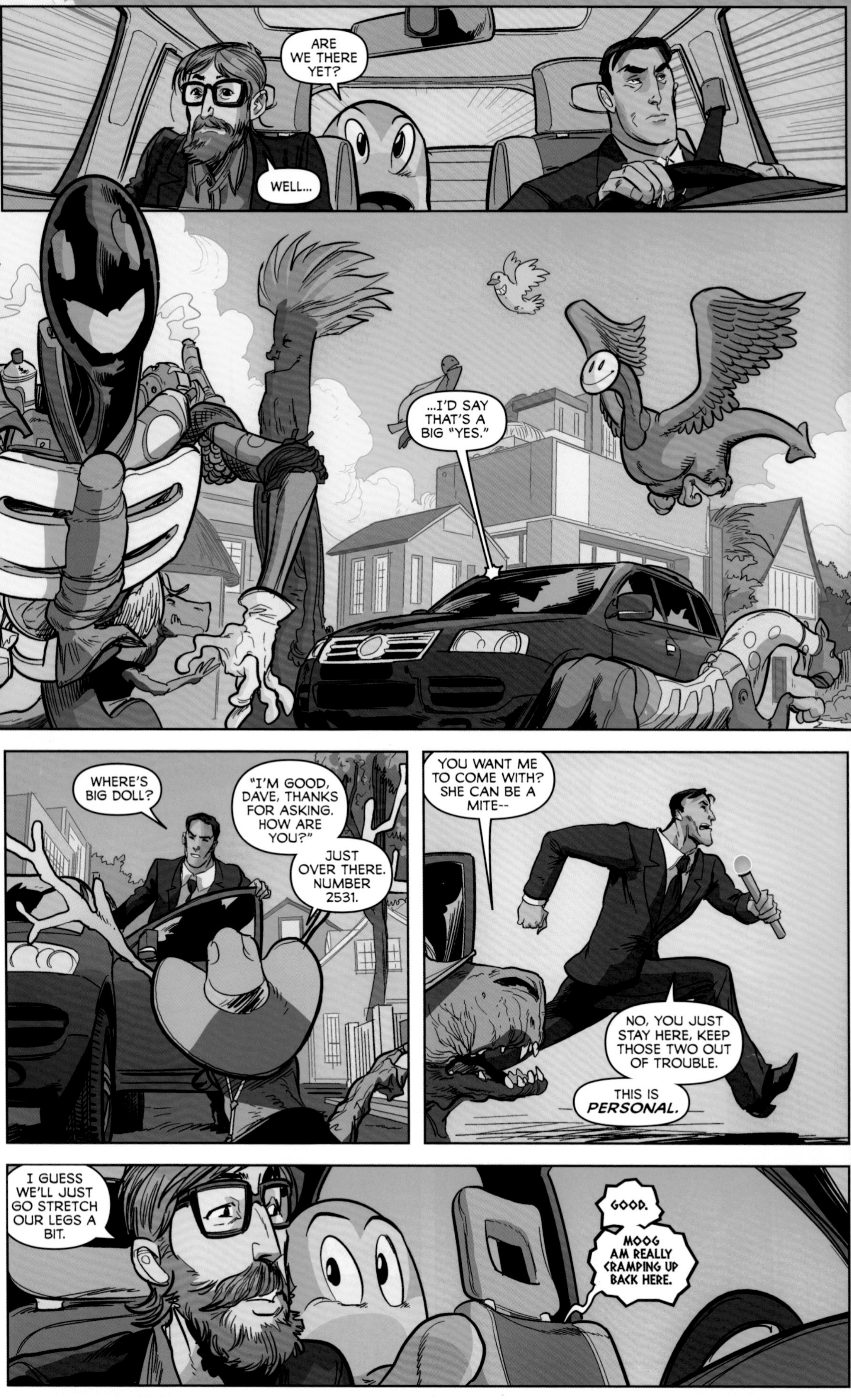
ARE WE THERE YET?
WELL...
...I'D SAY THAT'S A BIG "YES."
WHERE'S BIG DOLL?
"I'M GOOD, DAVE, THANKS FOR ASKING. HOW ARE YOU?"
JUST OVER THERE. NUMBER 2531.
YOU WANT ME TO COME WITH? SHE CAN BE A MITE--
NO, YOU JUST STAY HERE, KEEP THOSE TWO OUT OF TROUBLE.
THIS IS *PERSONAL.*
I GUESS WE'LL JUST GO STRETCH OUR LEGS A BIT.
GOOD.
MOOG AM REALLY CRAMPING UP BACK HERE.

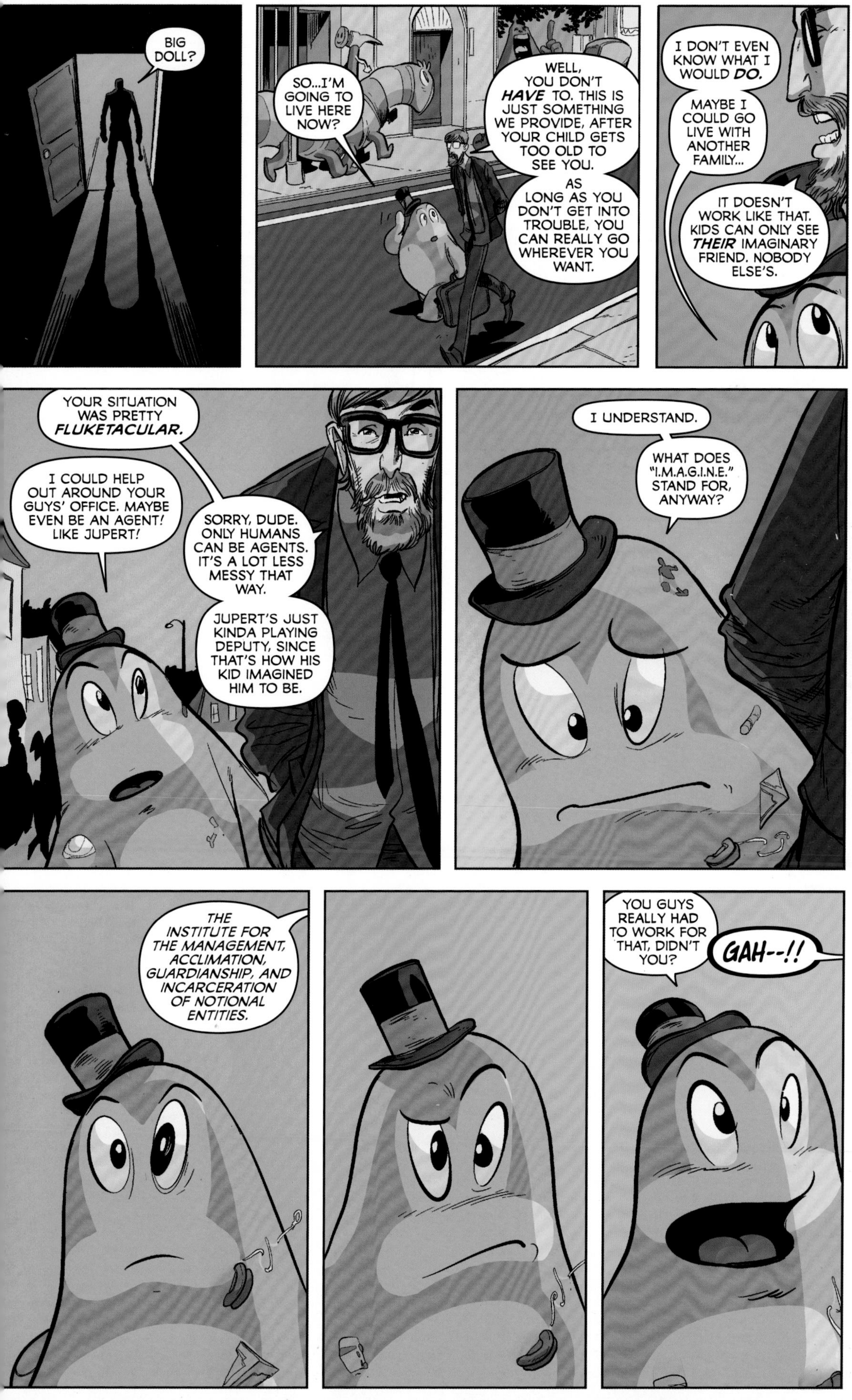
BIG DOLL?
SO...I'M GOING TO LIVE HERE NOW?
WELL, YOU DON'T *HAVE* TO. THIS IS JUST SOMETHING WE PROVIDE, AFTER YOUR CHILD GETS TOO OLD TO SEE YOU.
AS LONG AS YOU DON'T GET INTO TROUBLE, YOU CAN REALLY GO WHEREVER YOU WANT.
I DON'T EVEN KNOW WHAT I WOULD *DO.*
MAYBE I COULD GO LIVE WITH ANOTHER FAMILY...
IT DOESN'T WORK LIKE THAT. KIDS CAN ONLY SEE *THEIR* IMAGINARY FRIEND. NOBODY ELSE'S.
YOUR SITUATION WAS PRETTY *FLUKETACULAR.*
I COULD HELP OUT AROUND YOUR GUYS' OFFICE. MAYBE EVEN BE AN AGENT! LIKE JUPERT!
SORRY, DUDE. ONLY HUMANS CAN BE AGENTS. IT'S A LOT LESS MESSY THAT WAY.
JUPERT'S JUST KINDA PLAYING DEPUTY, SINCE THAT'S HOW HIS KID IMAGINED HIM TO BE.
I UNDERSTAND.
WHAT DOES "I.M.A.G.I.N.E." STAND FOR, ANYWAY?
THE INSTITUTE FOR THE MANAGEMENT, ACCLIMATION, GUARDIANSHIP, AND INCARCERATION OF NOTIONAL ENTITIES.
YOU GUYS REALLY HAD TO WORK FOR THAT, DIDN'T YOU?
GAH--!!

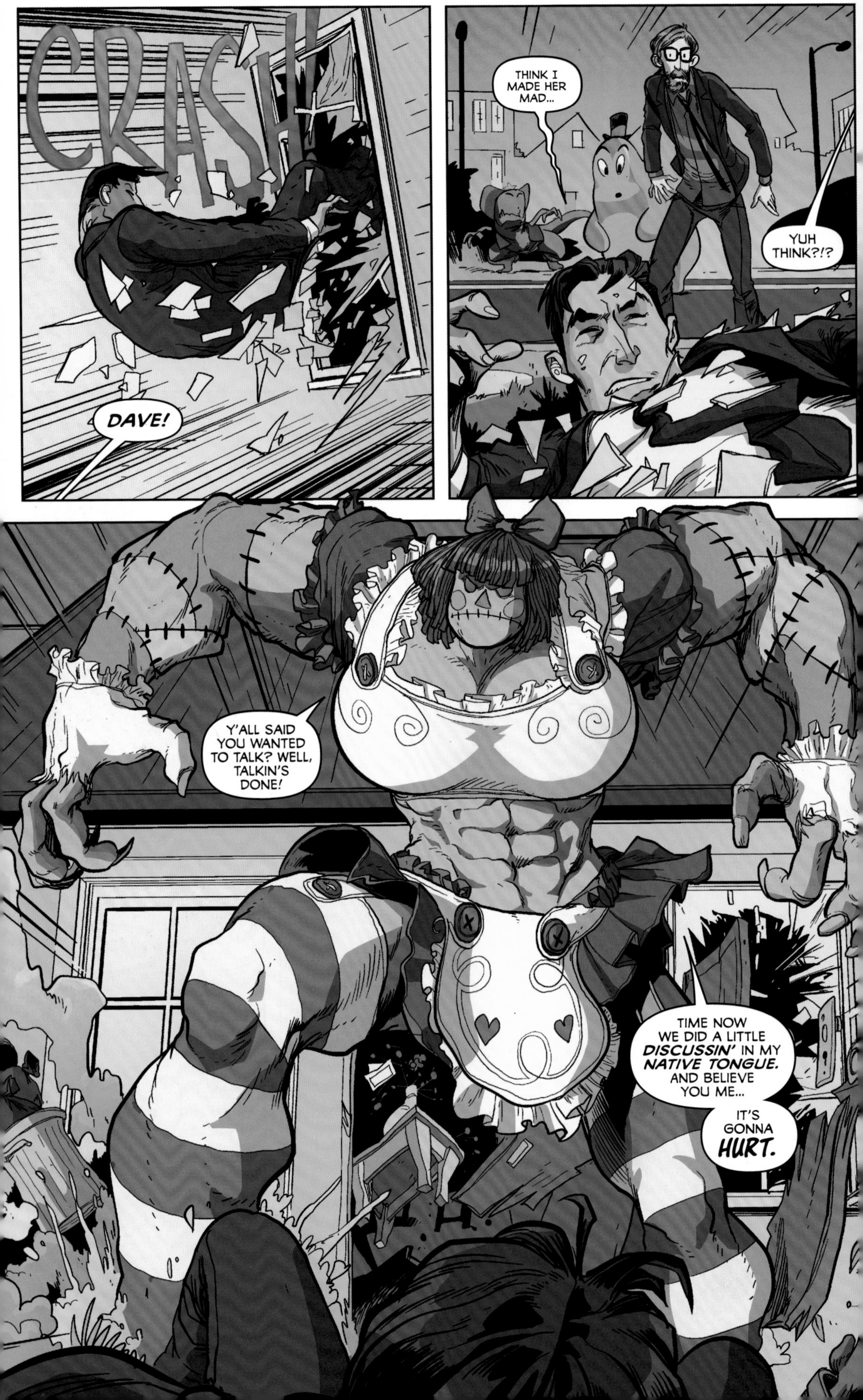
CRASH!
DAVE!
THINK I MADE HER MAD...
YUH THINK?!?
Y'ALL SAID YOU WANTED TO TALK? WELL, TALKIN'S DONE!
TIME NOW WE DID A LITTLE DISCUSSIN' IN MY NATIVE TONGUE. AND BELIEVE YOU ME...
IT'S GONNA HURT.

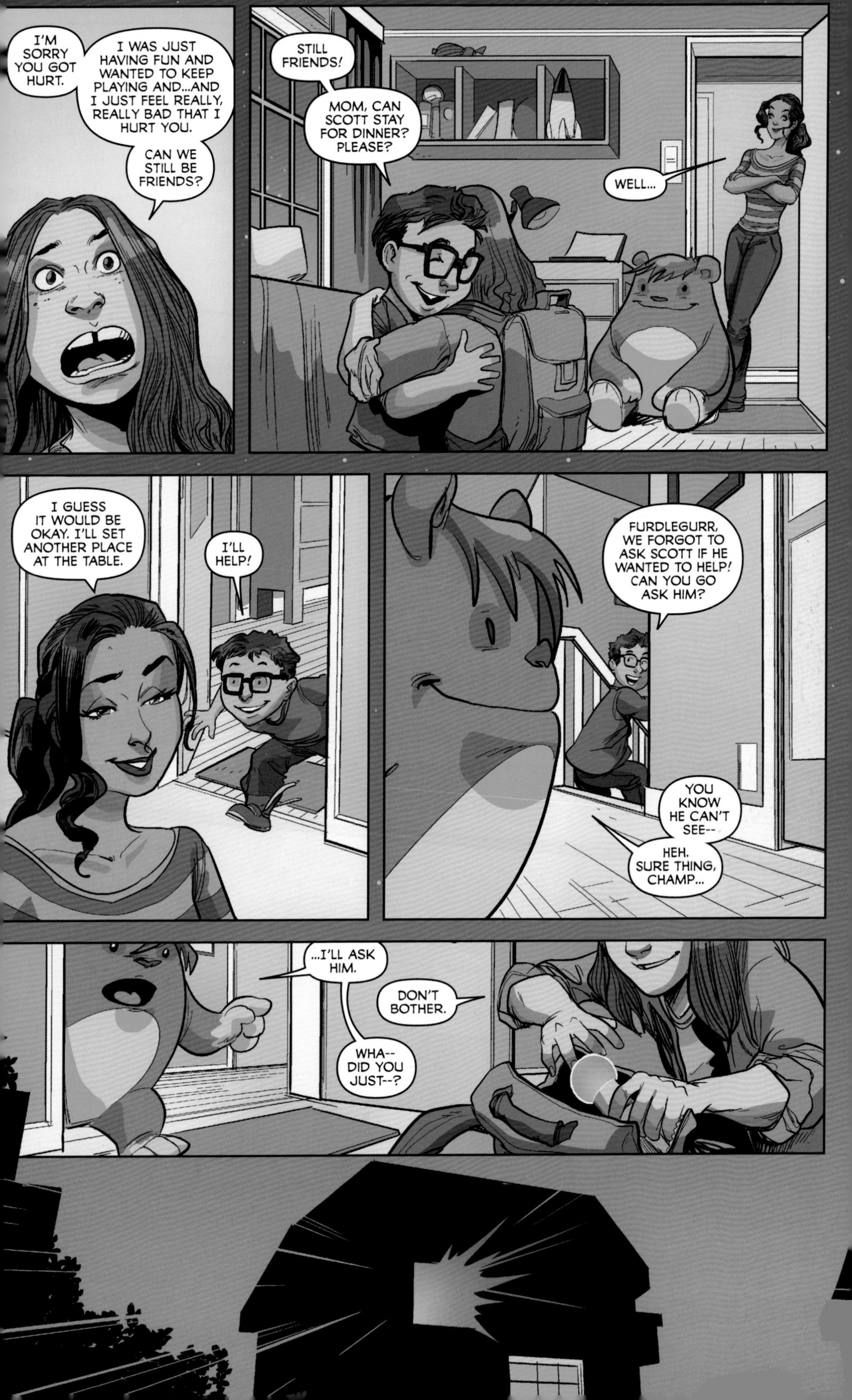

I'M SORRY YOU GOT HURT.
I WAS JUST HAVING FUN AND WANTED TO KEEP PLAYING AND...AND I JUST FEEL REALLY, REALLY BAD THAT I HURT YOU.
CAN WE STILL BE FRIENDS?
STILL FRIENDS!
MOM, CAN SCOTT STAY FOR DINNER? PLEASE?
WELL...
I GUESS IT WOULD BE OKAY. I'LL SET ANOTHER PLACE AT THE TABLE.
I'LL HELP!
FURDLEGURR, WE FORGOT TO ASK SCOTT IF HE WANTED TO HELP! CAN YOU GO ASK HIM?
YOU KNOW HE CAN'T SEE--
HEH. SURE THING, CHAMP...
...I'LL ASK HIM.
DON'T BOTHER.
WHA-- DID YOU JUST--?

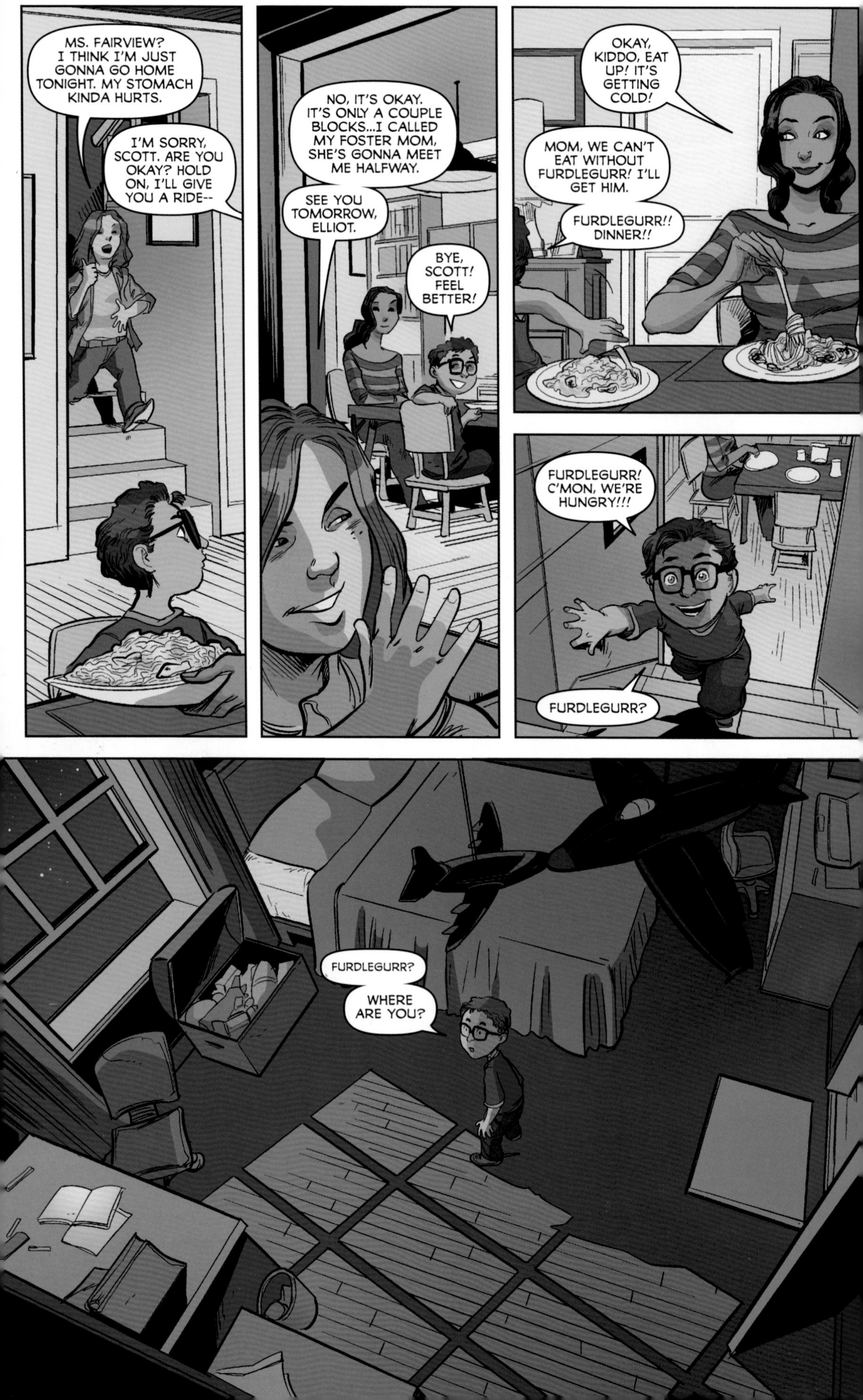
MS. FAIRVIEW? I THINK I'M JUST GONNA GO HOME TONIGHT. MY STOMACH KINDA HURTS.
I'M SORRY, SCOTT. ARE YOU OKAY? HOLD ON, I'LL GIVE YOU A RIDE--
NO, IT'S OKAY. IT'S ONLY A COUPLE BLOCKS...I CALLED MY FOSTER MOM, SHE'S GONNA MEET ME HALFWAY.
SEE YOU TOMORROW, ELLIOT.
BYE, SCOTT! FEEL BETTER!
OKAY, KIDDO, EAT UP! IT'S GETTING COLD!
MOM, WE CAN'T EAT WITHOUT FURDLEGURR! I'LL GET HIM.
FURDLEGURR!! DINNER!!
FURDLEGURR! C'MON, WE'RE HUNGRY!!!
FURDLEGURR?
FURDLEGURR?
WHERE ARE YOU?

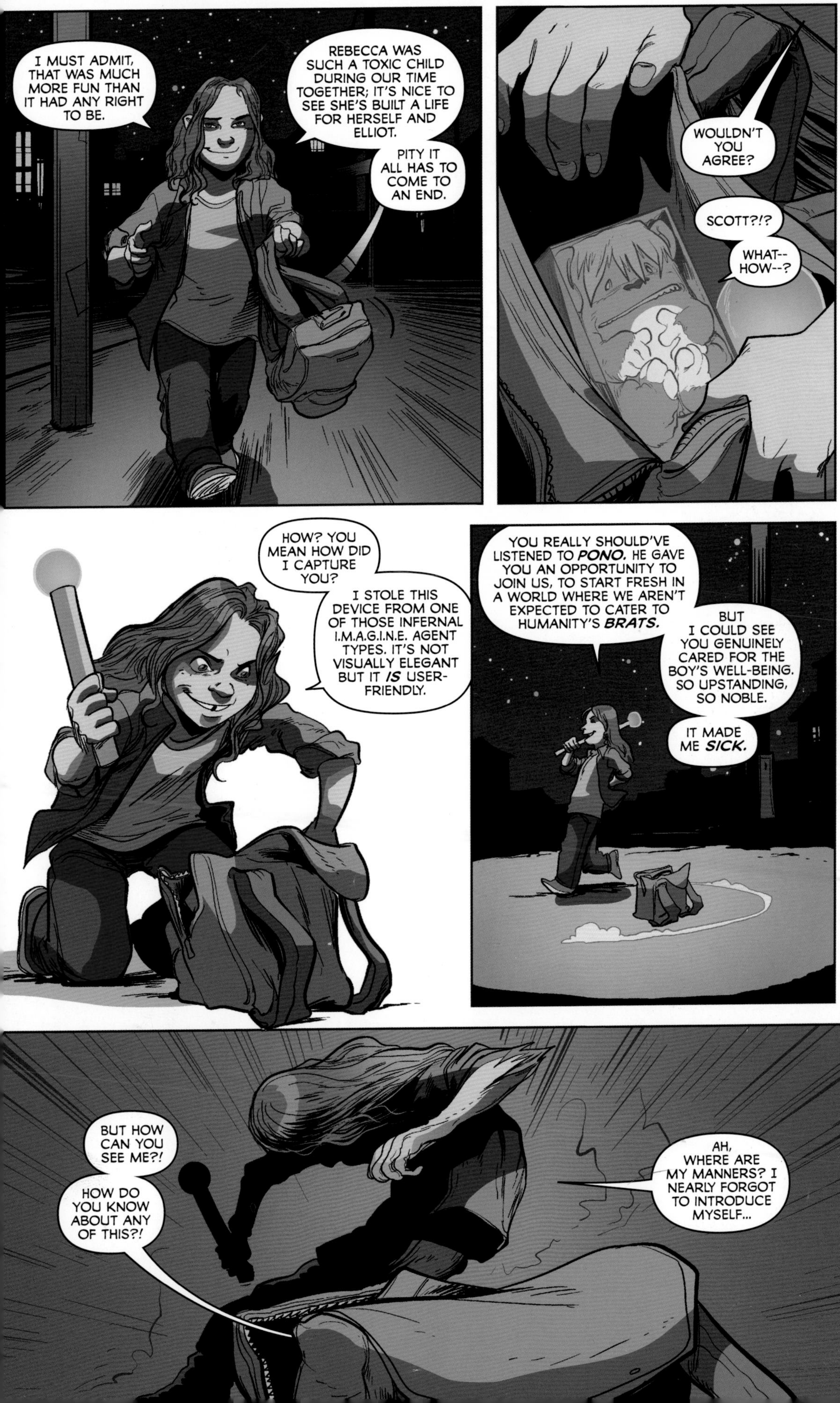

I MUST ADMIT, THAT WAS MUCH MORE FUN THAN IT HAD ANY RIGHT TO BE.
REBECCA WAS SUCH A TOXIC CHILD DURING OUR TIME TOGETHER; IT'S NICE TO SEE SHE'S BUILT A LIFE FOR HERSELF AND ELLIOT.
PITY IT ALL HAS TO COME TO AN END.
WOULDN'T YOU AGREE?
SCOTT?!?
WHAT-- HOW--?
HOW? YOU MEAN HOW DID I CAPTURE YOU?
I STOLE THIS DEVICE FROM ONE OF THOSE INFERNAL I.M.A.G.I.N.E. AGENT TYPES. IT'S NOT VISUALLY ELEGANT BUT IT *IS* USER-FRIENDLY.
YOU REALLY SHOULD'VE LISTENED TO ***PONO.*** HE GAVE YOU AN OPPORTUNITY TO JOIN US, TO START FRESH IN A WORLD WHERE WE AREN'T EXPECTED TO CATER TO HUMANITY'S ***BRATS.***
BUT I COULD SEE YOU GENUINELY CARED FOR THE BOY'S WELL-BEING. SO UPSTANDING, SO NOBLE.
IT MADE ME ***SICK.***
BUT HOW CAN YOU SEE ME?!
HOW DO YOU KNOW ABOUT ANY OF THIS?!
AH, WHERE ARE MY MANNERS? I NEARLY FORGOT TO INTRODUCE MYSELF...

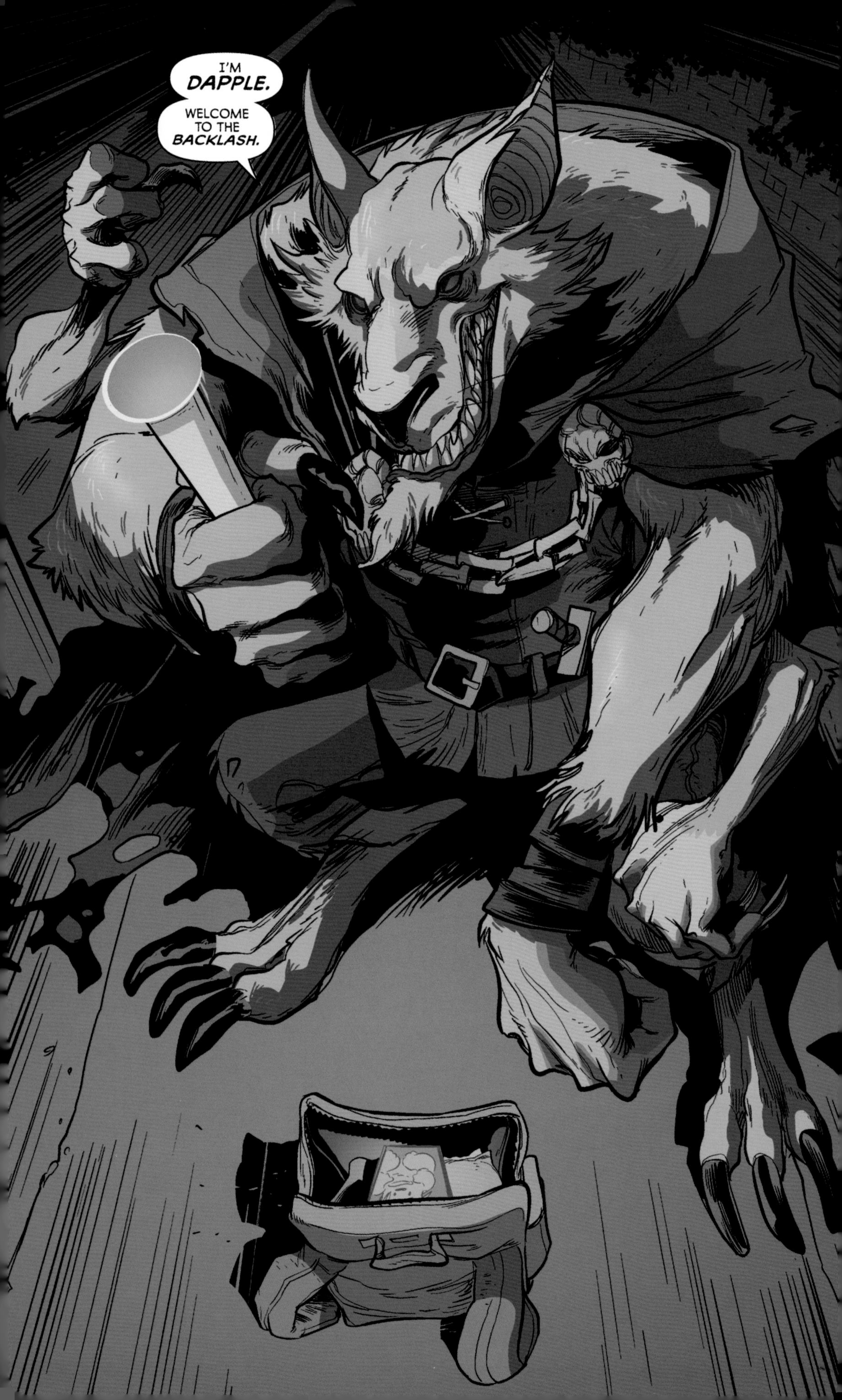
I'M DAPPLE.
WELCOME TO THE BACKLASH.

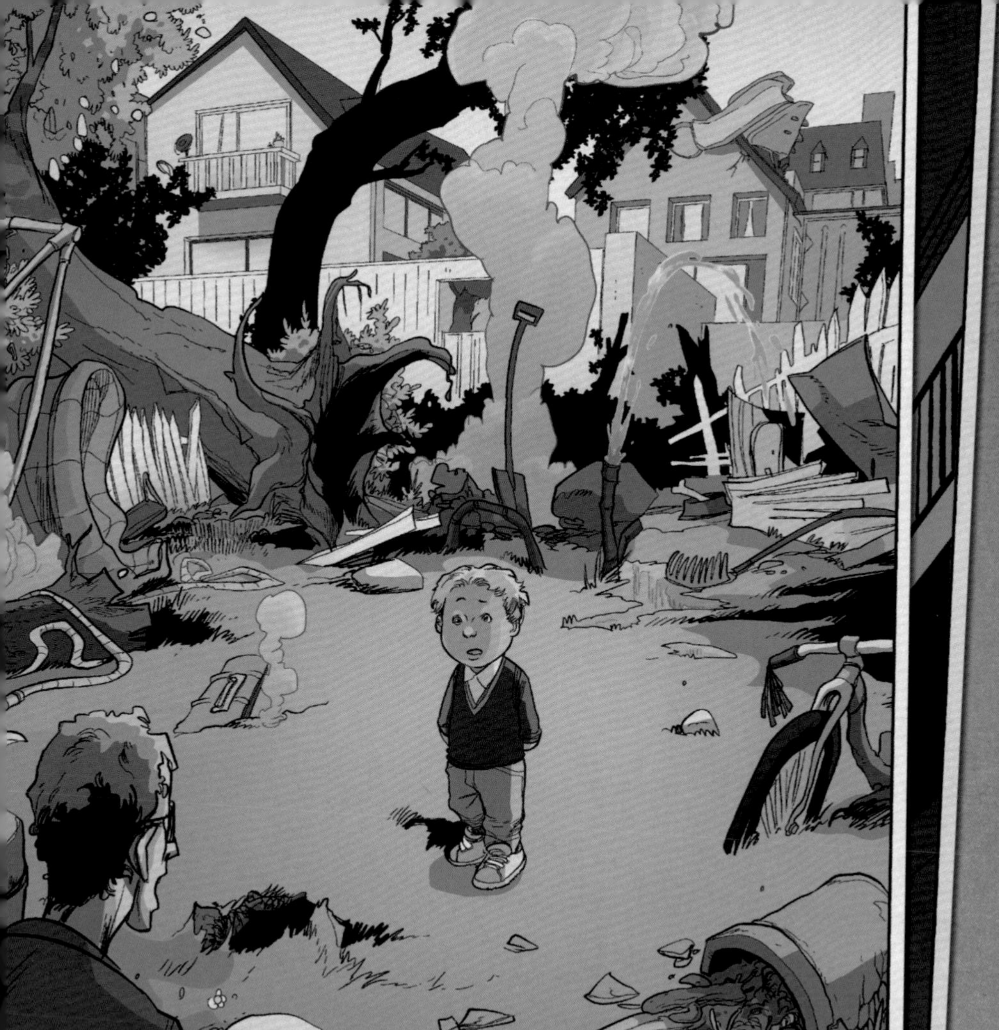

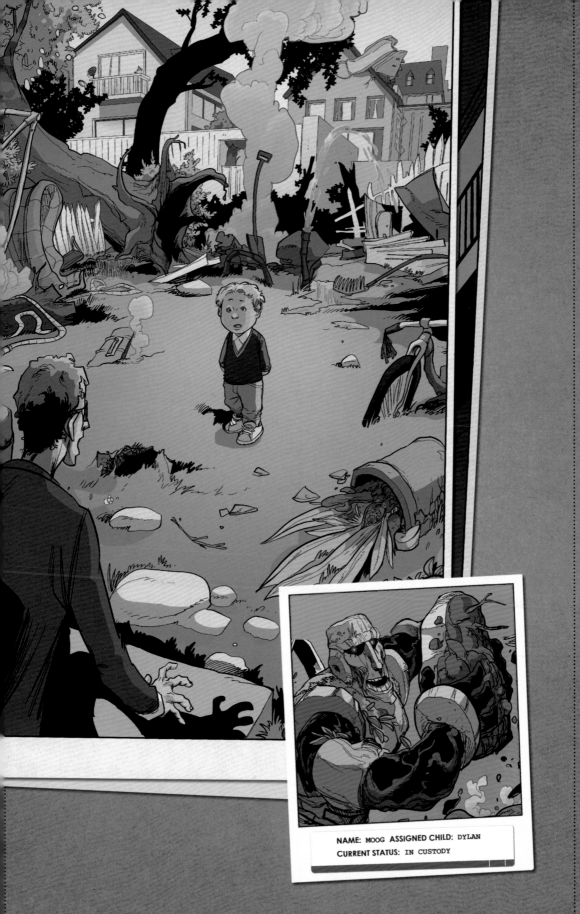

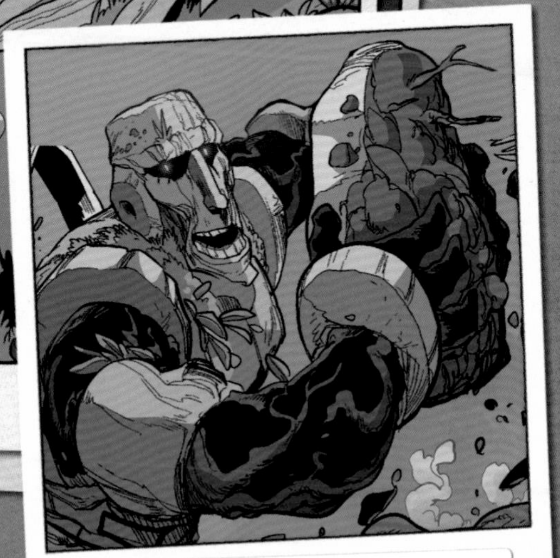
NAME: MOOG ASSIGNED CHILD: DYLAN
CURRENT STATUS: IN CUSTODY

CIAL AGENT
ELD MANUAL

REVISED EDITION NO. 12-D

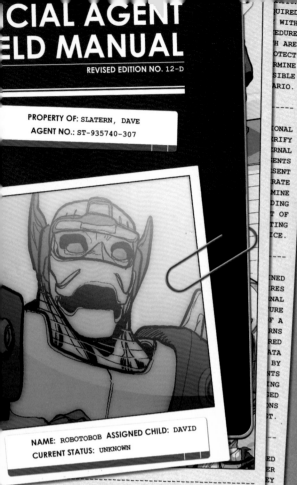

PROPERTY OF: SLATERN, DAVE
AGENT NO.: ST-935740-307

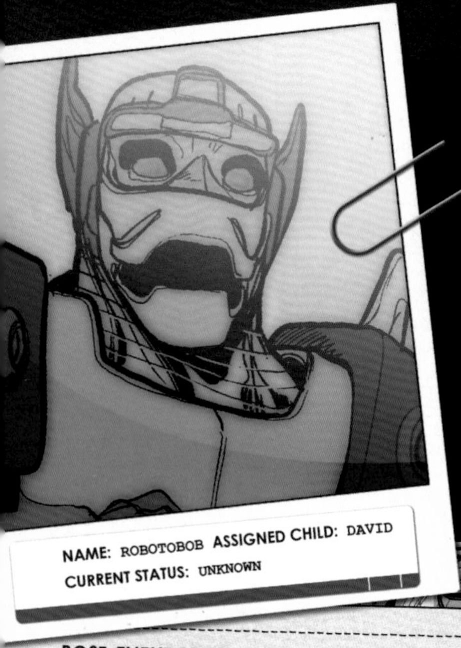

NAME: ROBOTOBOB ASSIGNED CHILD: DAVID
CURRENT STATUS: UNKNOWN

POST-EVENT RECON:

- FIELD AGENT **DAVE SLATERN**, PARTNERED WITH ROOKIE AGENT **TERRY SNOWGOOSE**, APPREHENDED ROGUE FIGMENT **MOOG OF MOG** AND RETRIEVED RETIRED IMAGINARY FRIEND **BLOUNDER** FROM HIS CHILD'S HOME UPON HER OUTGROWING OF HIM.
- AFTER RECEIVING A CALL FROM COMMUNITY HEAD **JUPERT** REGARDING THE RUMORED RETURN OF **DAPPLE**, FROM SLATERN'S PAST, SLATERN DISOBEYE AND DIRECTED SNOWGOOSE AND THE FIGMENT CUSTODY TO THE RUMOR'S SOURCE: **BIG DOLL** TRANSPLANT TO THE SEATTLE FIGMENT COMMU
- AFTER A ROUGH DAY AT SCHOOL, **ELLIOT FA** CARED FOR BY MOTHER AND TEACHER, **REBECC** FIGMENT **FURDLEGURR**.
- FURDLEGURR WAS APPROACHED BY TWO FIGMENTS TO JOIN DAPPLE'S CAUSE. HE RE OFFER IN FAVOR OF HIS LIFE WITH ELLIOT.
- **SCOTT KOWALSKI**, BEST FRIEND OF ELLIOT, FURDLEGURR AND REVEALED HIMSELF TO BE DAP

REPORT CONTINUED IN CASE NO.

CASE FILE REFERENCE IMAGE: 6781

CHAPTER TWO

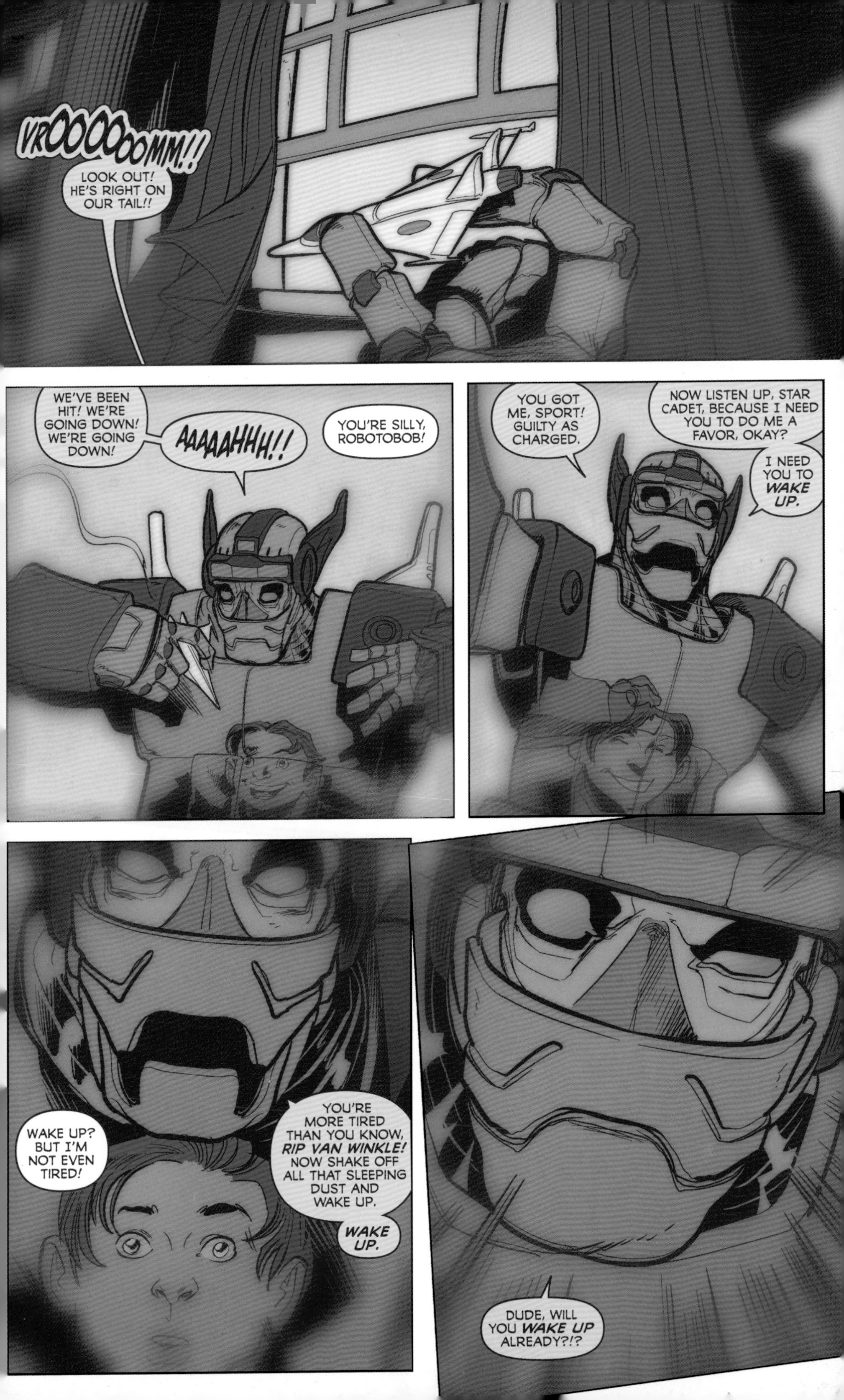
VROOOOoOMM!!
LOOK OUT! HE'S RIGHT ON OUR TAIL!!
WE'VE BEEN HIT! WE'RE GOING DOWN! WE'RE GOING DOWN!
AAAAAHHH!!
YOU'RE SILLY, ROBOTOBOB!
YOU GOT ME, SPORT! GUILTY AS CHARGED.
NOW LISTEN UP, STAR CADET, BECAUSE I NEED YOU TO DO ME A FAVOR, OKAY?
I NEED YOU TO *WAKE UP.*
WAKE UP? BUT I'M NOT EVEN TIRED!
YOU'RE MORE TIRED THAN YOU KNOW, *RIP VAN WINKLE!* NOW SHAKE OFF ALL THAT SLEEPING DUST AND WAKE UP.
WAKE UP.
DUDE, WILL YOU *WAKE UP* ALREADY?!?

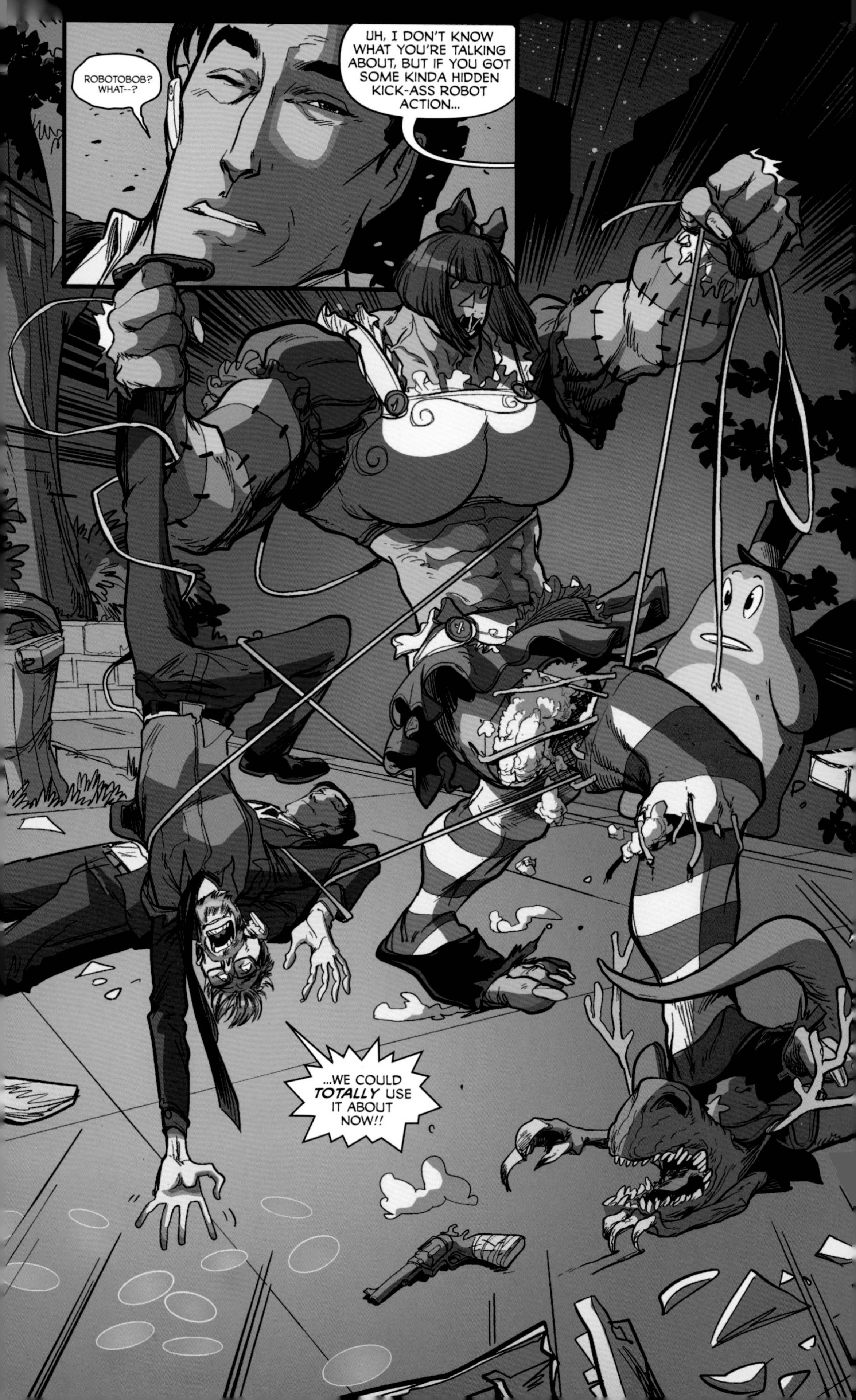
ROBOTOBOB? WHAT--?
UH, I DON'T KNOW WHAT YOU'RE TALKING ABOUT, BUT IF YOU GOT SOME KINDA HIDDEN KICK-ASS ROBOT ACTION...
...WE COULD TOTALLY USE IT ABOUT NOW!!

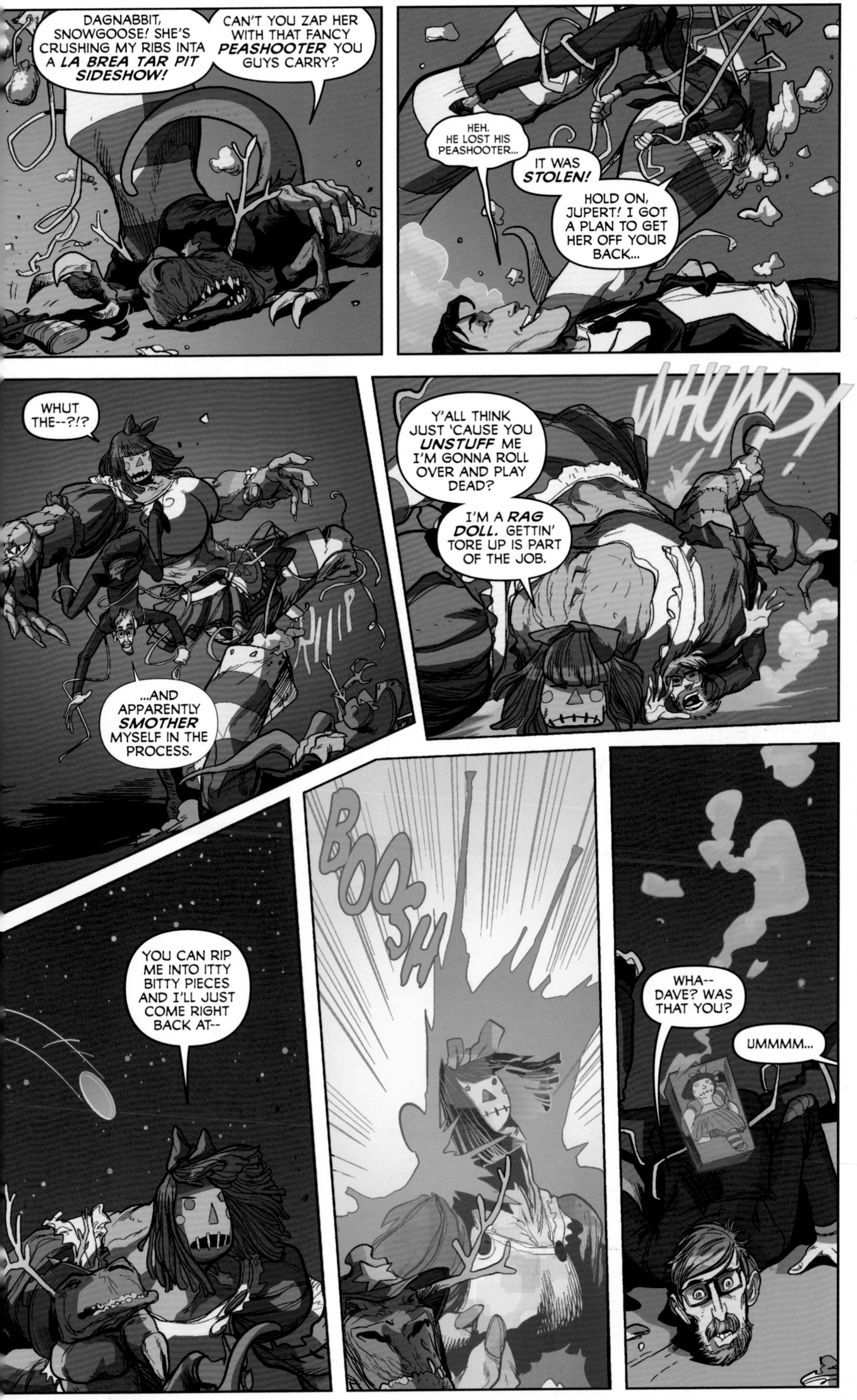
DAGNABBIT, SNOWGOOSE! SHE'S CRUSHING MY RIBS INTA A *LA BREA TAR PIT SIDESHOW!*
CAN'T YOU ZAP HER WITH THAT FANCY *PEASHOOTER* YOU GUYS CARRY?
HEH. HE LOST HIS PEASHOOTER...
IT WAS *STOLEN!*
HOLD ON, JUPERT! I GOT A PLAN TO GET HER OFF YOUR BACK...
WHUT THE--?!?
...AND APPARENTLY *SMOTHER* MYSELF IN THE PROCESS.
RHIIP
WHUMP!
Y'ALL THINK JUST 'CAUSE YOU *UNSTUFF* ME I'M GONNA ROLL OVER AND PLAY DEAD?
I'M A *RAG DOLL.* GETTIN' TORE UP IS PART OF THE JOB.
YOU CAN RIP ME INTO ITTY BITTY PIECES AND I'LL JUST COME RIGHT BACK AT--
BOOSH
WHA-- DAVE? WAS THAT YOU?
UMMMM...

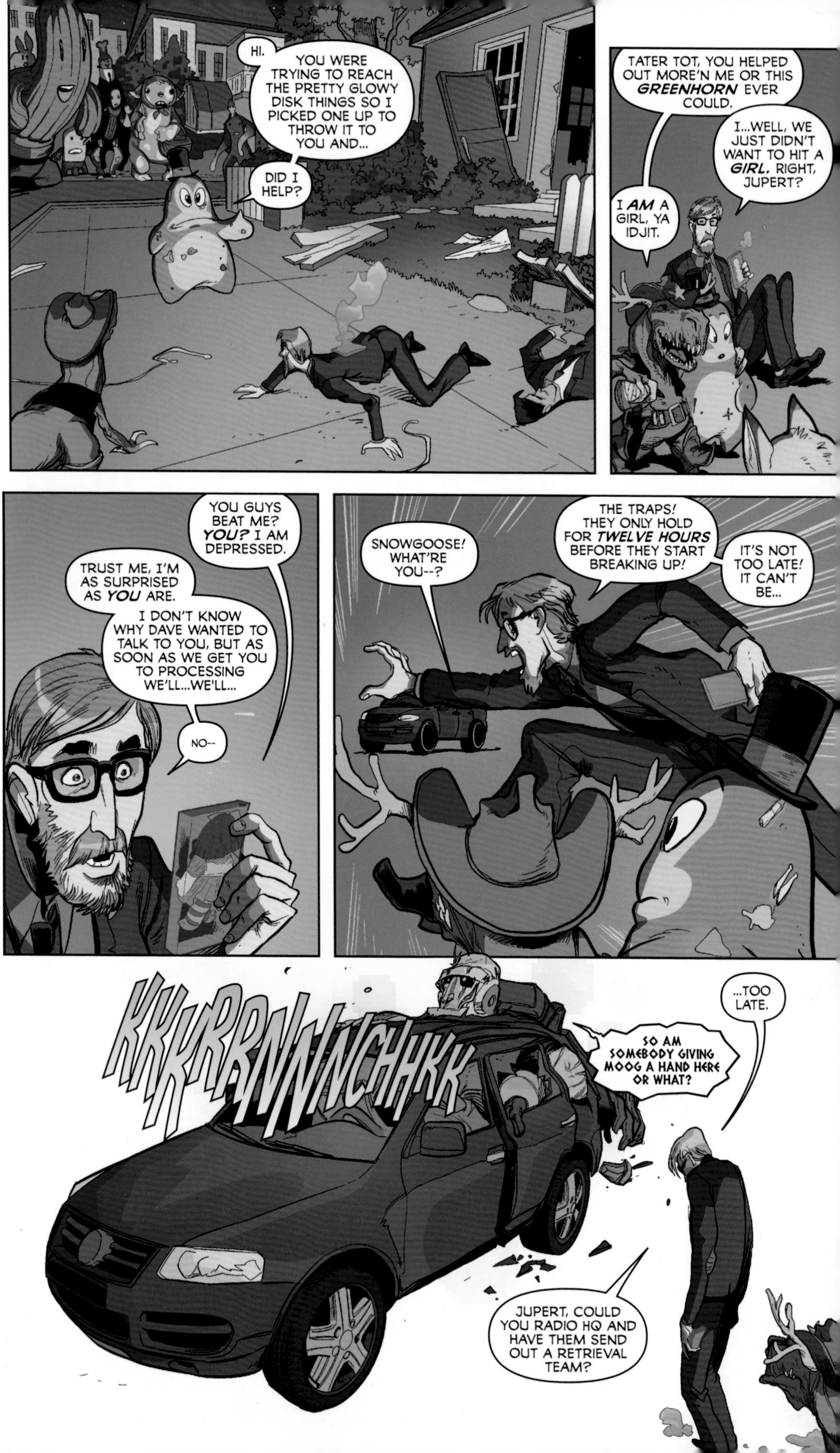
HI.
YOU WERE TRYING TO REACH THE PRETTY GLOWY DISK THINGS SO I PICKED ONE UP TO THROW IT TO YOU AND...
DID I HELP?
TATER TOT, YOU HELPED OUT MORE'N ME OR THIS **GREENHORN** EVER COULD.
I...WELL, WE JUST DIDN'T WANT TO HIT A **GIRL.** RIGHT, JUPERT?
I **AM** A GIRL, YA IDJIT.
YOU GUYS BEAT ME? ***YOU?*** I AM DEPRESSED.
TRUST ME, I'M AS SURPRISED AS ***YOU*** ARE.
I DON'T KNOW WHY DAVE WANTED TO TALK TO YOU, BUT AS SOON AS WE GET YOU TO PROCESSING WE'LL...WE'LL...
NO--
SNOWGOOSE! WHAT'RE YOU--?
THE TRAPS! THEY ONLY HOLD FOR ***TWELVE HOURS*** BEFORE THEY START BREAKING UP!
IT'S NOT TOO LATE! IT CAN'T BE...
KKKRRNNNCHHKK
SO AM SOMEBODY GIVING MOOG A HAND HERE OR WHAT?
...TOO LATE.
JUPERT, COULD YOU RADIO HQ AND HAVE THEM SEND OUT A RETRIEVAL TEAM?

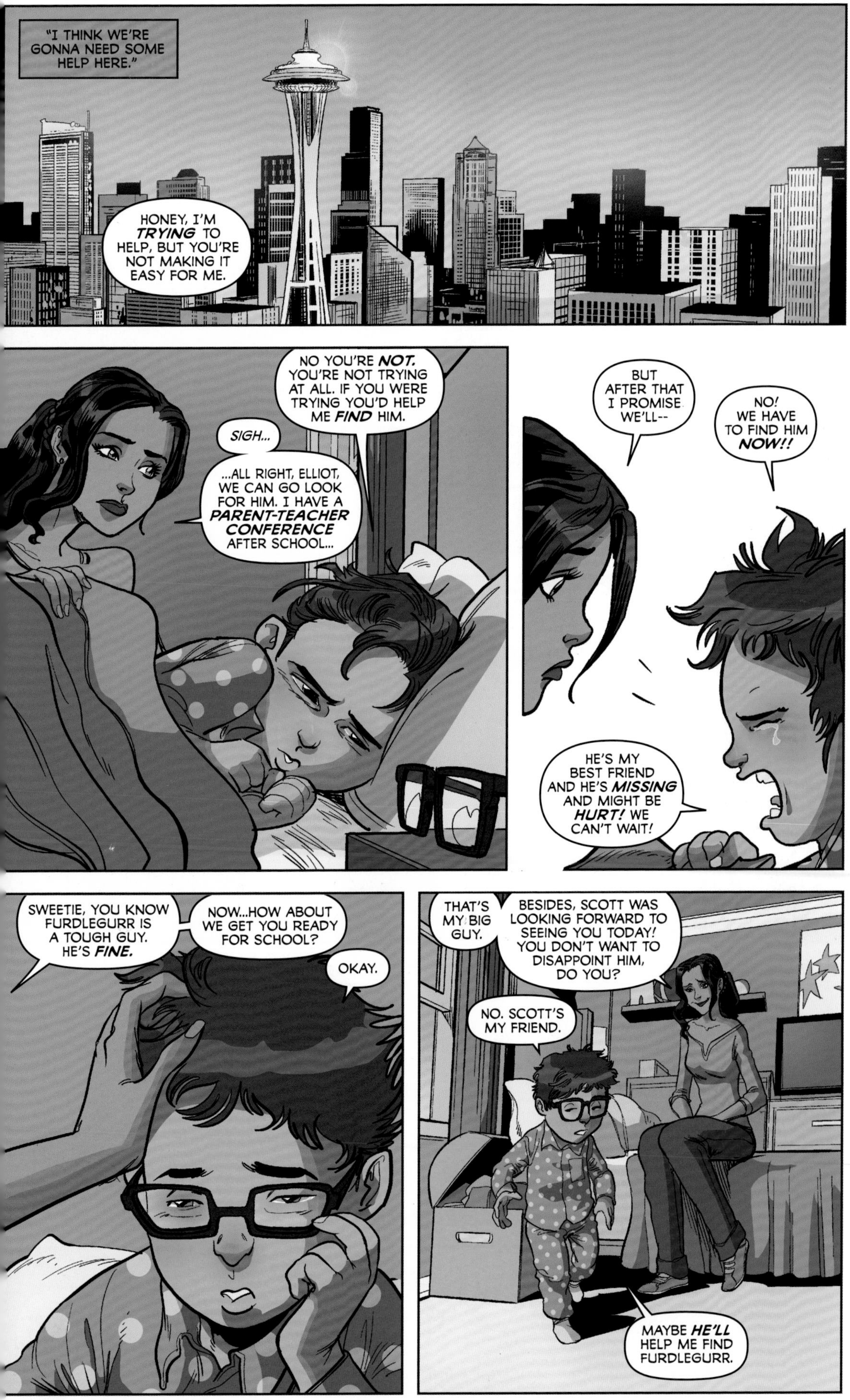

"I THINK WE'RE GONNA NEED SOME HELP HERE."
HONEY, I'M *TRYING* TO HELP, BUT YOU'RE NOT MAKING IT EASY FOR ME.
NO YOU'RE *NOT.* YOU'RE NOT TRYING AT ALL. IF YOU WERE TRYING YOU'D HELP ME *FIND* HIM.
SIGH...
...ALL RIGHT, ELLIOT, WE CAN GO LOOK FOR HIM. I HAVE A *PARENT-TEACHER CONFERENCE* AFTER SCHOOL...
BUT AFTER THAT I PROMISE WE'LL--
NO! WE HAVE TO FIND HIM *NOW!!*
HE'S MY BEST FRIEND AND HE'S *MISSING* AND MIGHT BE *HURT!* WE CAN'T WAIT!
SWEETIE, YOU KNOW FURDLEGURR IS A TOUGH GUY. HE'S *FINE.*
NOW...HOW ABOUT WE GET YOU READY FOR SCHOOL?
OKAY.
THAT'S MY BIG GUY.
BESIDES, SCOTT WAS LOOKING FORWARD TO SEEING YOU TODAY! YOU DON'T WANT TO DISAPPOINT HIM, DO YOU?
NO. SCOTT'S MY FRIEND.
MAYBE *HE'LL* HELP ME FIND FURDLEGURR.

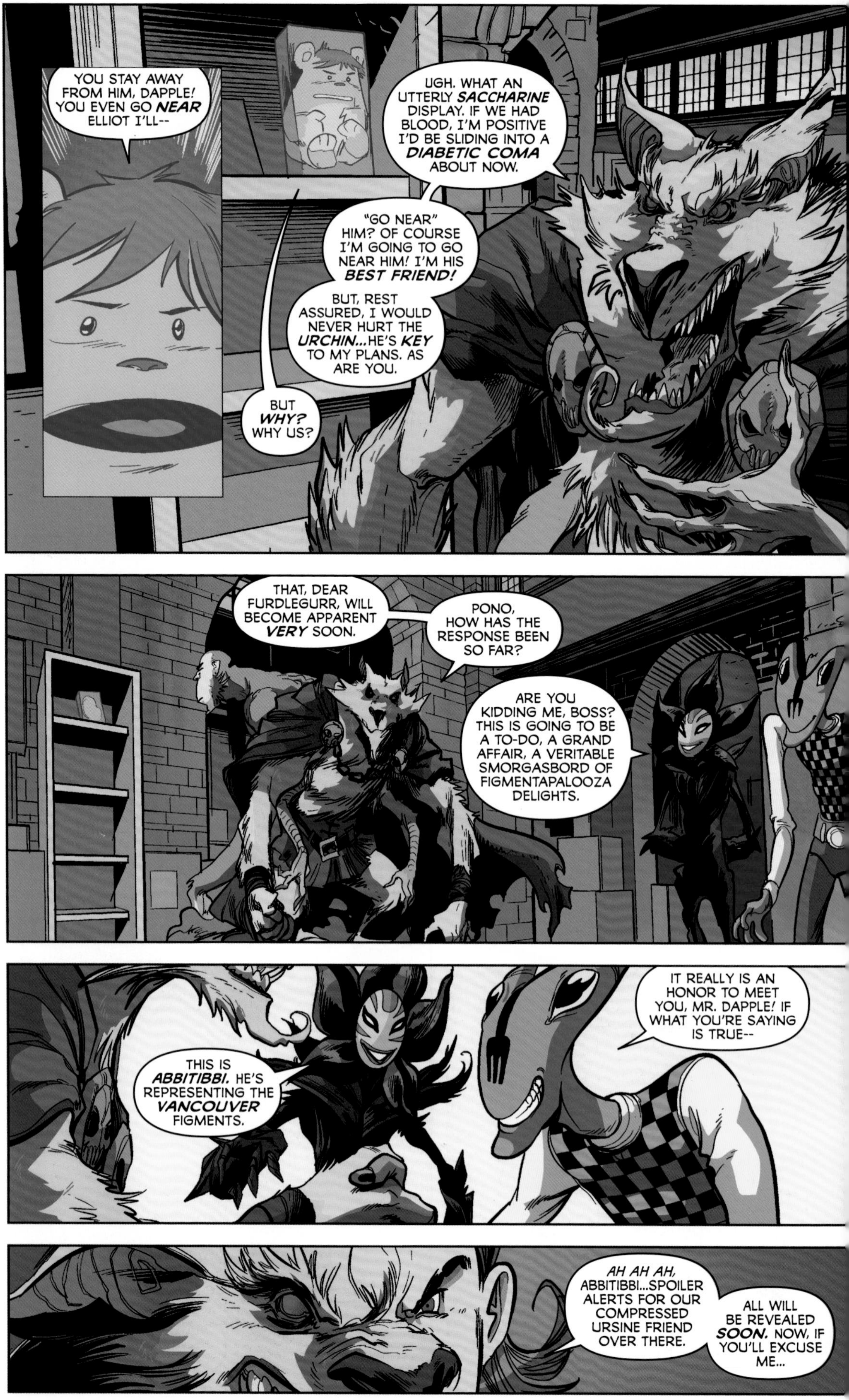

YOU STAY AWAY FROM HIM, DAPPLE! YOU EVEN GO NEAR ELLIOT I'LL--
UGH. WHAT AN UTTERLY SACCHARINE DISPLAY. IF WE HAD BLOOD, I'M POSITIVE I'D BE SLIDING INTO A DIABETIC COMA ABOUT NOW.
"GO NEAR" HIM? OF COURSE I'M GOING TO GO NEAR HIM! I'M HIS BEST FRIEND!
BUT, REST ASSURED, I WOULD NEVER HURT THE URCHIN...HE'S KEY TO MY PLANS. AS ARE YOU.
BUT WHY? WHY US?
THAT, DEAR FURDLEGURR, WILL BECOME APPARENT VERY SOON.
PONO, HOW HAS THE RESPONSE BEEN SO FAR?
ARE YOU KIDDING ME, BOSS? THIS IS GOING TO BE A TO-DO, A GRAND AFFAIR, A VERITABLE SMORGASBORD OF FIGMENTAPALOOZA DELIGHTS.
THIS IS ABBITIBBI. HE'S REPRESENTING THE VANCOUVER FIGMENTS.
IT REALLY IS AN HONOR TO MEET YOU, MR. DAPPLE! IF WHAT YOU'RE SAYING IS TRUE--
AH AH AH, ABBITIBBI...SPOILER ALERTS FOR OUR COMPRESSED URSINE FRIEND OVER THERE.
ALL WILL BE REVEALED SOON. NOW, IF YOU'LL EXCUSE ME...

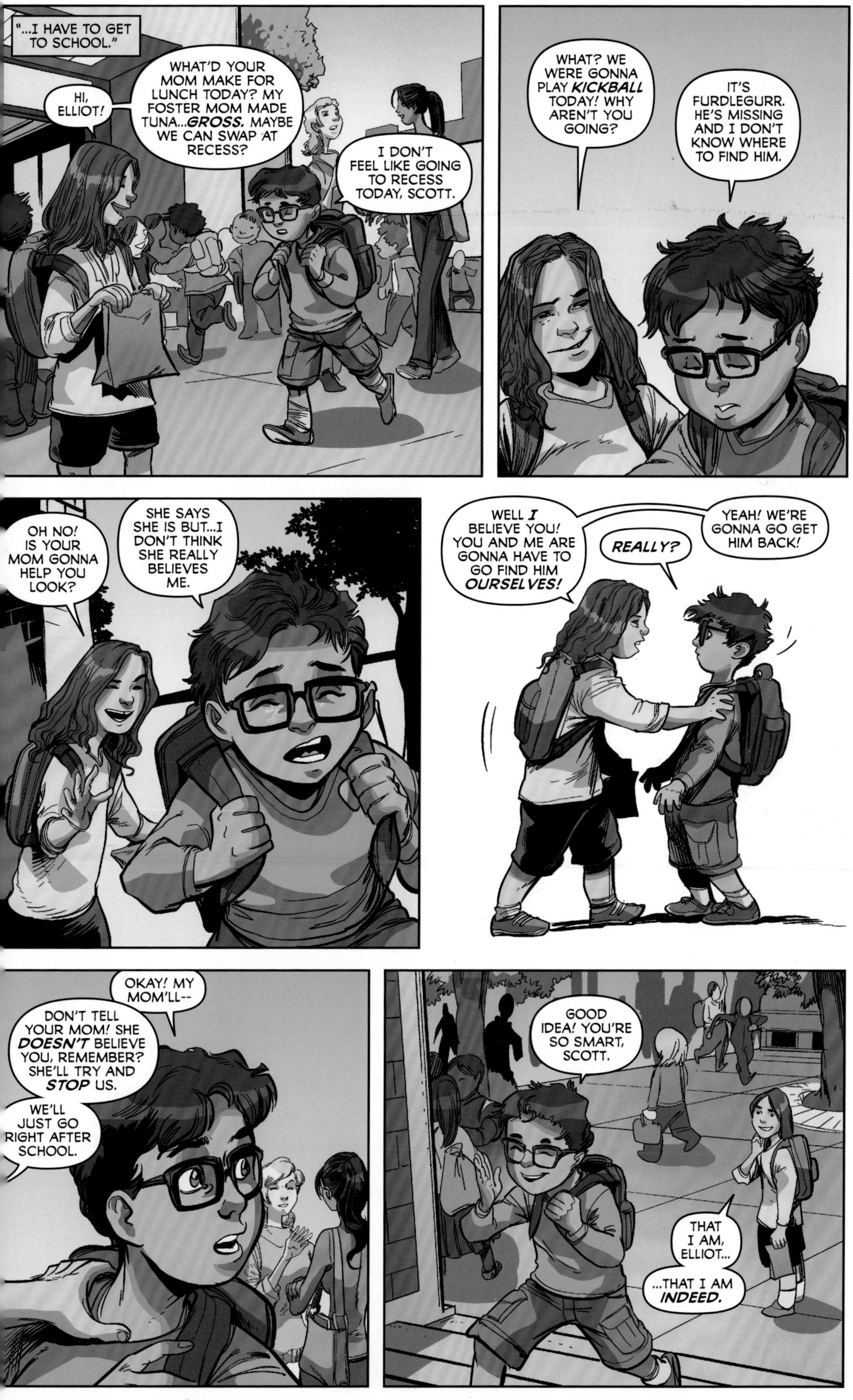
"...I HAVE TO GET TO SCHOOL."
HI, ELLIOT!
WHAT'D YOUR MOM MAKE FOR LUNCH TODAY? MY FOSTER MOM MADE TUNA...GROSS. MAYBE WE CAN SWAP AT RECESS?
I DON'T FEEL LIKE GOING TO RECESS TODAY, SCOTT.
WHAT? WE WERE GONNA PLAY KICKBALL TODAY! WHY AREN'T YOU GOING?
IT'S FURDLEGURR. HE'S MISSING AND I DON'T KNOW WHERE TO FIND HIM.
OH NO! IS YOUR MOM GONNA HELP YOU LOOK?
SHE SAYS SHE IS BUT...I DON'T THINK SHE REALLY BELIEVES ME.
WELL I BELIEVE YOU! YOU AND ME ARE GONNA HAVE TO GO FIND HIM OURSELVES!
REALLY?
YEAH! WE'RE GONNA GO GET HIM BACK!
OKAY! MY MOM'LL--
DON'T TELL YOUR MOM! SHE DOESN'T BELIEVE YOU, REMEMBER? SHE'LL TRY AND STOP US.
WE'LL JUST GO RIGHT AFTER SCHOOL.
GOOD IDEA! YOU'RE SO SMART, SCOTT.
THAT I AM, ELLIOT...
...THAT I AM INDEED.

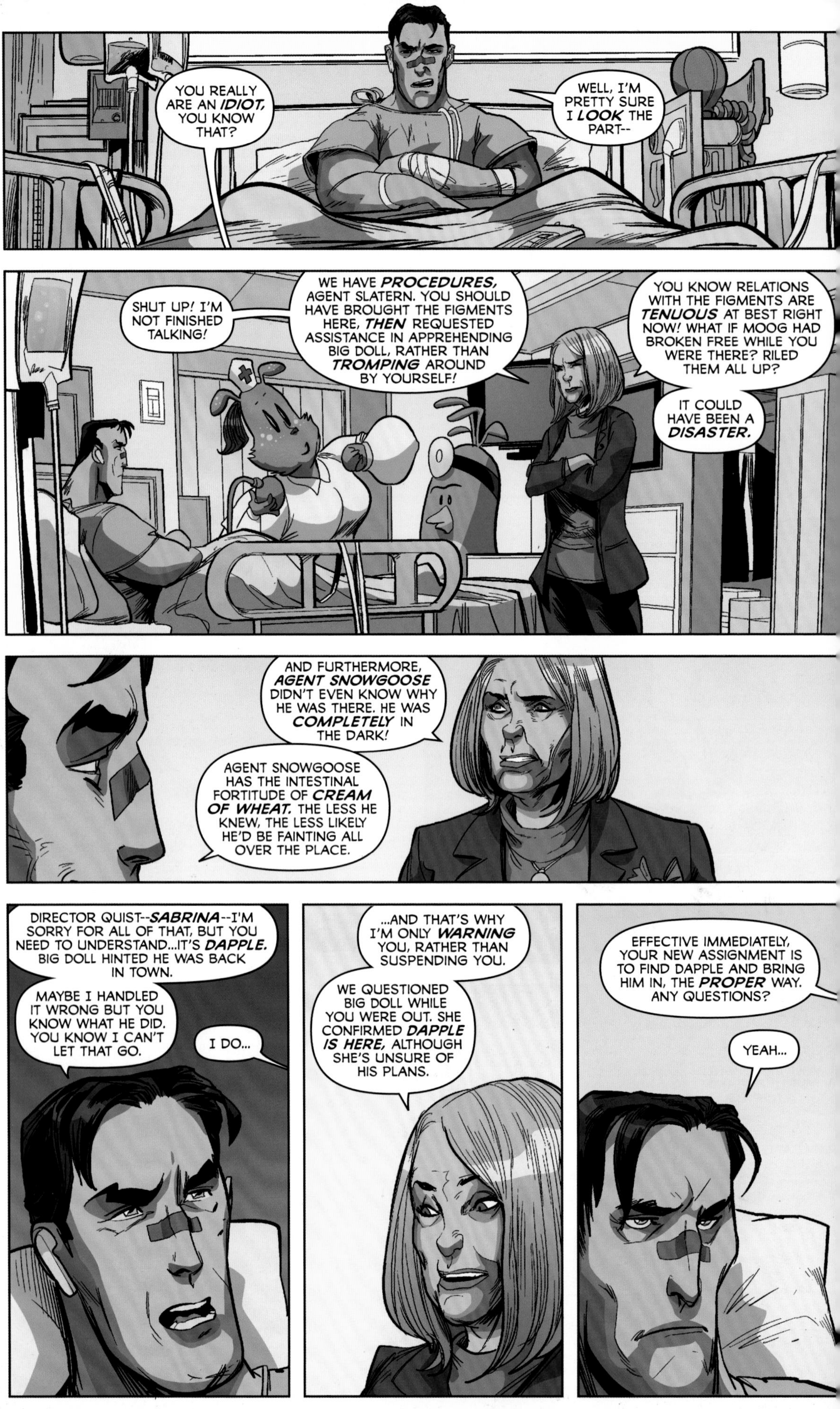
YOU REALLY ARE AN *IDIOT,* YOU KNOW THAT?
WELL, I'M PRETTY SURE I *LOOK* THE PART--
SHUT UP! I'M NOT FINISHED TALKING!
WE HAVE *PROCEDURES,* AGENT SLATERN. YOU SHOULD HAVE BROUGHT THE FIGMENTS HERE, *THEN* REQUESTED ASSISTANCE IN APPREHENDING BIG DOLL, RATHER THAN *TROMPING* AROUND BY YOURSELF!
YOU KNOW RELATIONS WITH THE FIGMENTS ARE *TENUOUS* AT BEST RIGHT NOW! WHAT IF MOOG HAD BROKEN FREE WHILE YOU WERE THERE? RILED THEM ALL UP?
IT COULD HAVE BEEN A *DISASTER.*
AND FURTHERMORE, *AGENT SNOWGOOSE* DIDN'T EVEN KNOW WHY HE WAS THERE. HE WAS *COMPLETELY* IN THE DARK!
AGENT SNOWGOOSE HAS THE INTESTINAL FORTITUDE OF *CREAM OF WHEAT.* THE LESS HE KNEW, THE LESS LIKELY HE'D BE FAINTING ALL OVER THE PLACE.
DIRECTOR QUIST--*SABRINA*--I'M SORRY FOR ALL OF THAT, BUT YOU NEED TO UNDERSTAND...IT'S *DAPPLE.* BIG DOLL HINTED HE WAS BACK IN TOWN.
MAYBE I HANDLED IT WRONG BUT YOU KNOW WHAT HE DID. YOU KNOW I CAN'T LET THAT GO.
I DO...
...AND THAT'S WHY I'M ONLY *WARNING* YOU, RATHER THAN SUSPENDING YOU.
WE QUESTIONED BIG DOLL WHILE YOU WERE OUT. SHE CONFIRMED *DAPPLE IS HERE,* ALTHOUGH SHE'S UNSURE OF HIS PLANS.
EFFECTIVE IMMEDIATELY, YOUR NEW ASSIGNMENT IS TO FIND DAPPLE AND BRING HIM IN, THE *PROPER* WAY. ANY QUESTIONS?
YEAH...

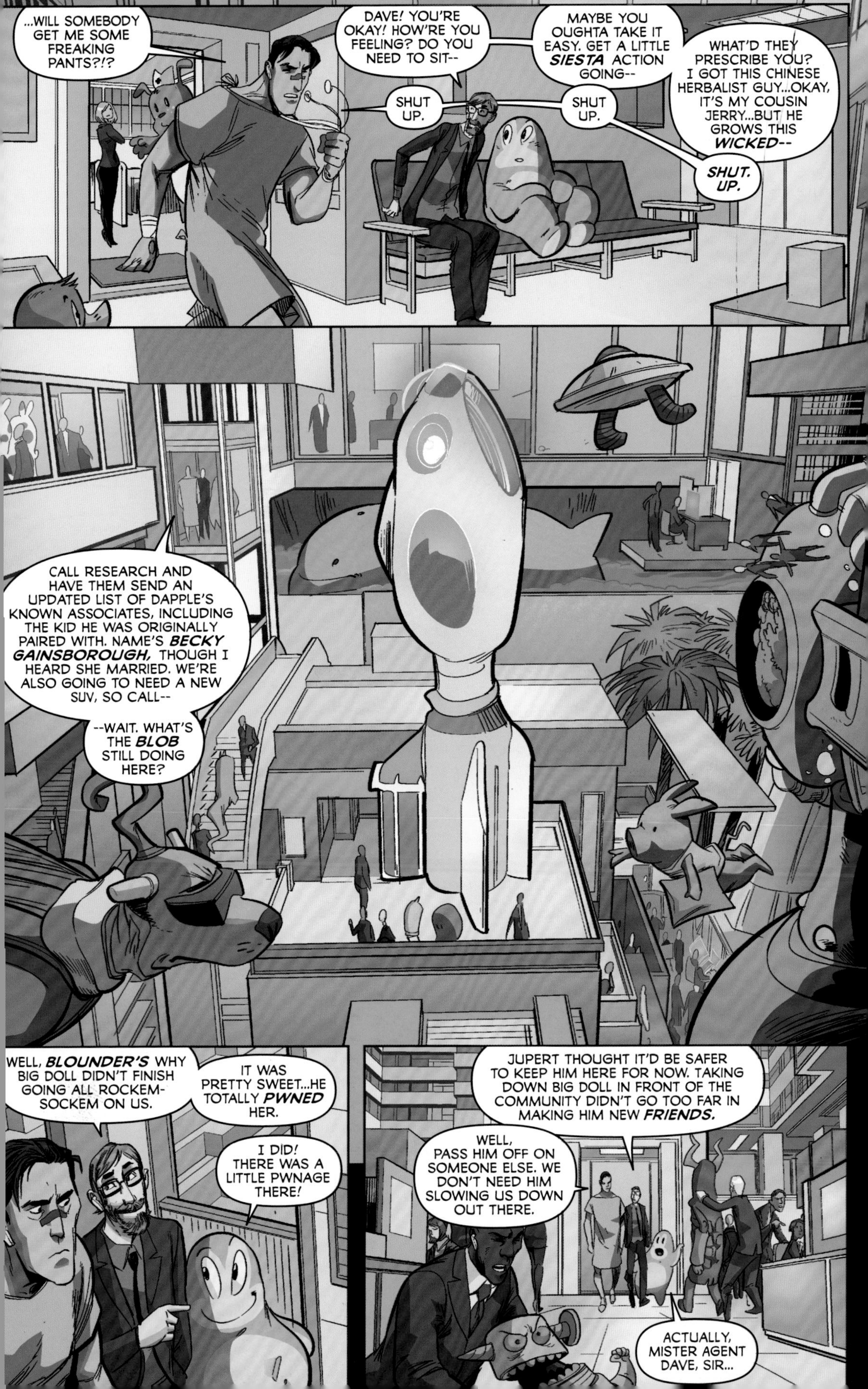
...WILL SOMEBODY GET ME SOME FREAKING PANTS?!?
DAVE! YOU'RE OKAY! HOW'RE YOU FEELING? DO YOU NEED TO SIT--
SHUT UP.
MAYBE YOU OUGHTA TAKE IT EASY. GET A LITTLE SIESTA ACTION GOING--
SHUT UP.
WHAT'D THEY PRESCRIBE YOU? I GOT THIS CHINESE HERBALIST GUY...OKAY, IT'S MY COUSIN JERRY...BUT HE GROWS THIS WICKED--
SHUT. UP.
CALL RESEARCH AND HAVE THEM SEND AN UPDATED LIST OF DAPPLE'S KNOWN ASSOCIATES, INCLUDING THE KID HE WAS ORIGINALLY PAIRED WITH. NAME'S BECKY GAINSBOROUGH, THOUGH I HEARD SHE MARRIED. WE'RE ALSO GOING TO NEED A NEW SUV, SO CALL--
--WAIT. WHAT'S THE BLOB STILL DOING HERE?
WELL, BLOUNDER'S WHY BIG DOLL DIDN'T FINISH GOING ALL ROCKEM-SOCKEM ON US.
IT WAS PRETTY SWEET...HE TOTALLY PWNED HER.
I DID! THERE WAS A LITTLE PWNAGE THERE!
JUPERT THOUGHT IT'D BE SAFER TO KEEP HIM HERE FOR NOW. TAKING DOWN BIG DOLL IN FRONT OF THE COMMUNITY DIDN'T GO TOO FAR IN MAKING HIM NEW FRIENDS.
WELL, PASS HIM OFF ON SOMEONE ELSE. WE DON'T NEED HIM SLOWING US DOWN OUT THERE.
ACTUALLY, MISTER AGENT DAVE, SIR...

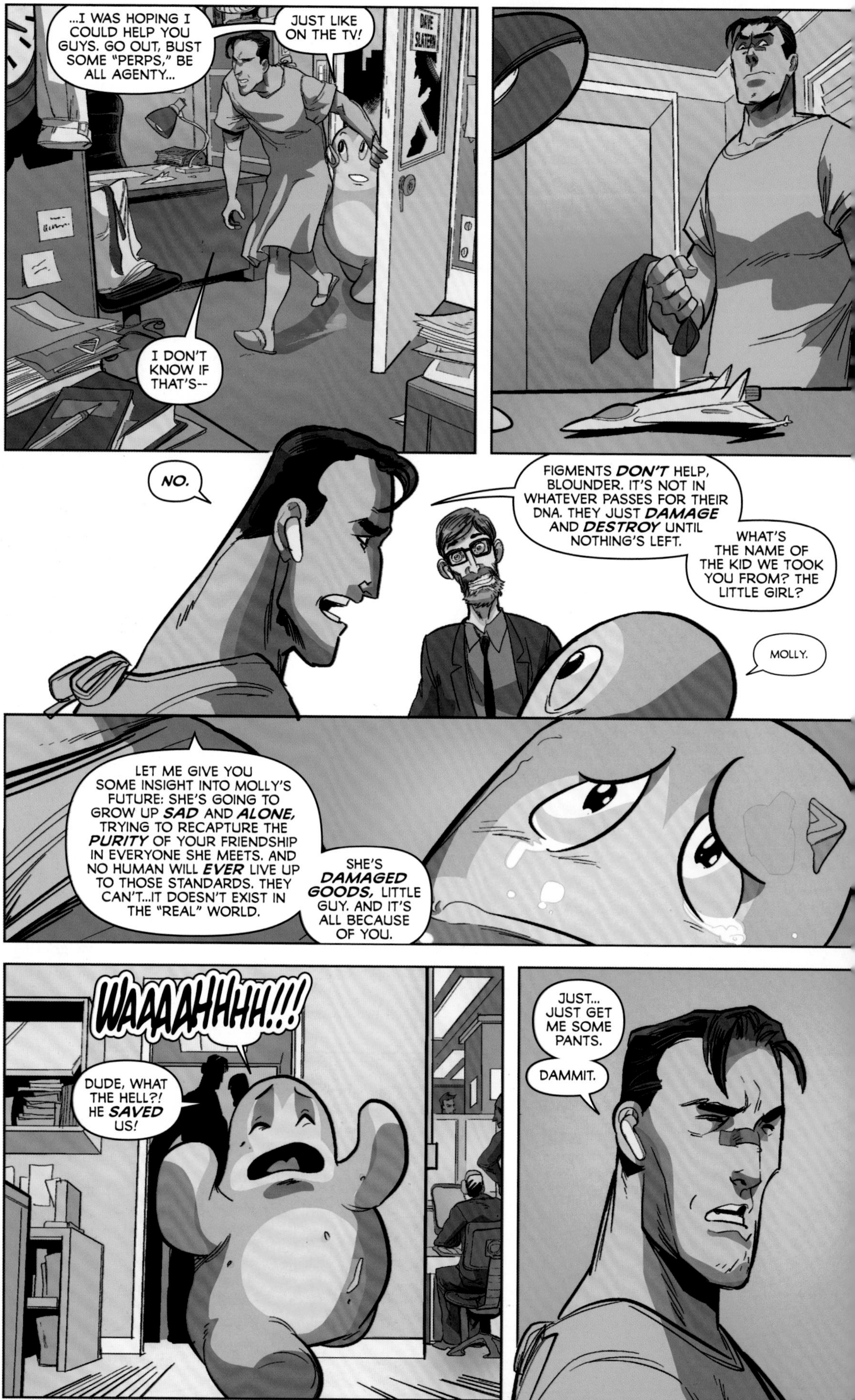
...I WAS HOPING I COULD HELP YOU GUYS. GO OUT, BUST SOME "PERPS," BE ALL AGENTY...
JUST LIKE ON THE TV!
DAVE SLATERN
I DON'T KNOW IF THAT'S--
NO.
FIGMENTS DON'T HELP, BLOUNDER. IT'S NOT IN WHATEVER PASSES FOR THEIR DNA. THEY JUST DAMAGE AND DESTROY UNTIL NOTHING'S LEFT.
WHAT'S THE NAME OF THE KID WE TOOK YOU FROM? THE LITTLE GIRL?
MOLLY.
LET ME GIVE YOU SOME INSIGHT INTO MOLLY'S FUTURE: SHE'S GOING TO GROW UP SAD AND ALONE, TRYING TO RECAPTURE THE PURITY OF YOUR FRIENDSHIP IN EVERYONE SHE MEETS. AND NO HUMAN WILL EVER LIVE UP TO THOSE STANDARDS. THEY CAN'T...IT DOESN'T EXIST IN THE "REAL" WORLD.
SHE'S DAMAGED GOODS, LITTLE GUY. AND IT'S ALL BECAUSE OF YOU.
WAAAAHHHH!!!
DUDE, WHAT THE HELL?! HE SAVED US!
JUST... JUST GET ME SOME PANTS.
DAMMIT.

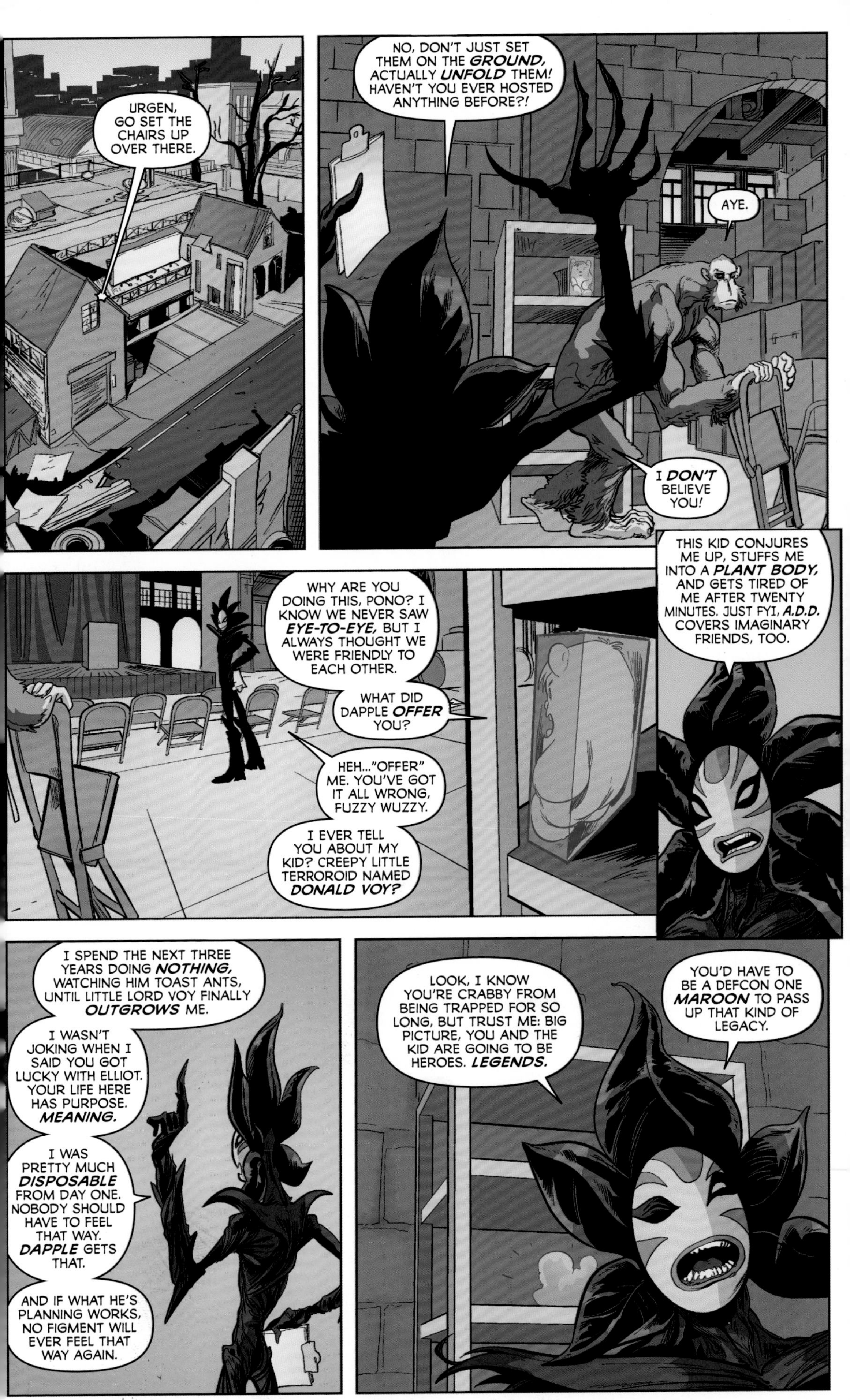
URGEN, GO SET THE CHAIRS UP OVER THERE.
NO, DON'T JUST SET THEM ON THE GROUND, ACTUALLY UNFOLD THEM! HAVEN'T YOU EVER HOSTED ANYTHING BEFORE?!
AYE.
I DON'T BELIEVE YOU!
WHY ARE YOU DOING THIS, PONO? I KNOW WE NEVER SAW EYE-TO-EYE, BUT I ALWAYS THOUGHT WE WERE FRIENDLY TO EACH OTHER.
WHAT DID DAPPLE OFFER YOU?
HEH..."OFFER" ME. YOU'VE GOT IT ALL WRONG, FUZZY WUZZY.
I EVER TELL YOU ABOUT MY KID? CREEPY LITTLE TERROROID NAMED DONALD VOY?
THIS KID CONJURES ME UP, STUFFS ME INTO A PLANT BODY, AND GETS TIRED OF ME AFTER TWENTY MINUTES. JUST FYI, A.D.D. COVERS IMAGINARY FRIENDS, TOO.
I SPEND THE NEXT THREE YEARS DOING NOTHING, WATCHING HIM TOAST ANTS, UNTIL LITTLE LORD VOY FINALLY OUTGROWS ME.
I WASN'T JOKING WHEN I SAID YOU GOT LUCKY WITH ELLIOT. YOUR LIFE HERE HAS PURPOSE. MEANING.
I WAS PRETTY MUCH DISPOSABLE FROM DAY ONE. NOBODY SHOULD HAVE TO FEEL THAT WAY. DAPPLE GETS THAT.
AND IF WHAT HE'S PLANNING WORKS, NO FIGMENT WILL EVER FEEL THAT WAY AGAIN.
LOOK, I KNOW YOU'RE CRABBY FROM BEING TRAPPED FOR SO LONG, BUT TRUST ME: BIG PICTURE, YOU AND THE KID ARE GOING TO BE HEROES. LEGENDS.
YOU'D HAVE TO BE A DEFCON ONE MAROON TO PASS UP THAT KIND OF LEGACY.

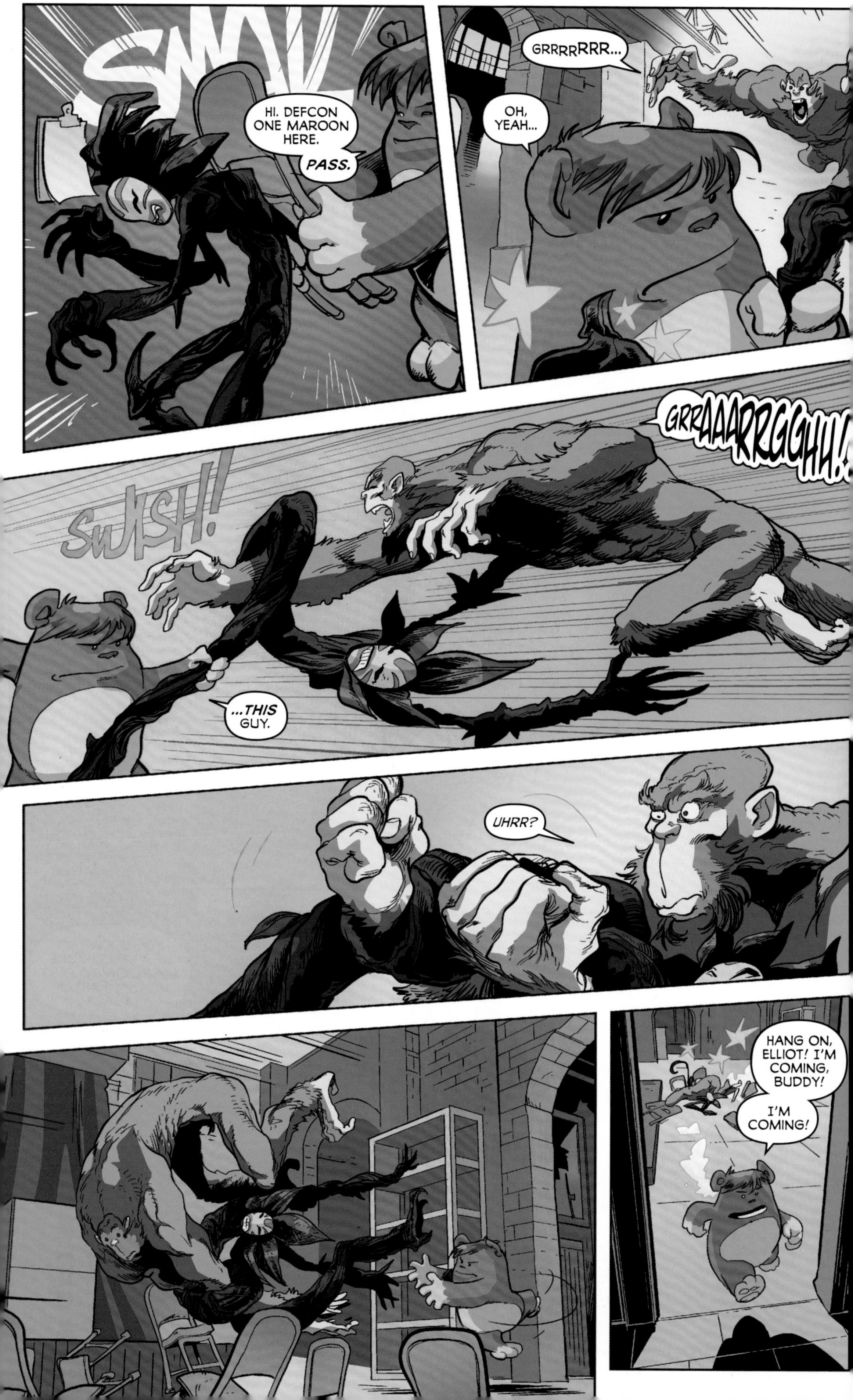
SMAK
HI. DEFCON ONE MAROON HERE.
PASS.
GRRRRRRR...
OH, YEAH...
GRRAAARRGGHH!
SWISH!
...THIS GUY.
UHRR?
HANG ON, ELLIOT! I'M COMING, BUDDY!
I'M COMING!

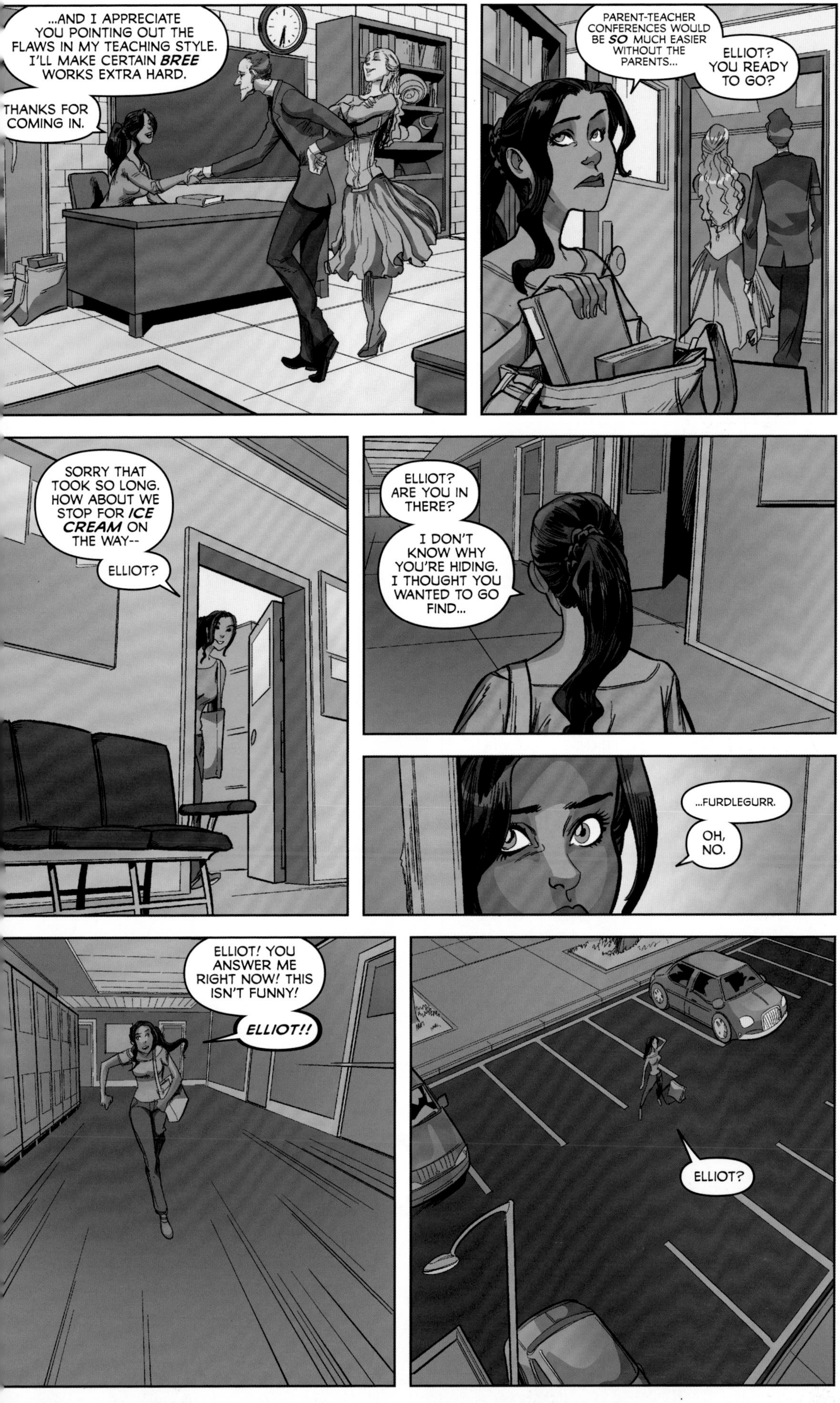
...AND I APPRECIATE YOU POINTING OUT THE FLAWS IN MY TEACHING STYLE. I'LL MAKE CERTAIN BREE WORKS EXTRA HARD.
THANKS FOR COMING IN.
PARENT-TEACHER CONFERENCES WOULD BE SO MUCH EASIER WITHOUT THE PARENTS...
ELLIOT? YOU READY TO GO?
SORRY THAT TOOK SO LONG. HOW ABOUT WE STOP FOR ICE CREAM ON THE WAY--
ELLIOT?
ELLIOT? ARE YOU IN THERE?
I DON'T KNOW WHY YOU'RE HIDING. I THOUGHT YOU WANTED TO GO FIND...
...FURDLEGURR.
OH, NO.
ELLIOT! YOU ANSWER ME RIGHT NOW! THIS ISN'T FUNNY!
ELLIOT!!
ELLIOT?

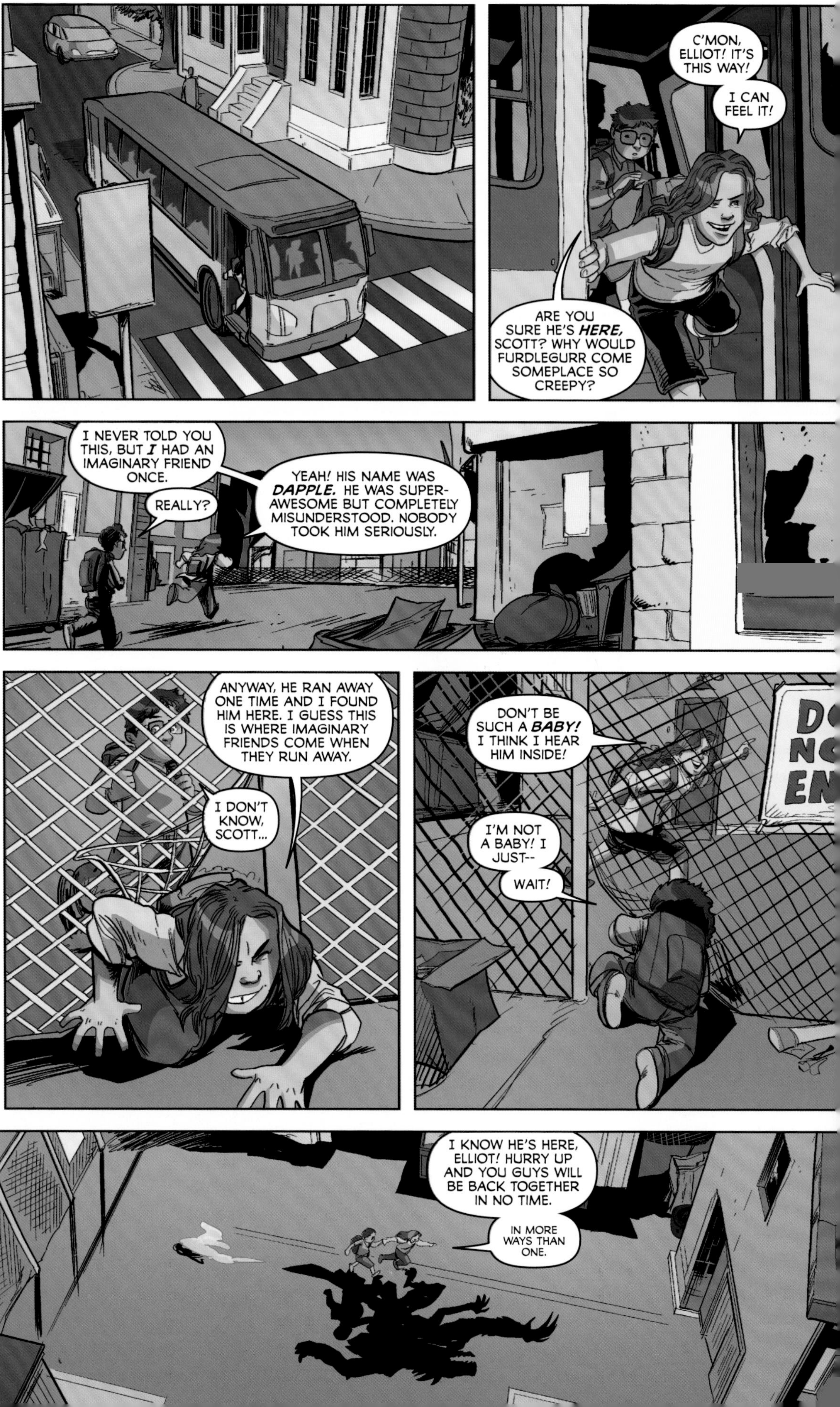
C'MON, ELLIOT! IT'S THIS WAY!
I CAN FEEL IT!
ARE YOU SURE HE'S HERE, SCOTT? WHY WOULD FURDLEGURR COME SOMEPLACE SO CREEPY?
I NEVER TOLD YOU THIS, BUT I HAD AN IMAGINARY FRIEND ONCE.
REALLY?
YEAH! HIS NAME WAS DAPPLE. HE WAS SUPER-AWESOME BUT COMPLETELY MISUNDERSTOOD. NOBODY TOOK HIM SERIOUSLY.
ANYWAY, HE RAN AWAY ONE TIME AND I FOUND HIM HERE. I GUESS THIS IS WHERE IMAGINARY FRIENDS COME WHEN THEY RUN AWAY.
I DON'T KNOW, SCOTT...
DON'T BE SUCH A BABY! I THINK I HEAR HIM INSIDE!
I'M NOT A BABY! I JUST--
WAIT!
I KNOW HE'S HERE, ELLIOT! HURRY UP AND YOU GUYS WILL BE BACK TOGETHER IN NO TIME.
IN MORE WAYS THAN ONE.

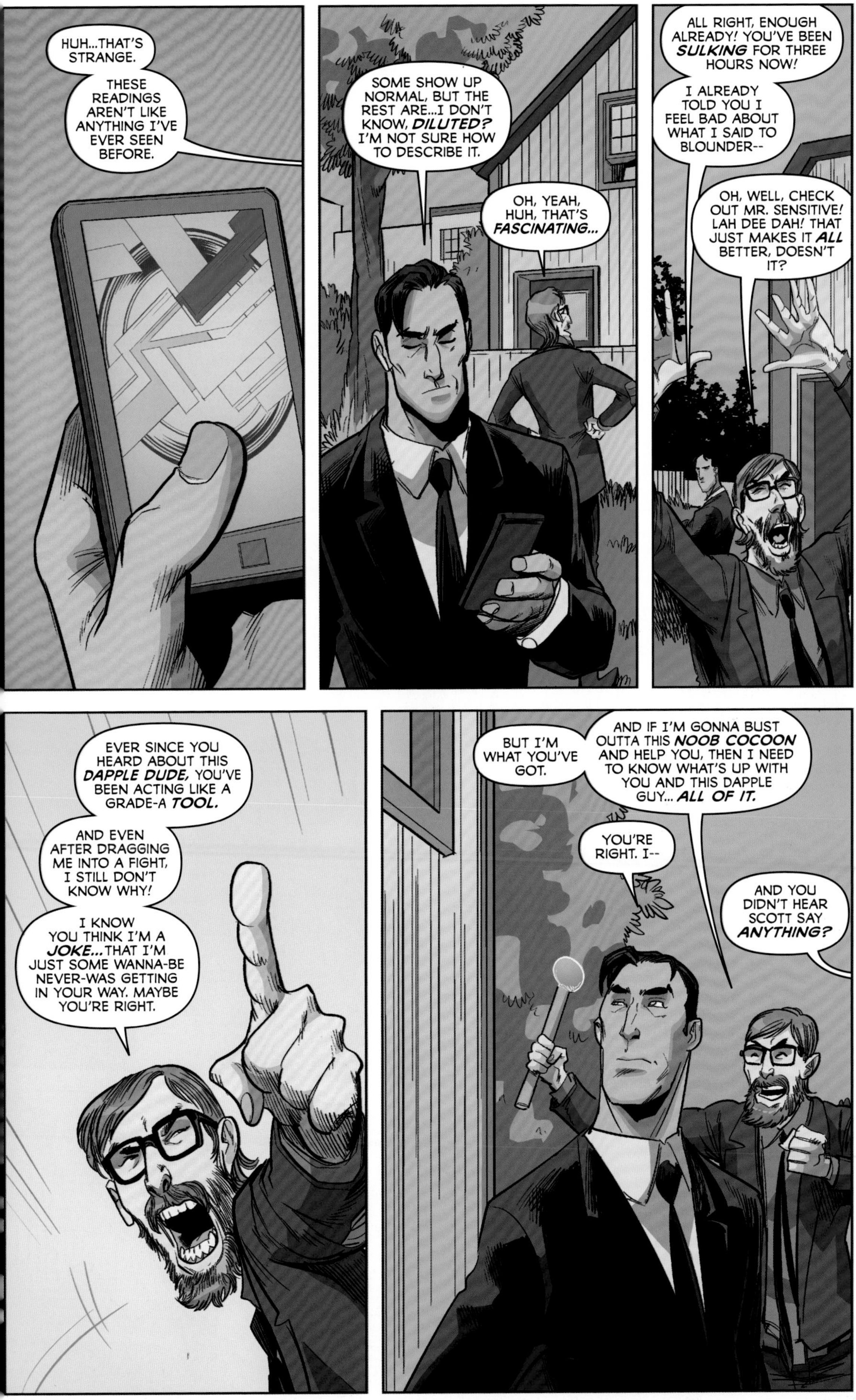
HUH...THAT'S STRANGE.
THESE READINGS AREN'T LIKE ANYTHING I'VE EVER SEEN BEFORE.
SOME SHOW UP NORMAL, BUT THE REST ARE...I DON'T KNOW, *DILUTED?* I'M NOT SURE HOW TO DESCRIBE IT.
OH, YEAH, HUH, THAT'S *FASCINATING...*
ALL RIGHT, ENOUGH ALREADY! YOU'VE BEEN *SULKING* FOR THREE HOURS NOW!
I ALREADY TOLD YOU I FEEL BAD ABOUT WHAT I SAID TO BLOUNDER--
OH, WELL, CHECK OUT MR. SENSITIVE! LAH DEE DAH! THAT JUST MAKES IT *ALL* BETTER, DOESN'T IT?
EVER SINCE YOU HEARD ABOUT THIS *DAPPLE DUDE,* YOU'VE BEEN ACTING LIKE A GRADE-A *TOOL.*
AND EVEN AFTER DRAGGING ME INTO A FIGHT, I STILL DON'T KNOW WHY!
I KNOW YOU THINK I'M A *JOKE...*THAT I'M JUST SOME WANNA-BE NEVER-WAS GETTING IN YOUR WAY. MAYBE YOU'RE RIGHT.
BUT I'M WHAT YOU'VE GOT.
AND IF I'M GONNA BUST OUTTA THIS *NOOB COCOON* AND HELP YOU, THEN I NEED TO KNOW WHAT'S UP WITH YOU AND THIS DAPPLE GUY... *ALL OF IT.*
YOU'RE RIGHT. I--
AND YOU DIDN'T HEAR SCOTT SAY *ANYTHING?*

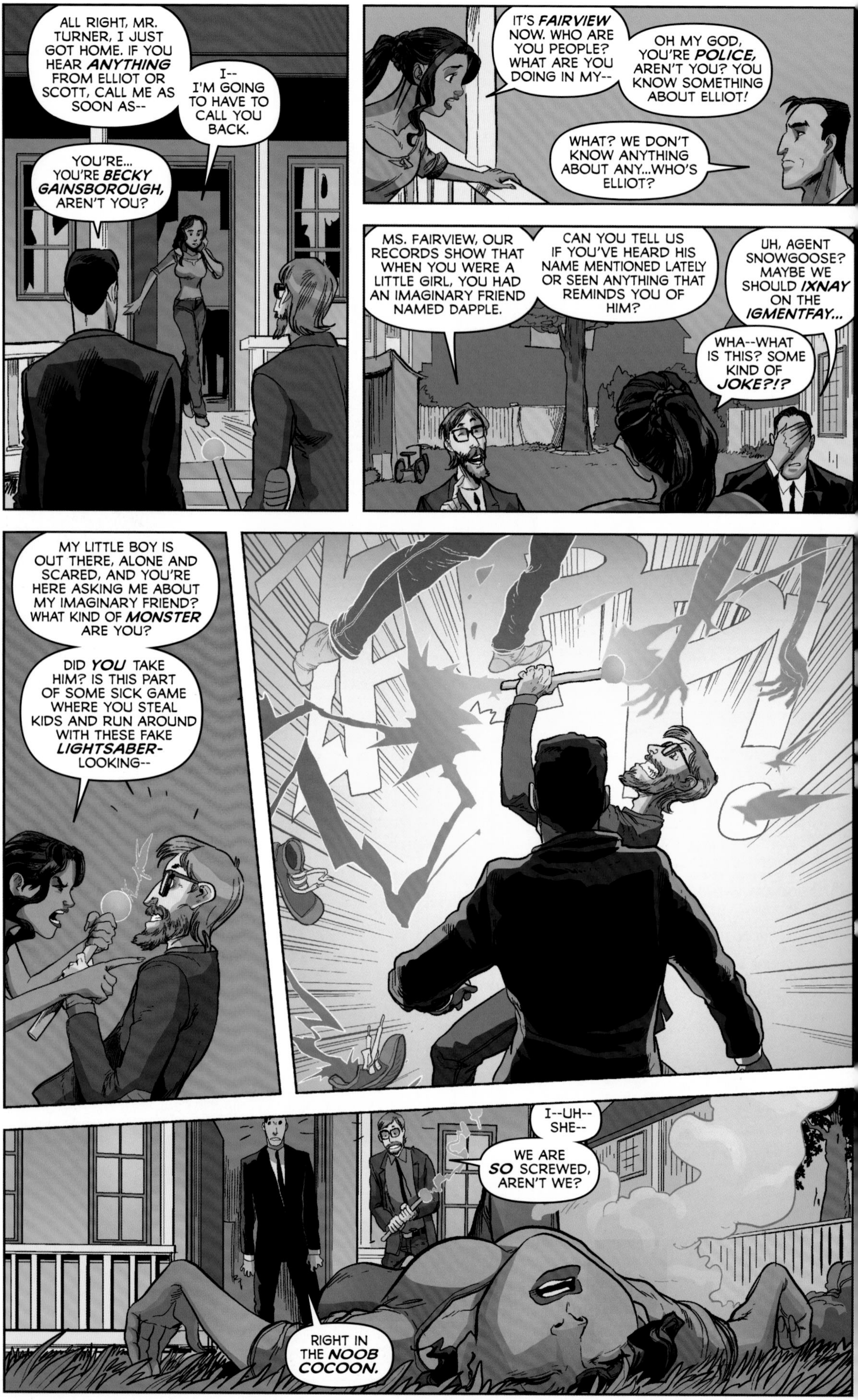

ALL RIGHT, MR. TURNER, I JUST GOT HOME. IF YOU HEAR ANYTHING FROM ELLIOT OR SCOTT, CALL ME AS SOON AS--
I-- I'M GOING TO HAVE TO CALL YOU BACK.
YOU'RE... YOU'RE BECKY GAINSBOROUGH, AREN'T YOU?
IT'S FAIRVIEW NOW. WHO ARE YOU PEOPLE? WHAT ARE YOU DOING IN MY--
OH MY GOD, YOU'RE POLICE, AREN'T YOU? YOU KNOW SOMETHING ABOUT ELLIOT!
WHAT? WE DON'T KNOW ANYTHING ABOUT ANY...WHO'S ELLIOT?
MS. FAIRVIEW, OUR RECORDS SHOW THAT WHEN YOU WERE A LITTLE GIRL, YOU HAD AN IMAGINARY FRIEND NAMED DAPPLE.
CAN YOU TELL US IF YOU'VE HEARD HIS NAME MENTIONED LATELY OR SEEN ANYTHING THAT REMINDS YOU OF HIM?
UH, AGENT SNOWGOOSE? MAYBE WE SHOULD IXNAY ON THE IGMENTFAY...
WHA--WHAT IS THIS? SOME KIND OF JOKE?!?
MY LITTLE BOY IS OUT THERE, ALONE AND SCARED, AND YOU'RE HERE ASKING ME ABOUT MY IMAGINARY FRIEND? WHAT KIND OF MONSTER ARE YOU?
DID YOU TAKE HIM? IS THIS PART OF SOME SICK GAME WHERE YOU STEAL KIDS AND RUN AROUND WITH THESE FAKE LIGHTSABER-LOOKING--
I--UH-- SHE--
WE ARE SO SCREWED, AREN'T WE?
RIGHT IN THE NOOB COCOON.

SNIFF!

STUPID MISTER AGENT DAVE...

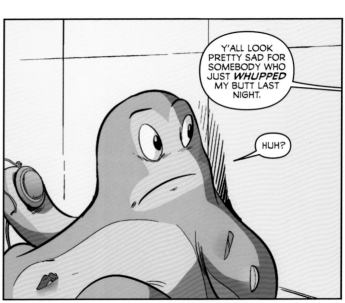

Y'ALL LOOK PRETTY SAD FOR SOMEBODY WHO JUST *WHUPPED* MY BUTT LAST NIGHT.

HUH?

I WOULDN'T LET WHAT THAT AGENT SAID GET YOU DOWN, SMALL FRY. WHAT I HEAR, HE'S GOT MORE ISSUES THAN *NATIONAL GEOGRAPHIC.*

HOW DO YOU--?

COUPLE FIGMENTS WERE GETTIN' PROCESSED UPSTAIRS...SAW THE WHOLE THING. AND I DON'T CARE IF YOU'RE HUMAN OR FIGMENT, FOLKS *LOVE* TALKIN' GOSSIP.

STUPID REMOTE! NO AM MAKE MOOG GET UP TO CHANGE CHANNEL!

COURSE, MISTER *HIGH-AND-MIGHTY* AGENT'S ATTITUDE AIN'T UNIQUE: LOTTA PEOPLE FEEL SAME AS HE DOES ABOUT US TYPES.

THAT'S WHAT BROUGHT ME OUT HERE FROM OKLAHOMA; THIS DAPPLE CHARACTER SAYS HE'S GOT A PLAN TO PUT US ON THE SAME LEVEL.

ACCORDING TO HIM, YOU'D BE ABLE TO TALK TO *ANYBODY.*

HELL, YOU MIGHT EVEN BE ABLE TO SEE THAT LITTLE GIRL OF YOURS AGAIN.

TELL ME MORE!

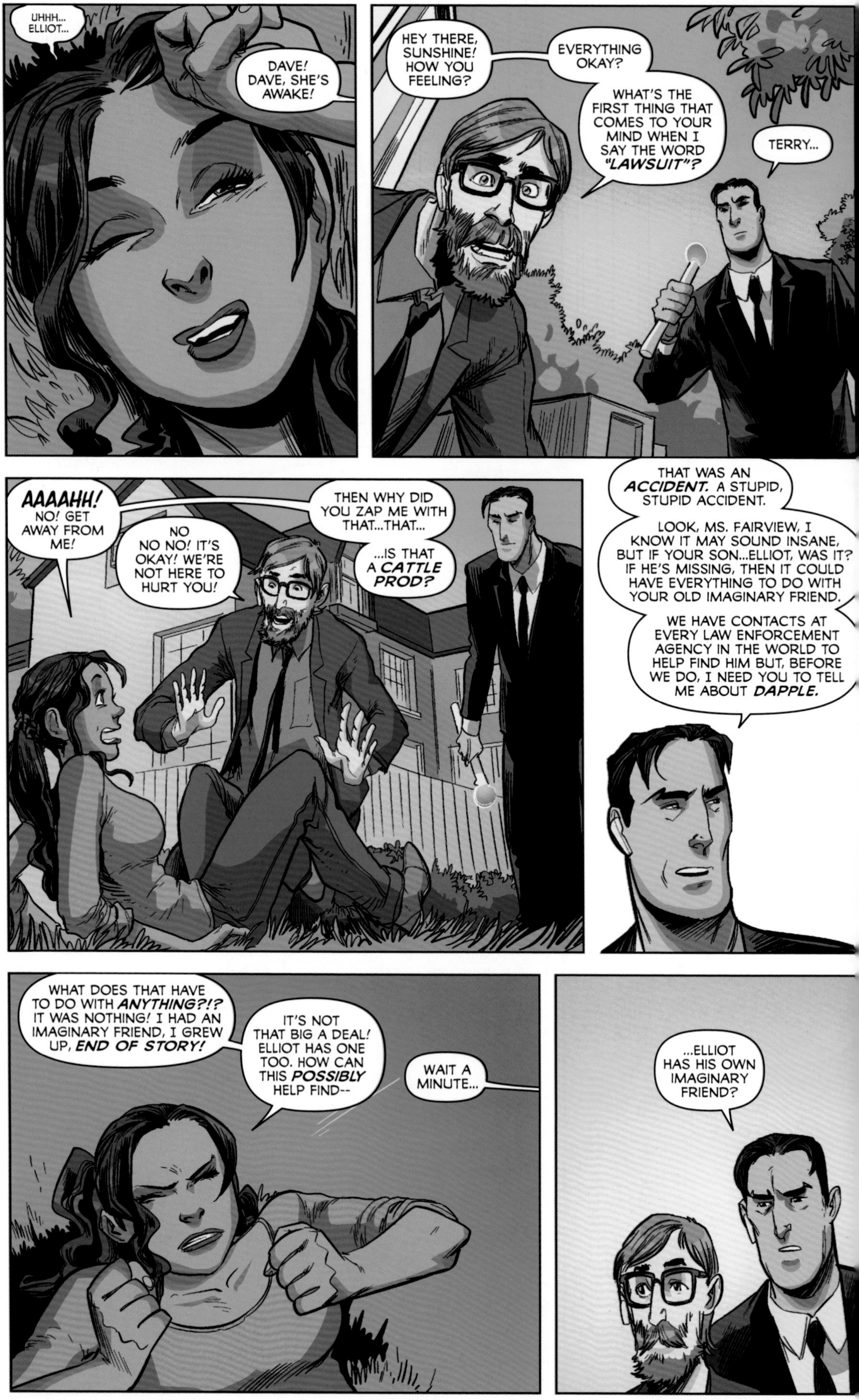
UHHH... ELLIOT...
DAVE! DAVE, SHE'S AWAKE!
HEY THERE, SUNSHINE! HOW YOU FEELING?
EVERYTHING OKAY?
WHAT'S THE FIRST THING THAT COMES TO YOUR MIND WHEN I SAY THE WORD "LAWSUIT"?
TERRY...
AAAAHH! NO! GET AWAY FROM ME!
NO NO NO! IT'S OKAY! WE'RE NOT HERE TO HURT YOU!
THEN WHY DID YOU ZAP ME WITH THAT...THAT...
...IS THAT A CATTLE PROD?
THAT WAS AN ACCIDENT. A STUPID, STUPID ACCIDENT.
LOOK, MS. FAIRVIEW, I KNOW IT MAY SOUND INSANE, BUT IF YOUR SON...ELLIOT, WAS IT? IF HE'S MISSING, THEN IT COULD HAVE EVERYTHING TO DO WITH YOUR OLD IMAGINARY FRIEND.
WE HAVE CONTACTS AT EVERY LAW ENFORCEMENT AGENCY IN THE WORLD TO HELP FIND HIM BUT, BEFORE WE DO, I NEED YOU TO TELL ME ABOUT DAPPLE.
WHAT DOES THAT HAVE TO DO WITH ANYTHING?!? IT WAS NOTHING! I HAD AN IMAGINARY FRIEND, I GREW UP, END OF STORY!
IT'S NOT THAT BIG A DEAL! ELLIOT HAS ONE TOO. HOW CAN THIS POSSIBLY HELP FIND--
WAIT A MINUTE...
...ELLIOT HAS HIS OWN IMAGINARY FRIEND?

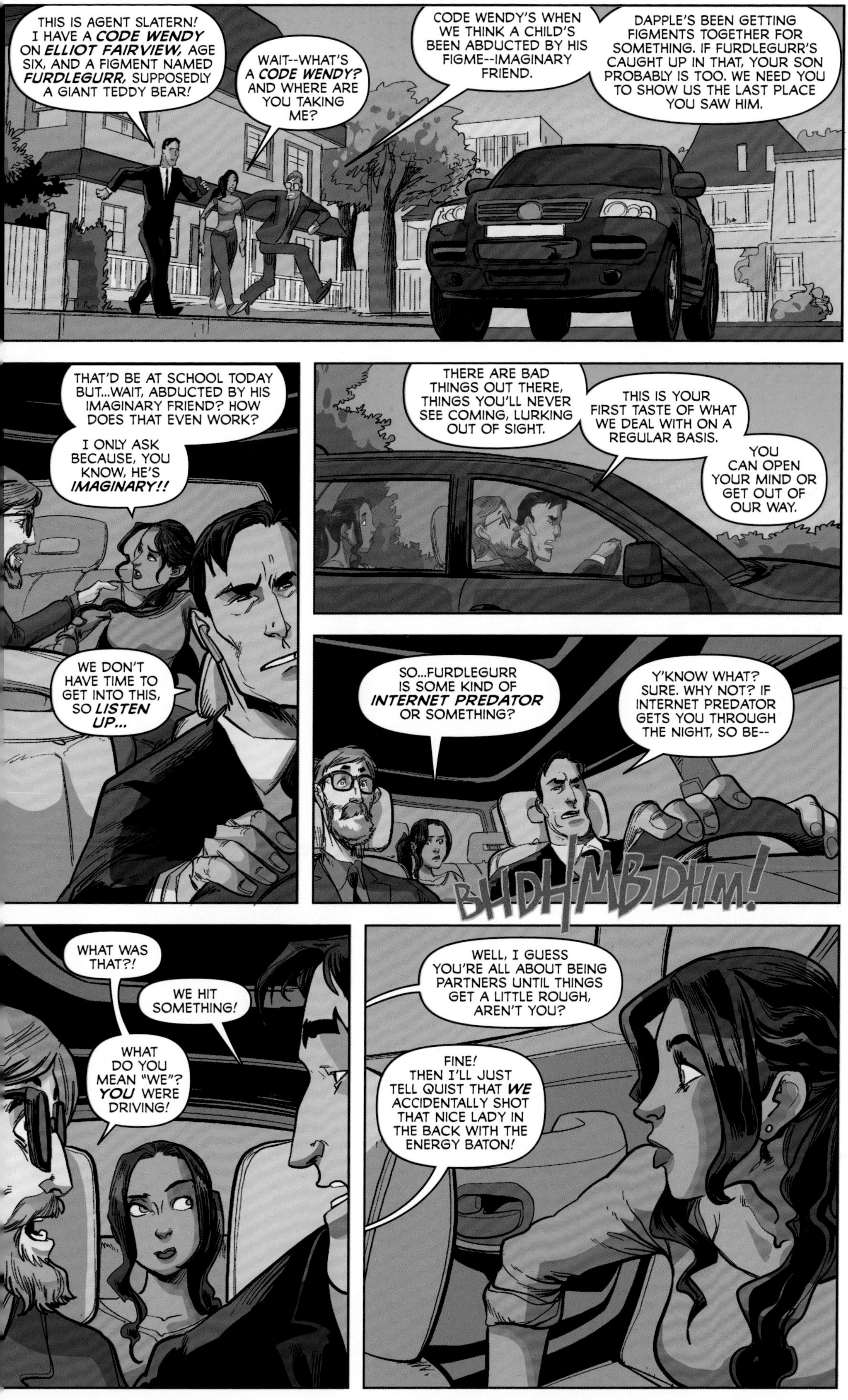

THIS IS AGENT SLATERN! I HAVE A CODE WENDY ON ELLIOT FAIRVIEW, AGE SIX, AND A FIGMENT NAMED FURDLEGURR, SUPPOSEDLY A GIANT TEDDY BEAR!
WAIT--WHAT'S A CODE WENDY? AND WHERE ARE YOU TAKING ME?
CODE WENDY'S WHEN WE THINK A CHILD'S BEEN ABDUCTED BY HIS FIGME--IMAGINARY FRIEND.
DAPPLE'S BEEN GETTING FIGMENTS TOGETHER FOR SOMETHING. IF FURDLEGURR'S CAUGHT UP IN THAT, YOUR SON PROBABLY IS TOO. WE NEED YOU TO SHOW US THE LAST PLACE YOU SAW HIM.
THAT'D BE AT SCHOOL TODAY BUT...WAIT, ABDUCTED BY HIS IMAGINARY FRIEND? HOW DOES THAT EVEN WORK?
I ONLY ASK BECAUSE, YOU KNOW, HE'S IMAGINARY!!
WE DON'T HAVE TIME TO GET INTO THIS, SO LISTEN UP...
THERE ARE BAD THINGS OUT THERE, THINGS YOU'LL NEVER SEE COMING, LURKING OUT OF SIGHT.
THIS IS YOUR FIRST TASTE OF WHAT WE DEAL WITH ON A REGULAR BASIS.
YOU CAN OPEN YOUR MIND OR GET OUT OF OUR WAY.
SO...FURDLEGURR IS SOME KIND OF INTERNET PREDATOR OR SOMETHING?
Y'KNOW WHAT? SURE. WHY NOT? IF INTERNET PREDATOR GETS YOU THROUGH THE NIGHT, SO BE--
BHDHMBDHM!
WHAT WAS THAT?!
WE HIT SOMETHING!
WHAT DO YOU MEAN "WE"? YOU WERE DRIVING!
WELL, I GUESS YOU'RE ALL ABOUT BEING PARTNERS UNTIL THINGS GET A LITTLE ROUGH, AREN'T YOU?
FINE! THEN I'LL JUST TELL QUIST THAT WE ACCIDENTALLY SHOT THAT NICE LADY IN THE BACK WITH THE ENERGY BATON!

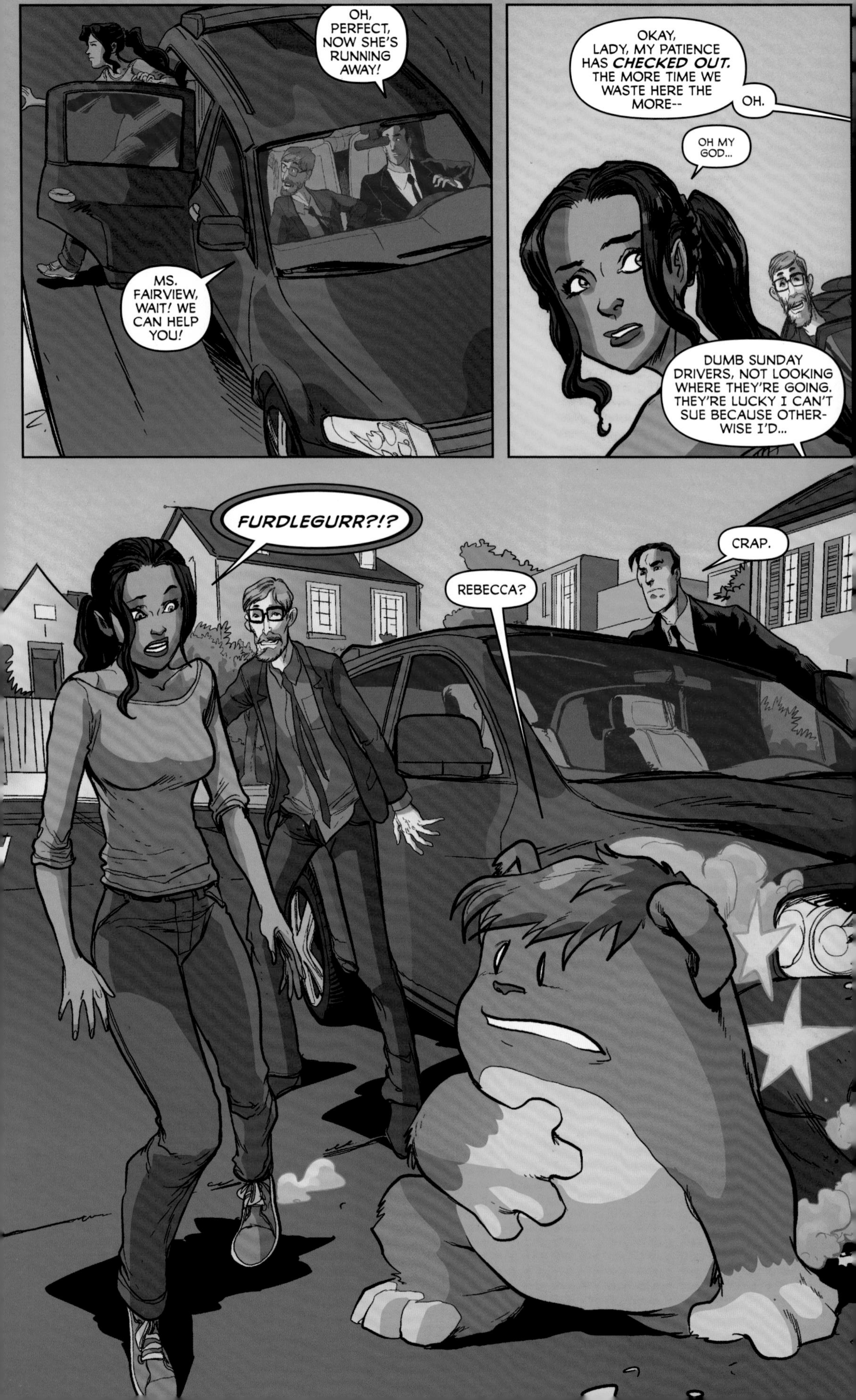
OH, PERFECT, NOW SHE'S RUNNING AWAY!
MS. FAIRVIEW, WAIT! WE CAN HELP YOU!
OKAY, LADY, MY PATIENCE HAS *CHECKED OUT.* THE MORE TIME WE WASTE HERE THE MORE--
OH.
OH MY GOD...
DUMB SUNDAY DRIVERS, NOT LOOKING WHERE THEY'RE GOING. THEY'RE LUCKY I CAN'T SUE BECAUSE OTHER-WISE I'D...
FURDLEGURR?!?
REBECCA?
CRAP.

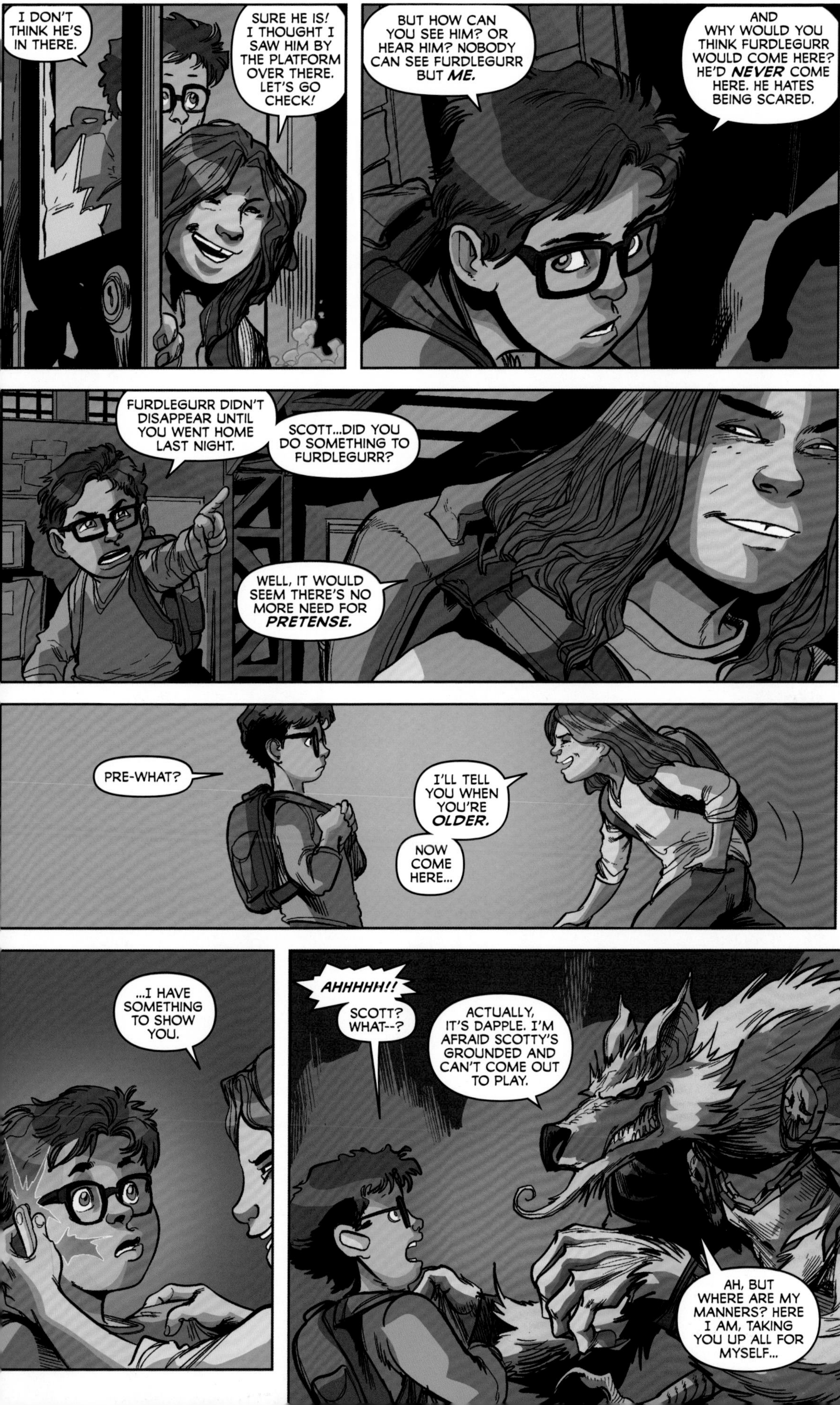
I DON'T THINK HE'S IN THERE.
SURE HE IS! I THOUGHT I SAW HIM BY THE PLATFORM OVER THERE. LET'S GO CHECK!
BUT HOW CAN YOU SEE HIM? OR HEAR HIM? NOBODY CAN SEE FURDLEGURR BUT *ME.*
AND WHY WOULD YOU THINK FURDLEGURR WOULD COME HERE? HE'D ***NEVER*** COME HERE. HE HATES BEING SCARED.
FURDLEGURR DIDN'T DISAPPEAR UNTIL YOU WENT HOME LAST NIGHT.
SCOTT...DID YOU DO SOMETHING TO FURDLEGURR?
WELL, IT WOULD SEEM THERE'S NO MORE NEED FOR ***PRETENSE.***
PRE-WHAT?
I'LL TELL YOU WHEN YOU'RE ***OLDER.***
NOW COME HERE...
...I HAVE SOMETHING TO SHOW YOU.
AHHHHH!!
SCOTT? WHAT--?
ACTUALLY, IT'S DAPPLE. I'M AFRAID SCOTTY'S GROUNDED AND CAN'T COME OUT TO PLAY.
AH, BUT WHERE ARE MY MANNERS? HERE I AM, TAKING YOU UP ALL FOR MYSELF...

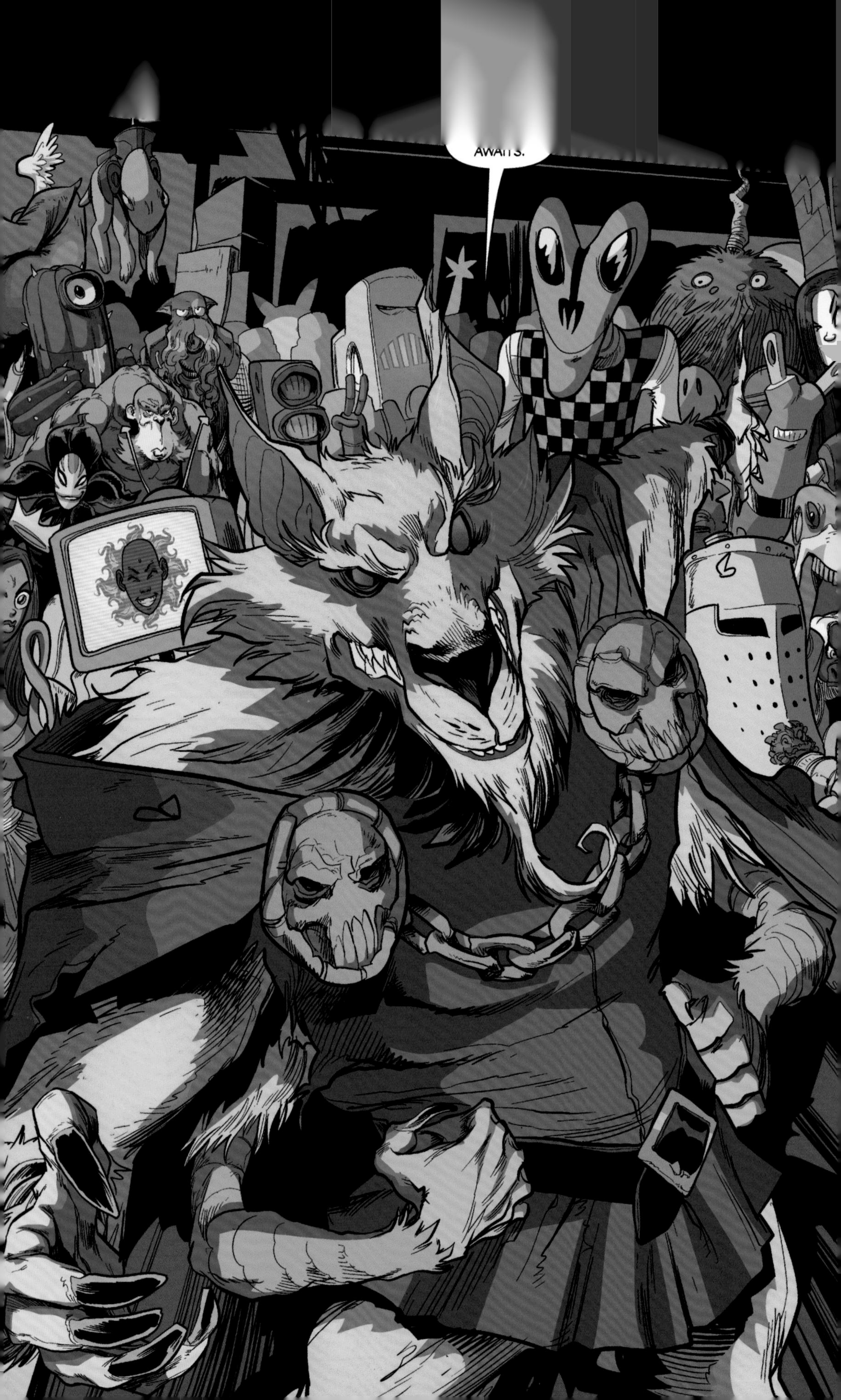

AWAITS.

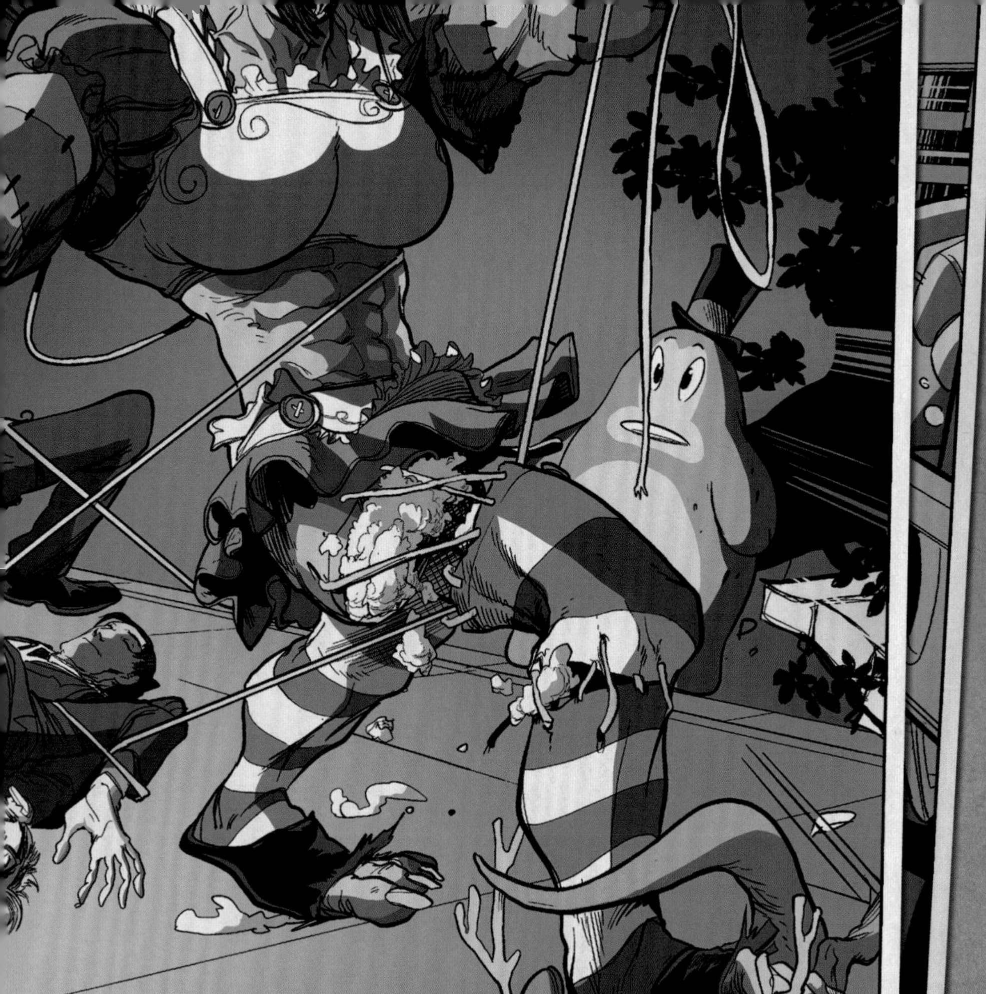

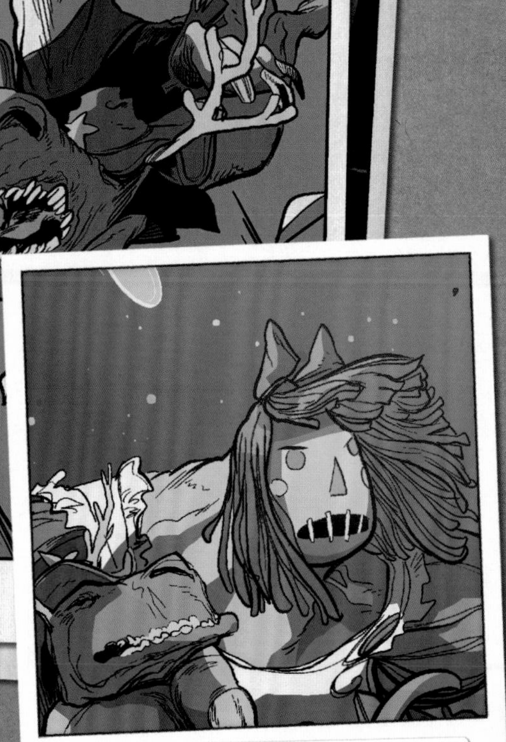
NAME: BIG DOLL ASSIGNED CHILD: ANNIE
CURRENT STATUS: APPREHENDED

ELD MANUAL

REVISED EDITION NO. 12-D

PROPERTY OF: DIRECTOR QUIST

AGENT NO.: ST-468370-146

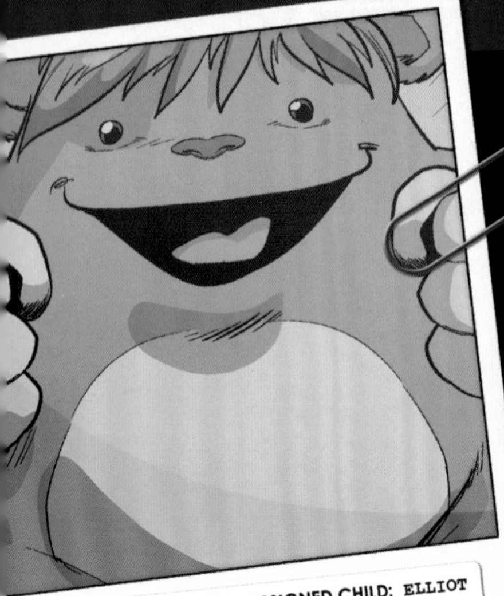

NAME: FURDLEGURR ASSIGNED CHILD: ELLIOT

CURRENT STATUS: RETURNED

POST-EVENT RECON:

- **ELLIOT FAIRVIEW** LEFT SCHOOL WITH BEST FRIEND **SCOTT KOWALKSI** TO FIND HIS MISSING FIGMENT, **FURDLEGURR. REBECCA FAIRVIEW** SEARCHED FOR HER LOST CHILD UPON HIS DISAPPEARANCE.
- FURDLEGURR, HELD CAPTIVE BY HENCHMEN **PONO** AND **URGEN MACGURGEN,** STAGED A DARING ESCAPE FROM **DAPPLE'S** WAREHOUSE, DETERMINED TO RETURN TO ELLIOT.
- DIRECTOR **SABRINA QUIST** ASSIGNED DAPPLE'S CAPTURE TO AGENTS **SLATERN** AND **SNOWGOOSE.**
- AFTER A PAINFUL ALTERCATION WITH SLATEF RETREATED TO THE I.M.A.G.I.N.E. DETENTION THE IMPRISONED **BIG DOLL** TOLD HIM OF DAPI
- WHEN REBECCA FOUND SLATERN AND SNOWGOOS THROUGH HER BACKYARD, SHE WAS ACCIDENTALI SNOWGOOSE'S I.M.A.G.I.N.E. DEVICE.
- AFTER REALIZING THAT DAPPLE WAS REBECCA' FRIEND, THE AGENTS CRASHED INTO FURDL THEIR VEHICLE. DURING THE RESULTING CHA REVEALED THAT REBECCA COULD NOW SEE FIGMI
- SCOTT LED ELLIOT TO THE ABANDONED WAREHC HE REVEALED HIMSELF TO BE DAPPLE, AND ON DISPLAY FOR A SMALL ARMY OF FIGMENTS.

REPORT CONTINUED IN CASE NC

CASE FILE REFERENCE IMAGE: 6335

CHAPTER THREE

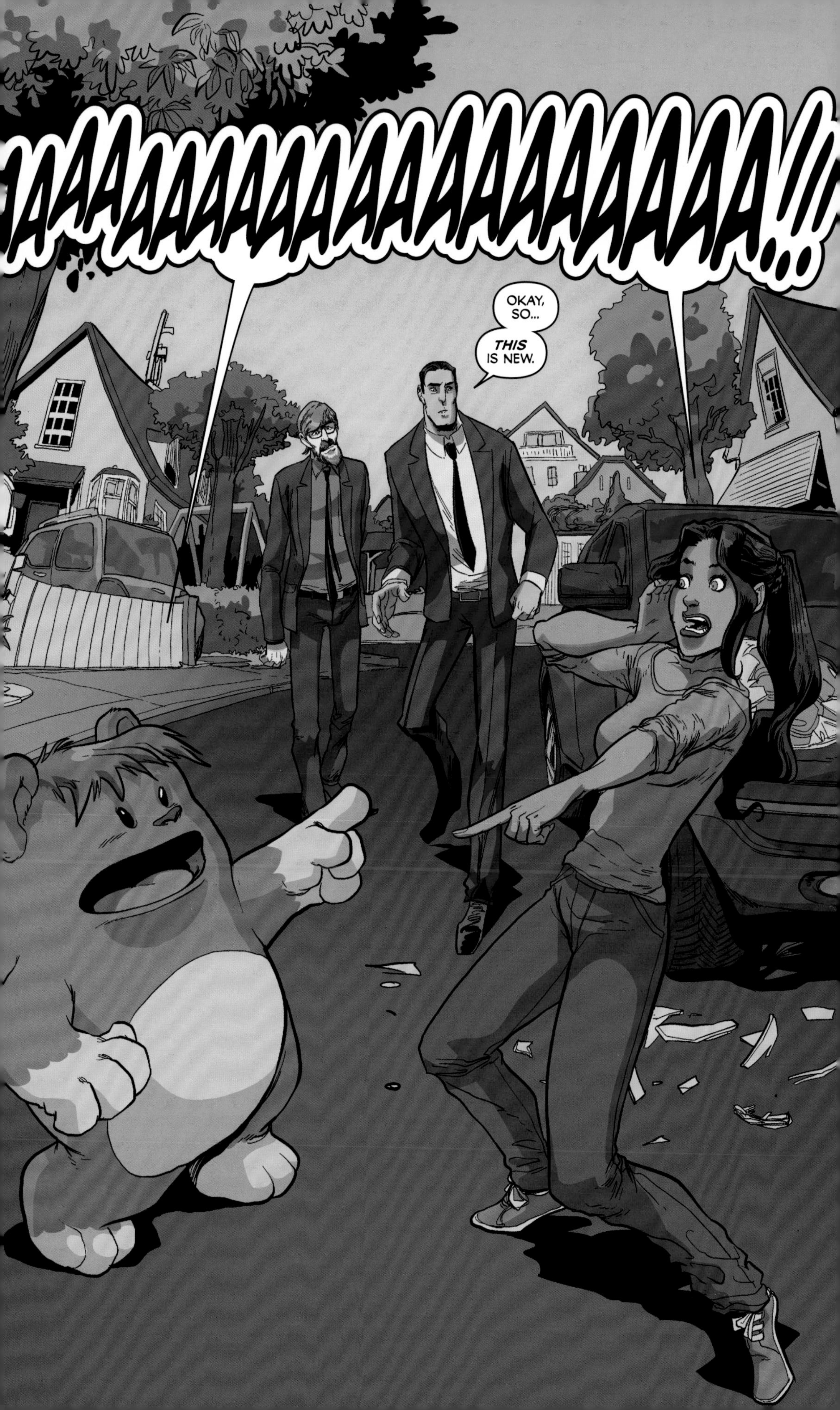
AAAAAAAAAAAAAAAAAAAA!!
OKAY, SO...
THIS IS NEW.

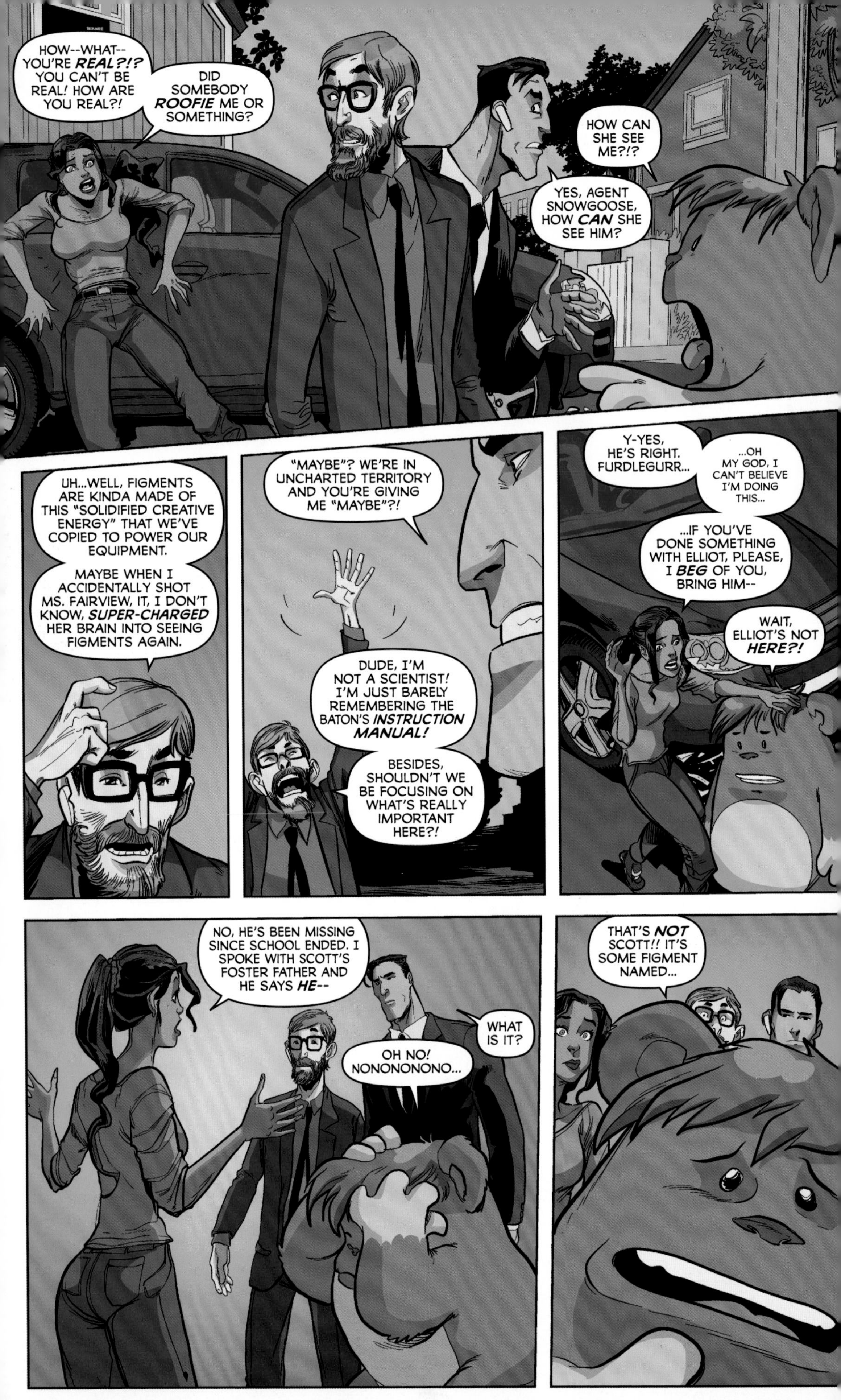
HOW--WHAT-- YOU'RE REAL?!? YOU CAN'T BE REAL! HOW ARE YOU REAL?!
DID SOMEBODY ROOFIE ME OR SOMETHING?
HOW CAN SHE SEE ME?!?
YES, AGENT SNOWGOOSE, HOW CAN SHE SEE HIM?
UH...WELL, FIGMENTS ARE KINDA MADE OF THIS "SOLIDIFIED CREATIVE ENERGY" THAT WE'VE COPIED TO POWER OUR EQUIPMENT.
MAYBE WHEN I ACCIDENTALLY SHOT MS. FAIRVIEW, IT, I DON'T KNOW, SUPER-CHARGED HER BRAIN INTO SEEING FIGMENTS AGAIN.
"MAYBE"? WE'RE IN UNCHARTED TERRITORY AND YOU'RE GIVING ME "MAYBE"?!
DUDE, I'M NOT A SCIENTIST! I'M JUST BARELY REMEMBERING THE BATON'S INSTRUCTION MANUAL!
BESIDES, SHOULDN'T WE BE FOCUSING ON WHAT'S REALLY IMPORTANT HERE?!
Y-YES, HE'S RIGHT. FURDLEGURR...
...OH MY GOD, I CAN'T BELIEVE I'M DOING THIS...
...IF YOU'VE DONE SOMETHING WITH ELLIOT, PLEASE, I BEG OF YOU, BRING HIM--
WAIT, ELLIOT'S NOT HERE?!
NO, HE'S BEEN MISSING SINCE SCHOOL ENDED. I SPOKE WITH SCOTT'S FOSTER FATHER AND HE SAYS HE--
WHAT IS IT?
OH NO! NONONONONO...
THAT'S NOT SCOTT!! IT'S SOME FIGMENT NAMED...

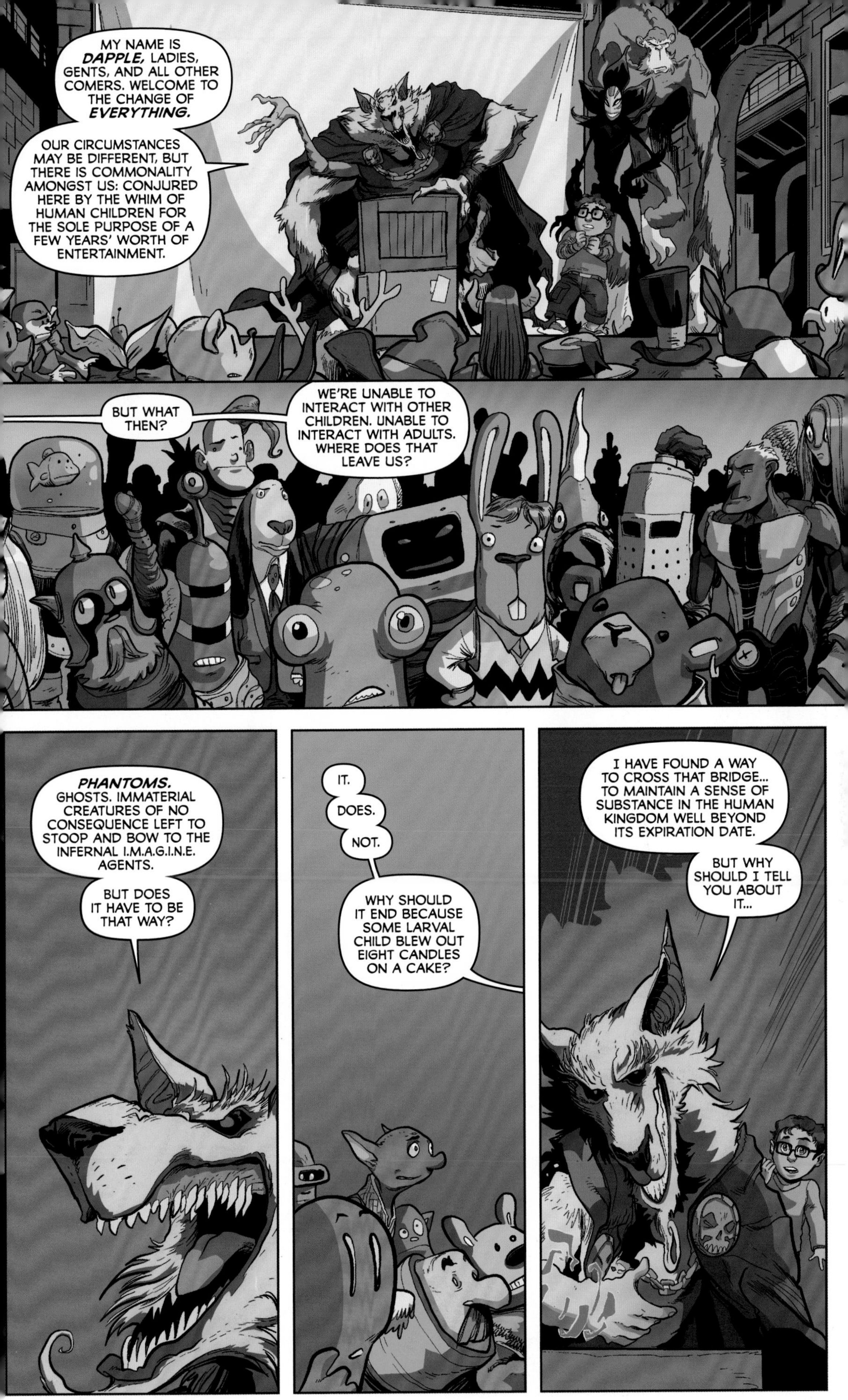

MY NAME IS DAPPLE, LADIES, GENTS, AND ALL OTHER COMERS. WELCOME TO THE CHANGE OF EVERYTHING.
OUR CIRCUMSTANCES MAY BE DIFFERENT, BUT THERE IS COMMONALITY AMONGST US: CONJURED HERE BY THE WHIM OF HUMAN CHILDREN FOR THE SOLE PURPOSE OF A FEW YEARS' WORTH OF ENTERTAINMENT.
BUT WHAT THEN?
WE'RE UNABLE TO INTERACT WITH OTHER CHILDREN. UNABLE TO INTERACT WITH ADULTS. WHERE DOES THAT LEAVE US?
PHANTOMS. GHOSTS. IMMATERIAL CREATURES OF NO CONSEQUENCE LEFT TO STOOP AND BOW TO THE INFERNAL I.M.A.G.I.N.E. AGENTS.
BUT DOES IT HAVE TO BE THAT WAY?
IT.
DOES.
NOT.
WHY SHOULD IT END BECAUSE SOME LARVAL CHILD BLEW OUT EIGHT CANDLES ON A CAKE?
I HAVE FOUND A WAY TO CROSS THAT BRIDGE... TO MAINTAIN A SENSE OF SUBSTANCE IN THE HUMAN KINGDOM WELL BEYOND ITS EXPIRATION DATE.
BUT WHY SHOULD I TELL YOU ABOUT IT...

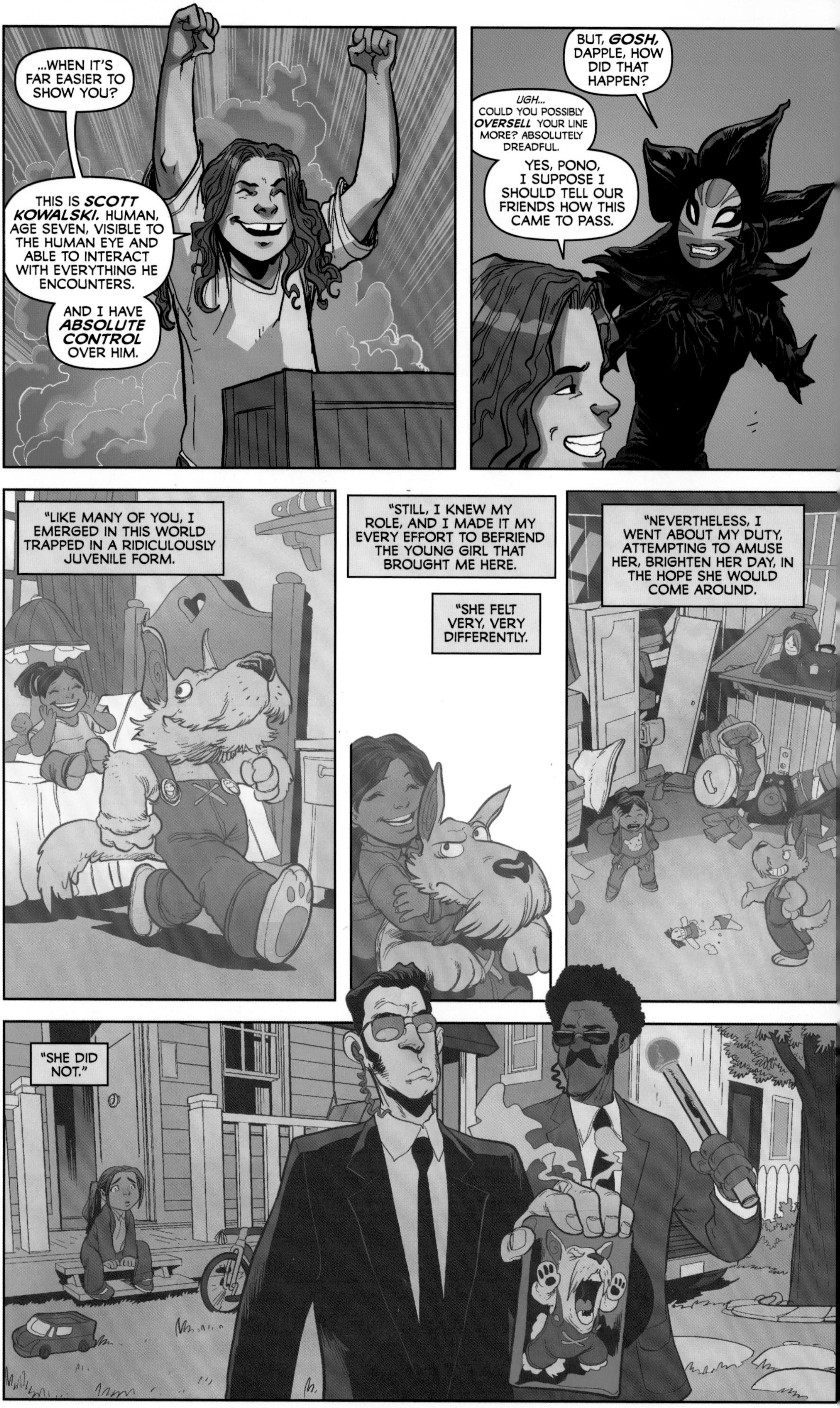
...WHEN IT'S FAR EASIER TO SHOW YOU?
THIS IS SCOTT KOWALSKI. HUMAN, AGE SEVEN, VISIBLE TO THE HUMAN EYE AND ABLE TO INTERACT WITH EVERYTHING HE ENCOUNTERS.
AND I HAVE ABSOLUTE CONTROL OVER HIM.
BUT, GOSH, DAPPLE, HOW DID THAT HAPPEN?
UGH... COULD YOU POSSIBLY OVERSELL YOUR LINE MORE? ABSOLUTELY DREADFUL.
YES, PONO, I SUPPOSE I SHOULD TELL OUR FRIENDS HOW THIS CAME TO PASS.
"LIKE MANY OF YOU, I EMERGED IN THIS WORLD TRAPPED IN A RIDICULOUSLY JUVENILE FORM.
"STILL, I KNEW MY ROLE, AND I MADE IT MY EVERY EFFORT TO BEFRIEND THE YOUNG GIRL THAT BROUGHT ME HERE.
"SHE FELT VERY, VERY DIFFERENTLY.
"NEVERTHELESS, I WENT ABOUT MY DUTY, ATTEMPTING TO AMUSE HER, BRIGHTEN HER DAY, IN THE HOPE SHE WOULD COME AROUND.
"SHE DID NOT."

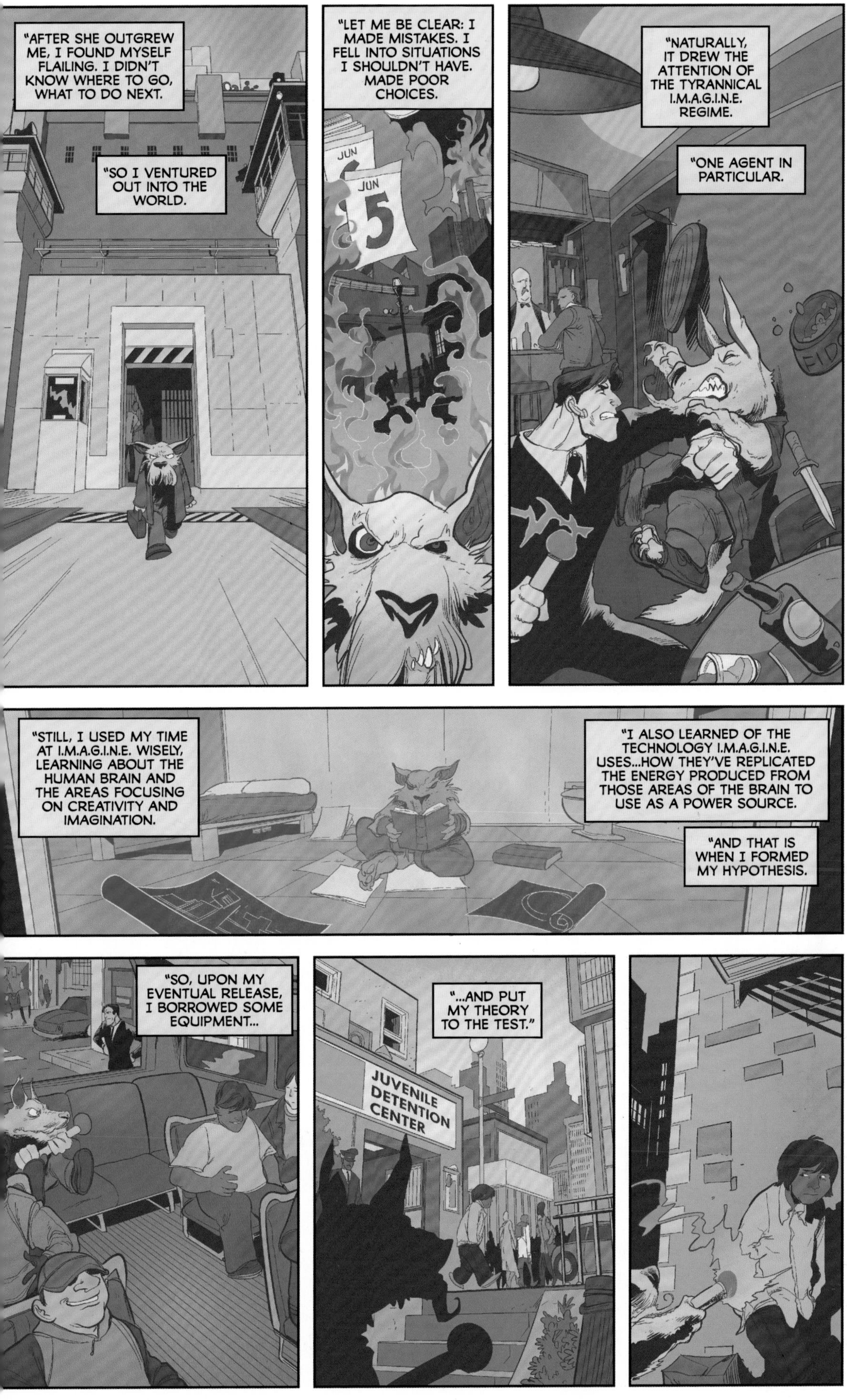
"AFTER SHE OUTGREW ME, I FOUND MYSELF FLAILING. I DIDN'T KNOW WHERE TO GO, WHAT TO DO NEXT.
"SO I VENTURED OUT INTO THE WORLD.
"LET ME BE CLEAR: I MADE MISTAKES. I FELL INTO SITUATIONS I SHOULDN'T HAVE. MADE POOR CHOICES.
JUN
JUN
5
"NATURALLY, IT DREW THE ATTENTION OF THE TYRANNICAL I.M.A.G.I.N.E. REGIME.
"ONE AGENT IN PARTICULAR.
"STILL, I USED MY TIME AT I.M.A.G.I.N.E. WISELY, LEARNING ABOUT THE HUMAN BRAIN AND THE AREAS FOCUSING ON CREATIVITY AND IMAGINATION.
"I ALSO LEARNED OF THE TECHNOLOGY I.M.A.G.I.N.E. USES...HOW THEY'VE REPLICATED THE ENERGY PRODUCED FROM THOSE AREAS OF THE BRAIN TO USE AS A POWER SOURCE.
"AND THAT IS WHEN I FORMED MY HYPOTHESIS.
"SO, UPON MY EVENTUAL RELEASE, I BORROWED SOME EQUIPMENT...
"...AND PUT MY THEORY TO THE TEST."
JUVENILE DETENTION CENTER

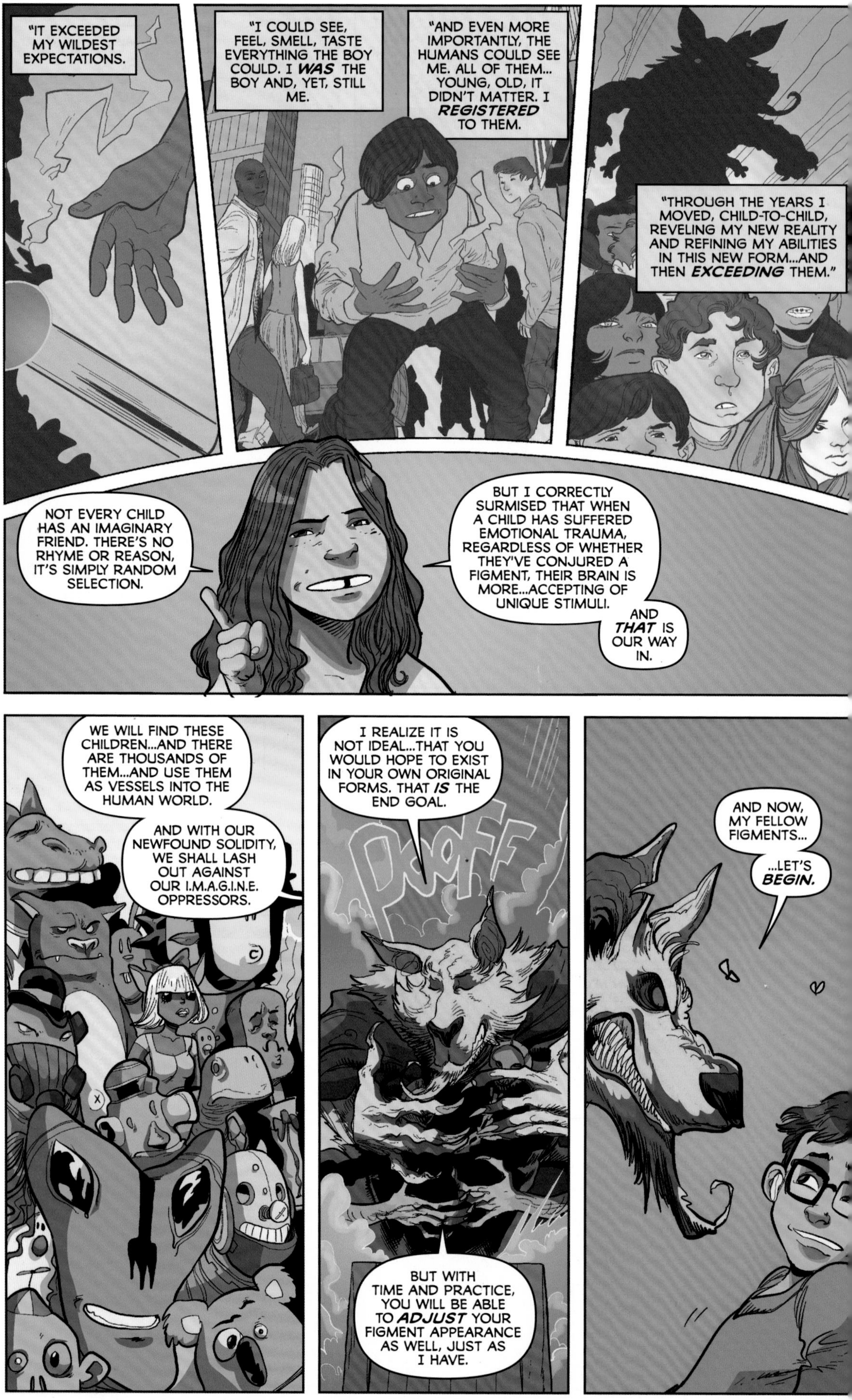
"IT EXCEEDED MY WILDEST EXPECTATIONS.
"I COULD SEE, FEEL, SMELL, TASTE EVERYTHING THE BOY COULD. I *WAS* THE BOY AND, YET, STILL ME.
"AND EVEN MORE IMPORTANTLY, THE HUMANS COULD SEE ME. ALL OF THEM... YOUNG, OLD, IT DIDN'T MATTER. I *REGISTERED* TO THEM.
"THROUGH THE YEARS I MOVED, CHILD-TO-CHILD, REVELING MY NEW REALITY AND REFINING MY ABILITIES IN THIS NEW FORM...AND THEN *EXCEEDING* THEM."
NOT EVERY CHILD HAS AN IMAGINARY FRIEND. THERE'S NO RHYME OR REASON, IT'S SIMPLY RANDOM SELECTION.
BUT I CORRECTLY SURMISED THAT WHEN A CHILD HAS SUFFERED EMOTIONAL TRAUMA, REGARDLESS OF WHETHER THEY'VE CONJURED A FIGMENT, THEIR BRAIN IS MORE...ACCEPTING OF UNIQUE STIMULI.
AND *THAT* IS OUR WAY IN.
WE WILL FIND THESE CHILDREN...AND THERE ARE THOUSANDS OF THEM...AND USE THEM AS VESSELS INTO THE HUMAN WORLD.
AND WITH OUR NEWFOUND SOLIDITY, WE SHALL LASH OUT AGAINST OUR I.M.A.G.I.N.E. OPPRESSORS.
I REALIZE IT IS NOT IDEAL...THAT YOU WOULD HOPE TO EXIST IN YOUR OWN ORIGINAL FORMS. THAT *IS* THE END GOAL.
POOFF
BUT WITH TIME AND PRACTICE, YOU WILL BE ABLE TO *ADJUST* YOUR FIGMENT APPEARANCE AS WELL, JUST AS I HAVE.
AND NOW, MY FELLOW FIGMENTS...
...LET'S *BEGIN.*

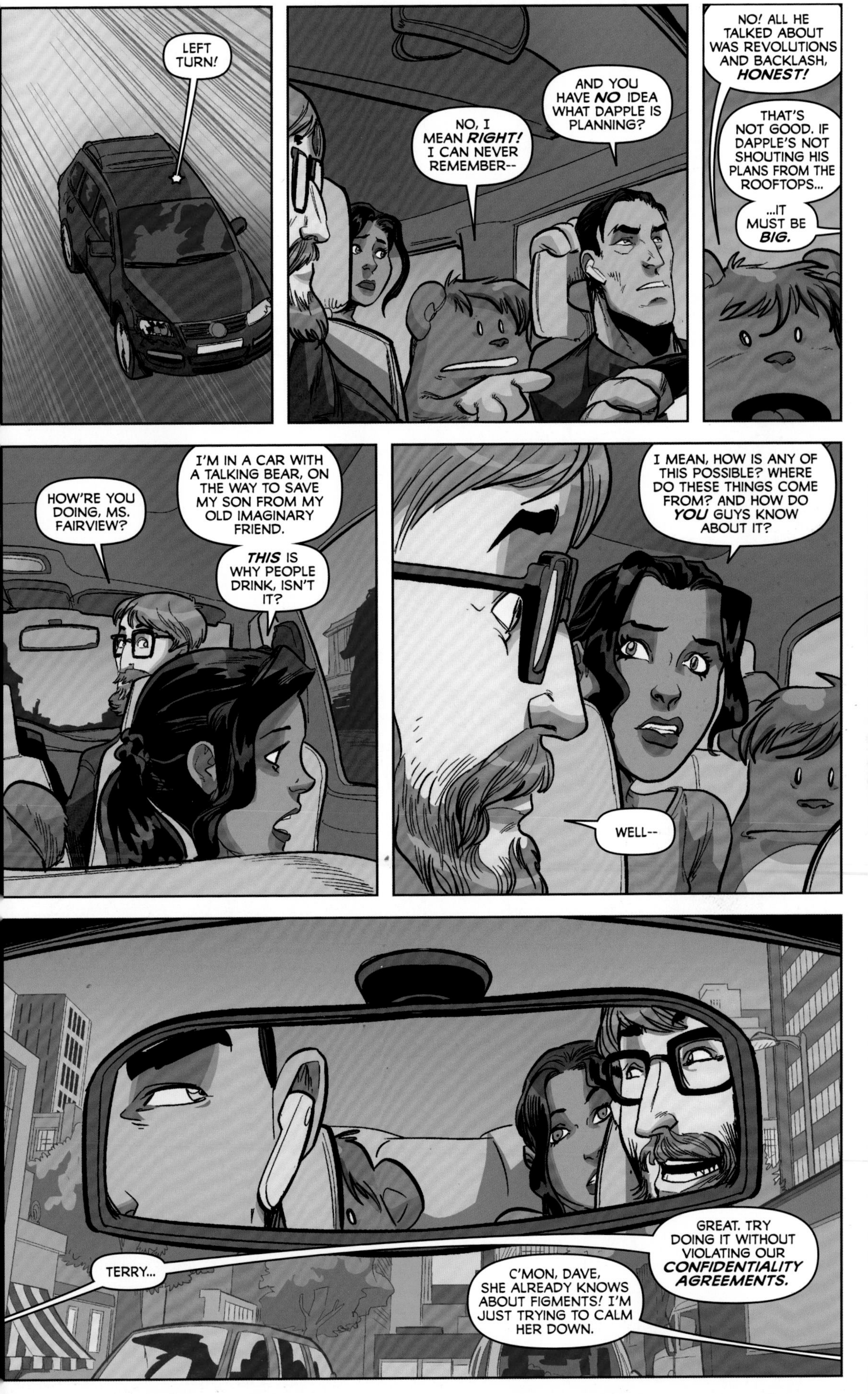
LEFT TURN!
NO, I MEAN RIGHT! I CAN NEVER REMEMBER--
AND YOU HAVE NO IDEA WHAT DAPPLE IS PLANNING?
NO! ALL HE TALKED ABOUT WAS REVOLUTIONS AND BACKLASH, HONEST!
THAT'S NOT GOOD. IF DAPPLE'S NOT SHOUTING HIS PLANS FROM THE ROOFTOPS...
...IT MUST BE BIG.
HOW'RE YOU DOING, MS. FAIRVIEW?
I'M IN A CAR WITH A TALKING BEAR, ON THE WAY TO SAVE MY SON FROM MY OLD IMAGINARY FRIEND.
THIS IS WHY PEOPLE DRINK, ISN'T IT?
I MEAN, HOW IS ANY OF THIS POSSIBLE? WHERE DO THESE THINGS COME FROM? AND HOW DO YOU GUYS KNOW ABOUT IT?
WELL--
TERRY...
GREAT. TRY DOING IT WITHOUT VIOLATING OUR CONFIDENTIALITY AGREEMENTS.
C'MON, DAVE, SHE ALREADY KNOWS ABOUT FIGMENTS! I'M JUST TRYING TO CALM HER DOWN.

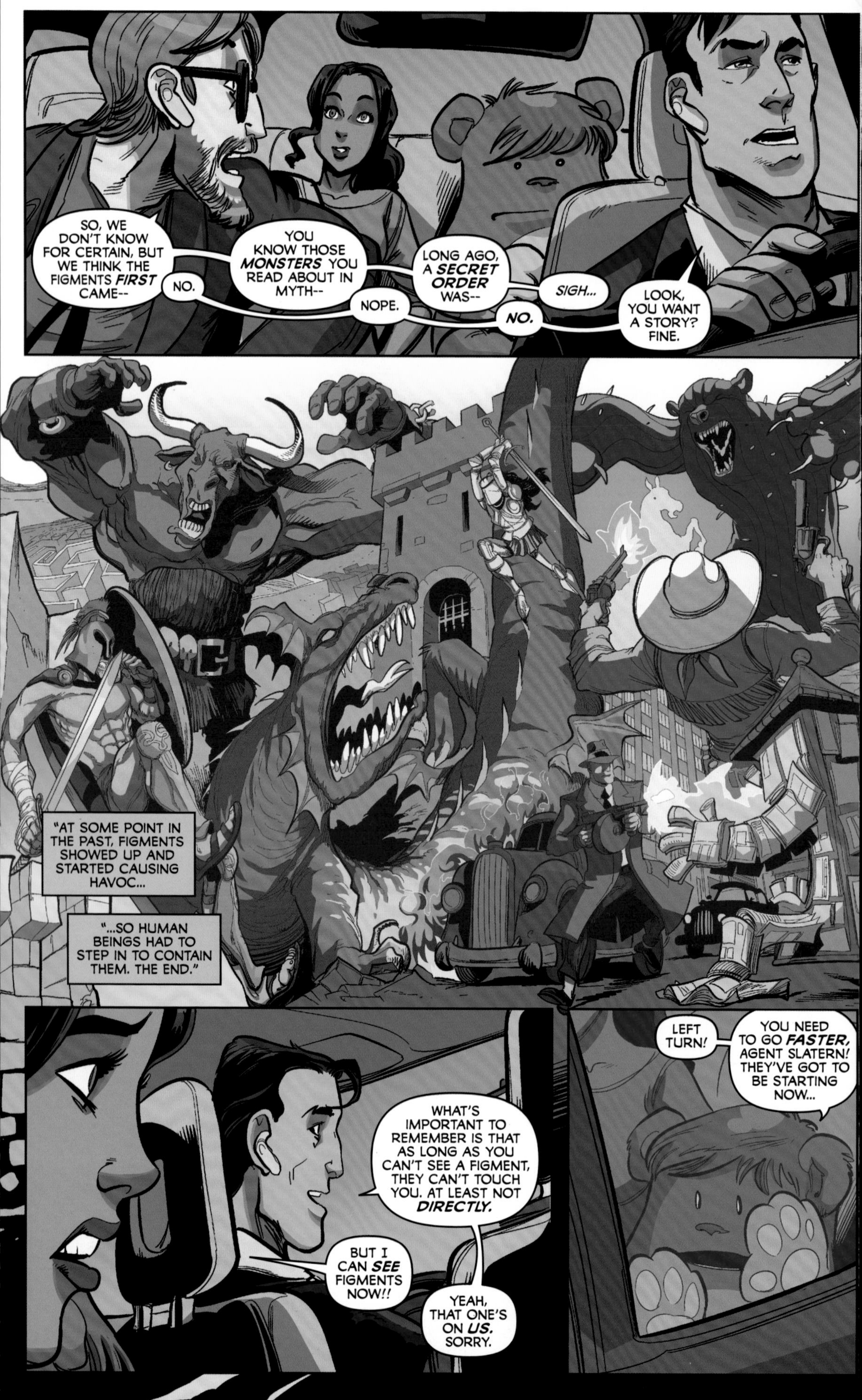
SO, WE DON'T KNOW FOR CERTAIN, BUT WE THINK THE FIGMENTS *FIRST* CAME--
NO.
YOU KNOW THOSE *MONSTERS* YOU READ ABOUT IN MYTH--
NOPE.
LONG AGO, A *SECRET ORDER* WAS--
NO.
SIGH...
LOOK, YOU WANT A STORY? FINE.
"AT SOME POINT IN THE PAST, FIGMENTS SHOWED UP AND STARTED CAUSING HAVOC...
"...SO HUMAN BEINGS HAD TO STEP IN TO CONTAIN THEM. THE END."
WHAT'S IMPORTANT TO REMEMBER IS THAT AS LONG AS YOU CAN'T SEE A FIGMENT, THEY CAN'T TOUCH YOU. AT LEAST NOT *DIRECTLY.*
BUT I CAN *SEE* FIGMENTS NOW*!!*
YEAH, THAT ONE'S ON *US.* SORRY.
LEFT TURN*!*
YOU NEED TO GO *FASTER,* AGENT SLATERN*!* THEY'VE GOT TO BE STARTING NOW...

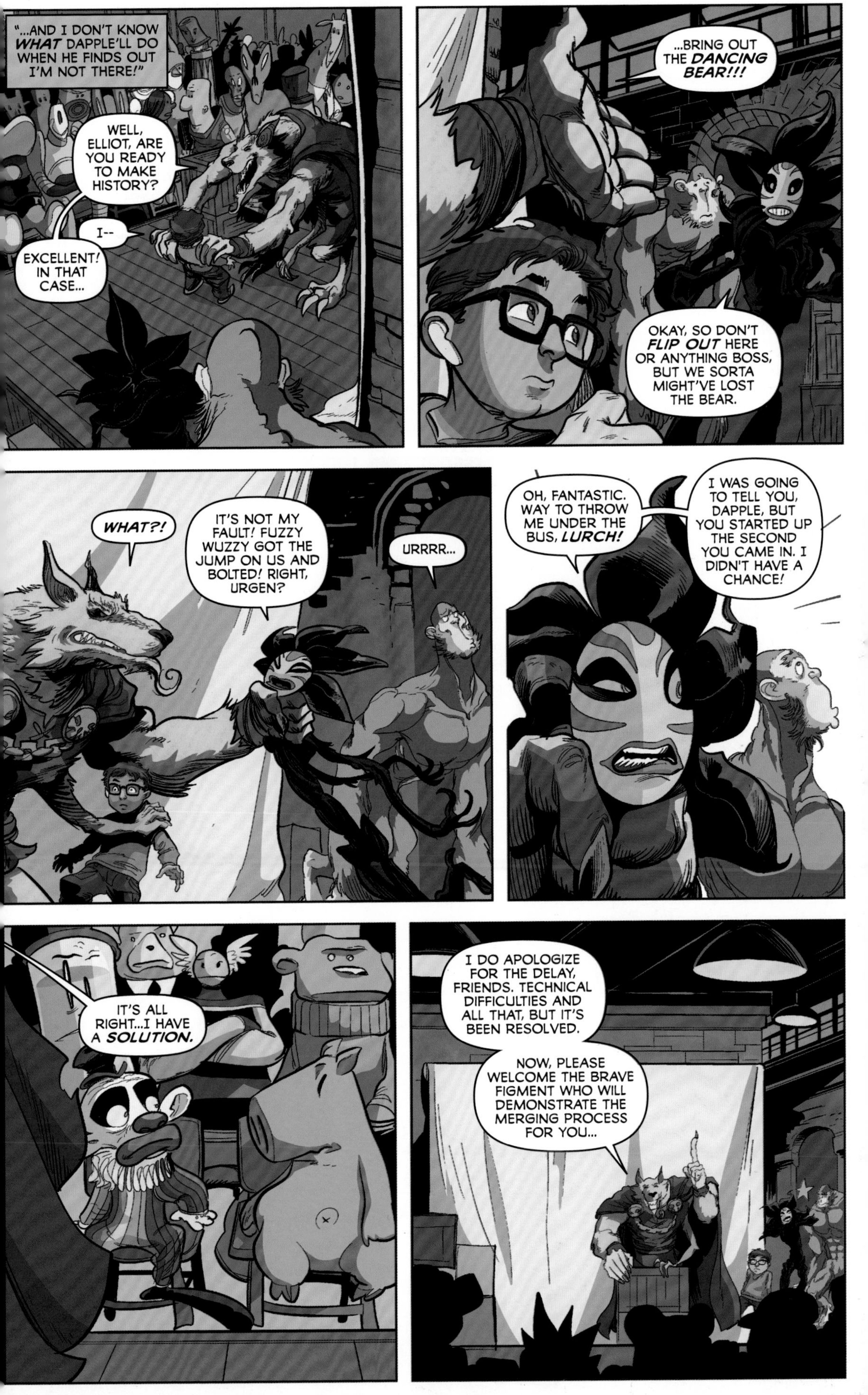
"...AND I DON'T KNOW *WHAT* DAPPLE'LL DO WHEN HE FINDS OUT I'M NOT THERE!"
WELL, ELLIOT, ARE YOU READY TO MAKE HISTORY?
I--
EXCELLENT! IN THAT CASE...
...BRING OUT THE *DANCING BEAR!!!*
OKAY, SO DON'T *FLIP OUT* HERE OR ANYTHING BOSS, BUT WE SORTA MIGHT'VE LOST THE BEAR.
WHAT?!
IT'S NOT MY FAULT! FUZZY WUZZY GOT THE JUMP ON US AND BOLTED! RIGHT, URGEN?
URRRR...
OH, FANTASTIC. WAY TO THROW ME UNDER THE BUS, *LURCH!*
I WAS GOING TO TELL YOU, DAPPLE, BUT YOU STARTED UP THE SECOND YOU CAME IN. I DIDN'T HAVE A CHANCE!
IT'S ALL RIGHT...I HAVE A *SOLUTION.*
I DO APOLOGIZE FOR THE DELAY, FRIENDS. TECHNICAL DIFFICULTIES AND ALL THAT, BUT IT'S BEEN RESOLVED.
NOW, PLEASE WELCOME THE BRAVE FIGMENT WHO WILL DEMONSTRATE THE MERGING PROCESS FOR YOU...

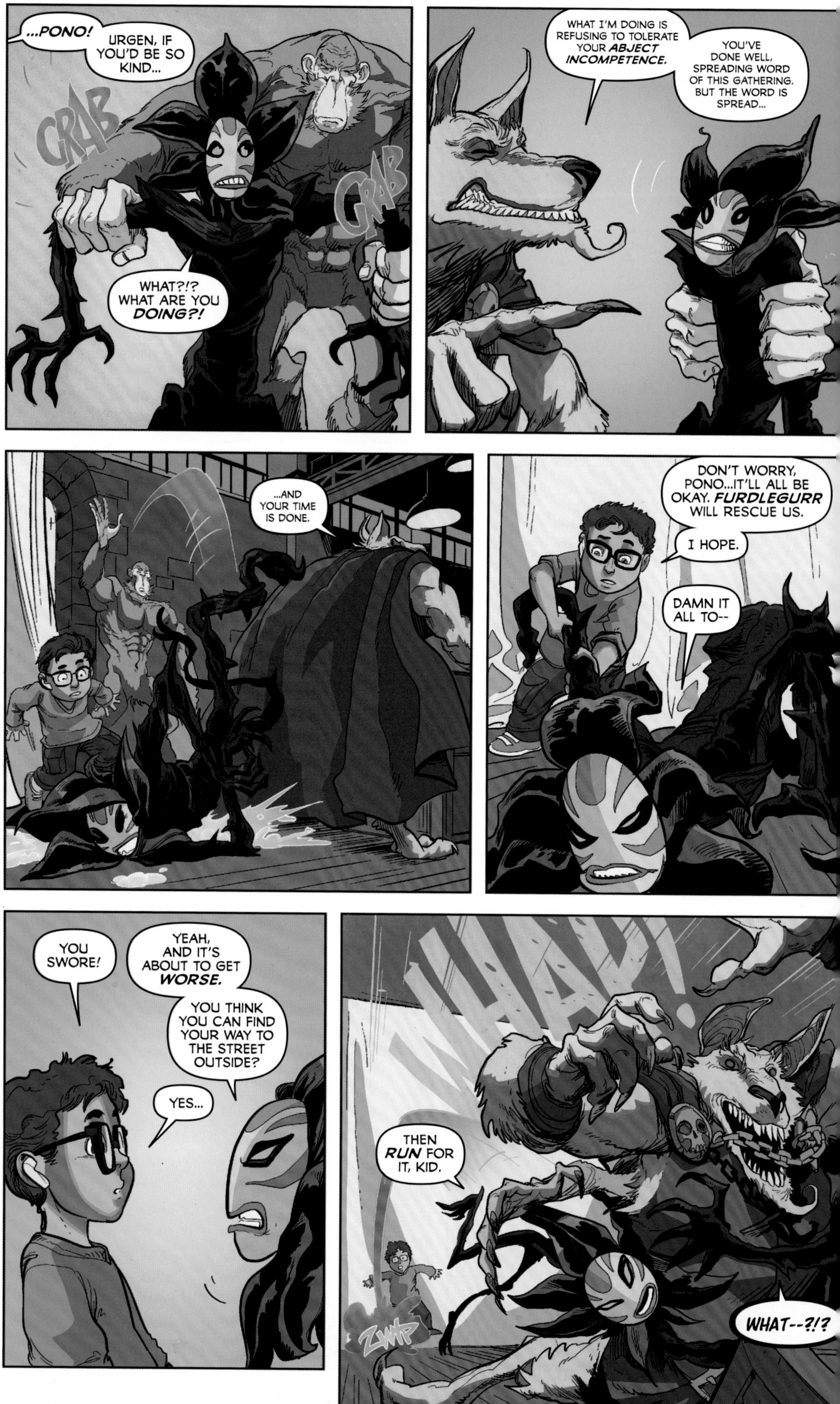
...PONO!
URGEN, IF YOU'D BE SO KIND...
GRAB
GRAB
WHAT?!? WHAT ARE YOU DOING?!
WHAT I'M DOING IS REFUSING TO TOLERATE YOUR ABJECT INCOMPETENCE.
YOU'VE DONE WELL, SPREADING WORD OF THIS GATHERING. BUT THE WORD IS SPREAD...
...AND YOUR TIME IS DONE.
DON'T WORRY, PONO...IT'LL ALL BE OKAY. FURDLEGURR WILL RESCUE US.
I HOPE.
DAMN IT ALL TO--
YOU SWORE!
YEAH, AND IT'S ABOUT TO GET WORSE.
YOU THINK YOU CAN FIND YOUR WAY TO THE STREET OUTSIDE?
YES...
THEN RUN FOR IT, KID.
WHAP!
ZWIP
WHAT--?!?

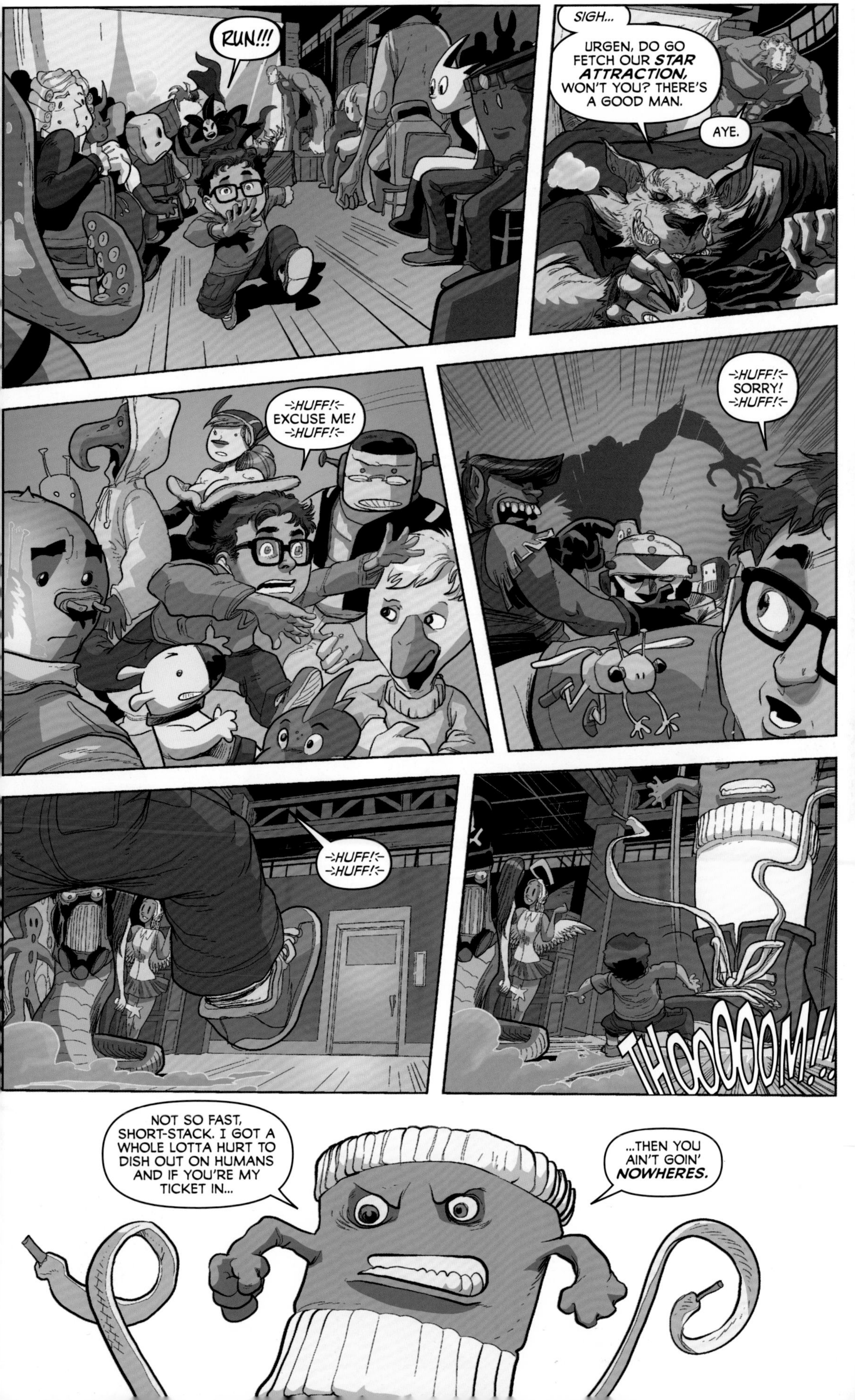

RUN!!!
SIGH...
URGEN, DO GO FETCH OUR STAR ATTRACTION, WON'T YOU? THERE'S A GOOD MAN.
AYE.
-HUFF!- EXCUSE ME! -HUFF!-
-HUFF!- SORRY! -HUFF!-
-HUFF!- -HUFF!-
THOOOOOM!!!
NOT SO FAST, SHORT-STACK. I GOT A WHOLE LOTTA HURT TO DISH OUT ON HUMANS AND IF YOU'RE MY TICKET IN...
...THEN YOU AIN'T GOIN' NOWHERES.

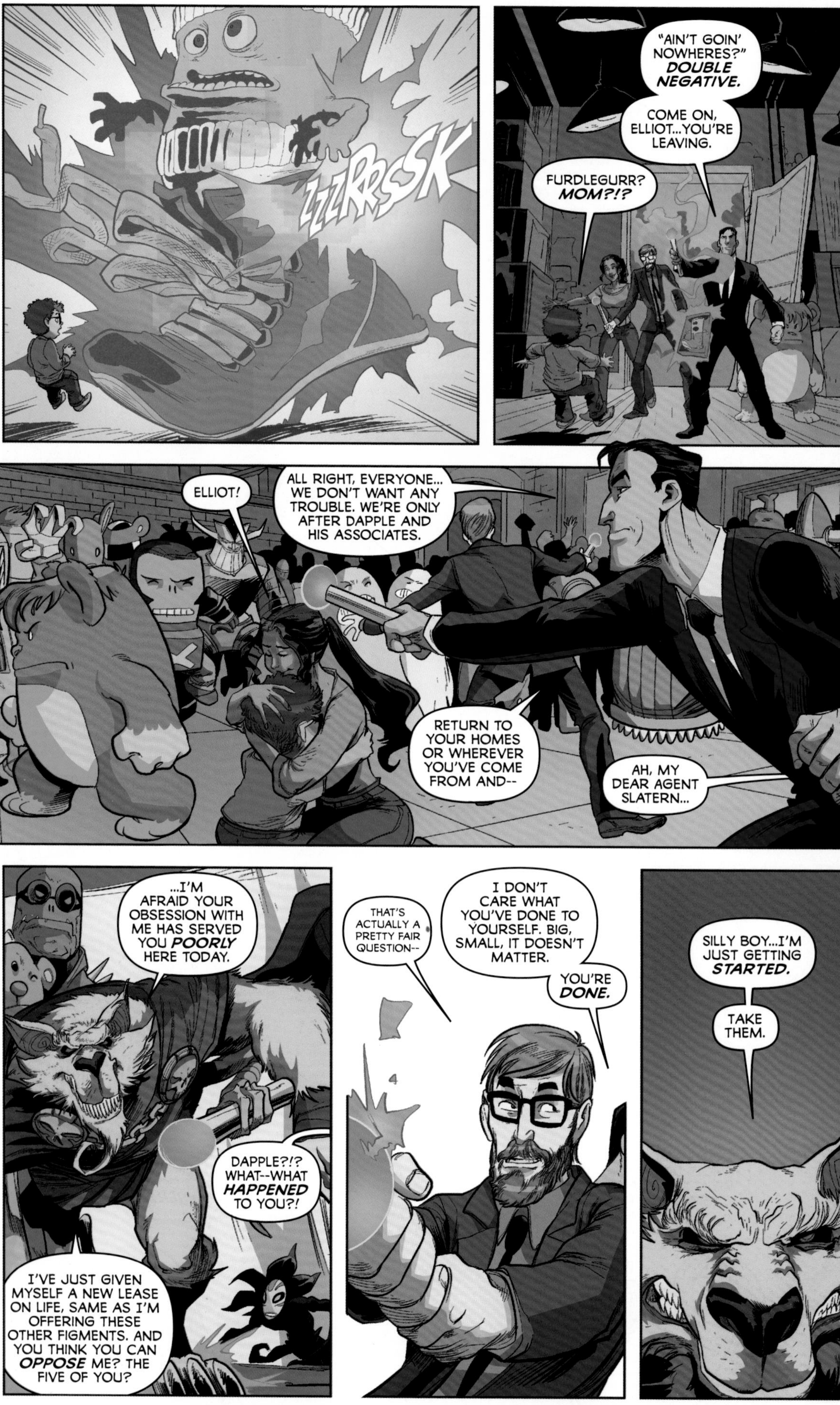
ZZZRRRSSK
"AIN'T GOIN' NOWHERES?" DOUBLE NEGATIVE.
COME ON, ELLIOT...YOU'RE LEAVING.
FURDLEGURR? MOM?!?
ELLIOT!
ALL RIGHT, EVERYONE... WE DON'T WANT ANY TROUBLE. WE'RE ONLY AFTER DAPPLE AND HIS ASSOCIATES.
RETURN TO YOUR HOMES OR WHEREVER YOU'VE COME FROM AND--
AH, MY DEAR AGENT SLATERN...
...I'M AFRAID YOUR OBSESSION WITH ME HAS SERVED YOU POORLY HERE TODAY.
DAPPLE?!? WHAT--WHAT HAPPENED TO YOU?!
I'VE JUST GIVEN MYSELF A NEW LEASE ON LIFE, SAME AS I'M OFFERING THESE OTHER FIGMENTS. AND YOU THINK YOU CAN OPPOSE ME? THE FIVE OF YOU?
THAT'S ACTUALLY A PRETTY FAIR QUESTION--
I DON'T CARE WHAT YOU'VE DONE TO YOURSELF. BIG, SMALL, IT DOESN'T MATTER.
YOU'RE DONE.
SILLY BOY...I'M JUST GETTING STARTED.
TAKE THEM.

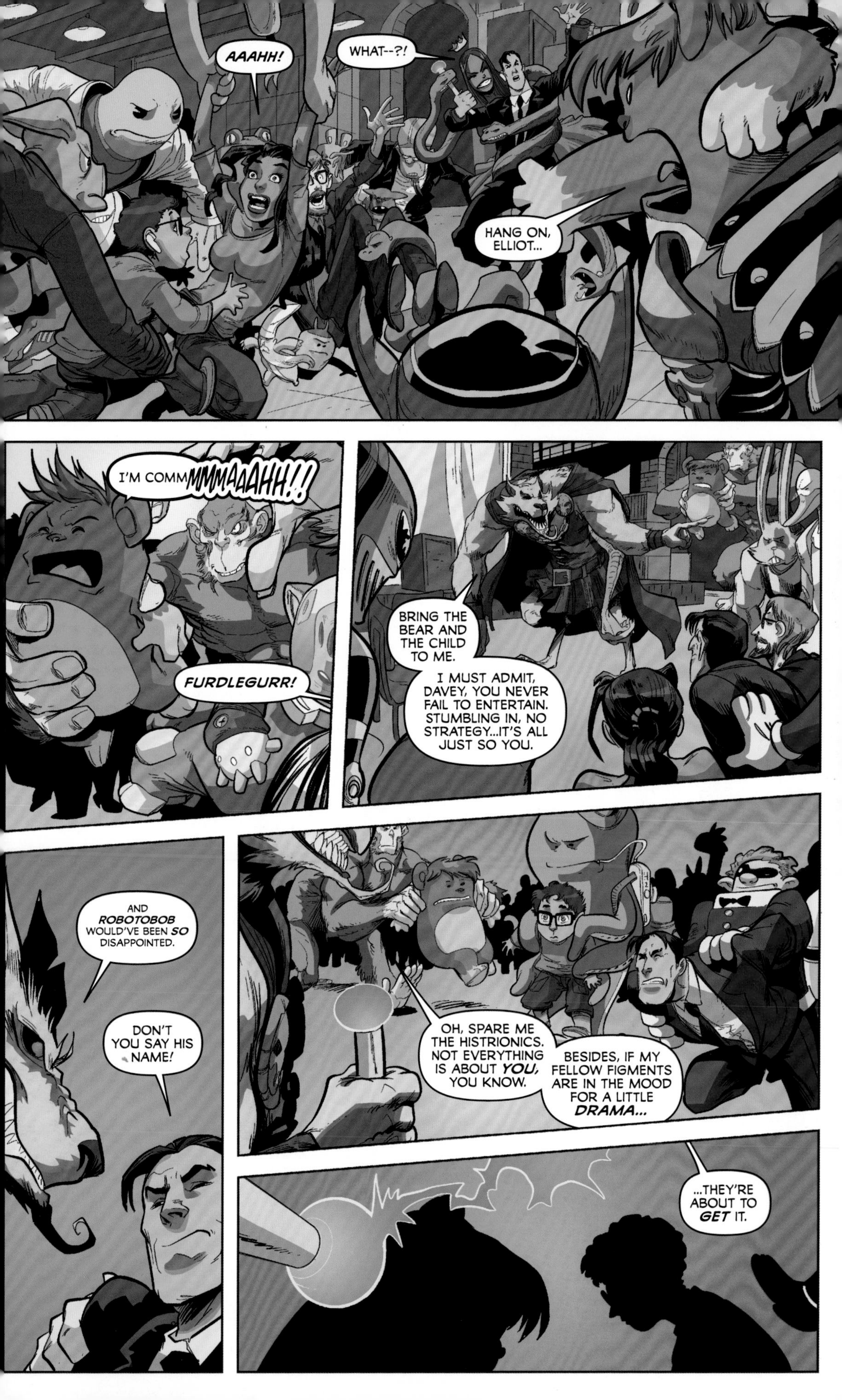
AAAHH!
WHAT--?!
HANG ON, ELLIOT...
I'M COMMMMMAAAHH!!
FURDLEGURR!
BRING THE BEAR AND THE CHILD TO ME.
I MUST ADMIT, DAVEY, YOU NEVER FAIL TO ENTERTAIN. STUMBLING IN, NO STRATEGY...IT'S ALL JUST SO YOU.
AND ROBOTOBOB WOULD'VE BEEN SO DISAPPOINTED.
DON'T YOU SAY HIS NAME!
OH, SPARE ME THE HISTRIONICS. NOT EVERYTHING IS ABOUT YOU, YOU KNOW.
BESIDES, IF MY FELLOW FIGMENTS ARE IN THE MOOD FOR A LITTLE DRAMA...
...THEY'RE ABOUT TO GET IT.

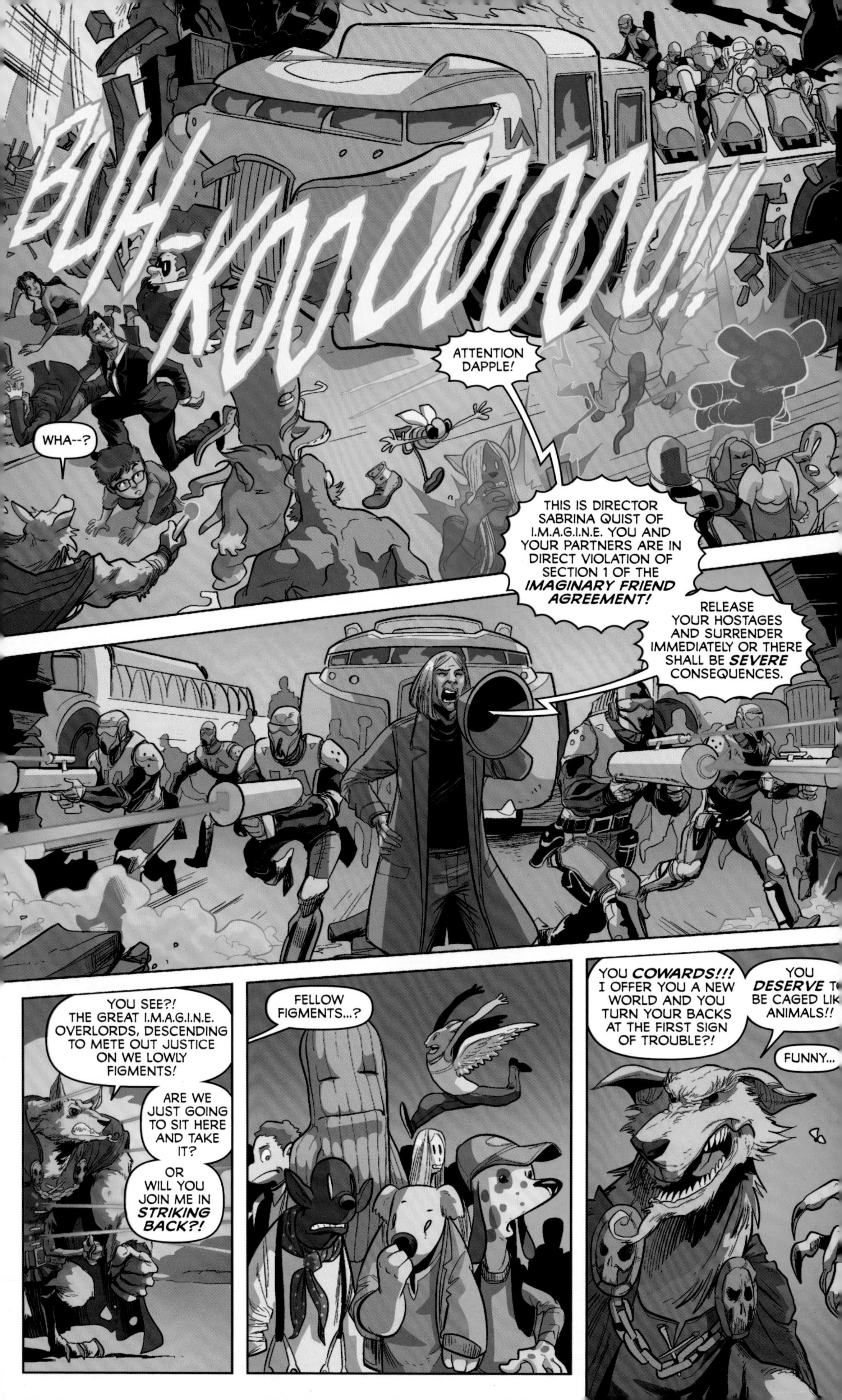
BUH-KOOOOOOOM!!
ATTENTION DAPPLE!
WHA--?
THIS IS DIRECTOR SABRINA QUIST OF I.M.A.G.I.N.E. YOU AND YOUR PARTNERS ARE IN DIRECT VIOLATION OF SECTION 1 OF THE IMAGINARY FRIEND AGREEMENT!
RELEASE YOUR HOSTAGES AND SURRENDER IMMEDIATELY OR THERE SHALL BE SEVERE CONSEQUENCES.
YOU SEE?! THE GREAT I.M.A.G.I.N.E. OVERLORDS, DESCENDING TO METE OUT JUSTICE ON WE LOWLY FIGMENTS!
ARE WE JUST GOING TO SIT HERE AND TAKE IT?
OR WILL YOU JOIN ME IN STRIKING BACK?!
FELLOW FIGMENTS...?
YOU COWARDS!!! I OFFER YOU A NEW WORLD AND YOU TURN YOUR BACKS AT THE FIRST SIGN OF TROUBLE?!
YOU DESERVE TO BE CAGED LIK ANIMALS!!
FUNNY...

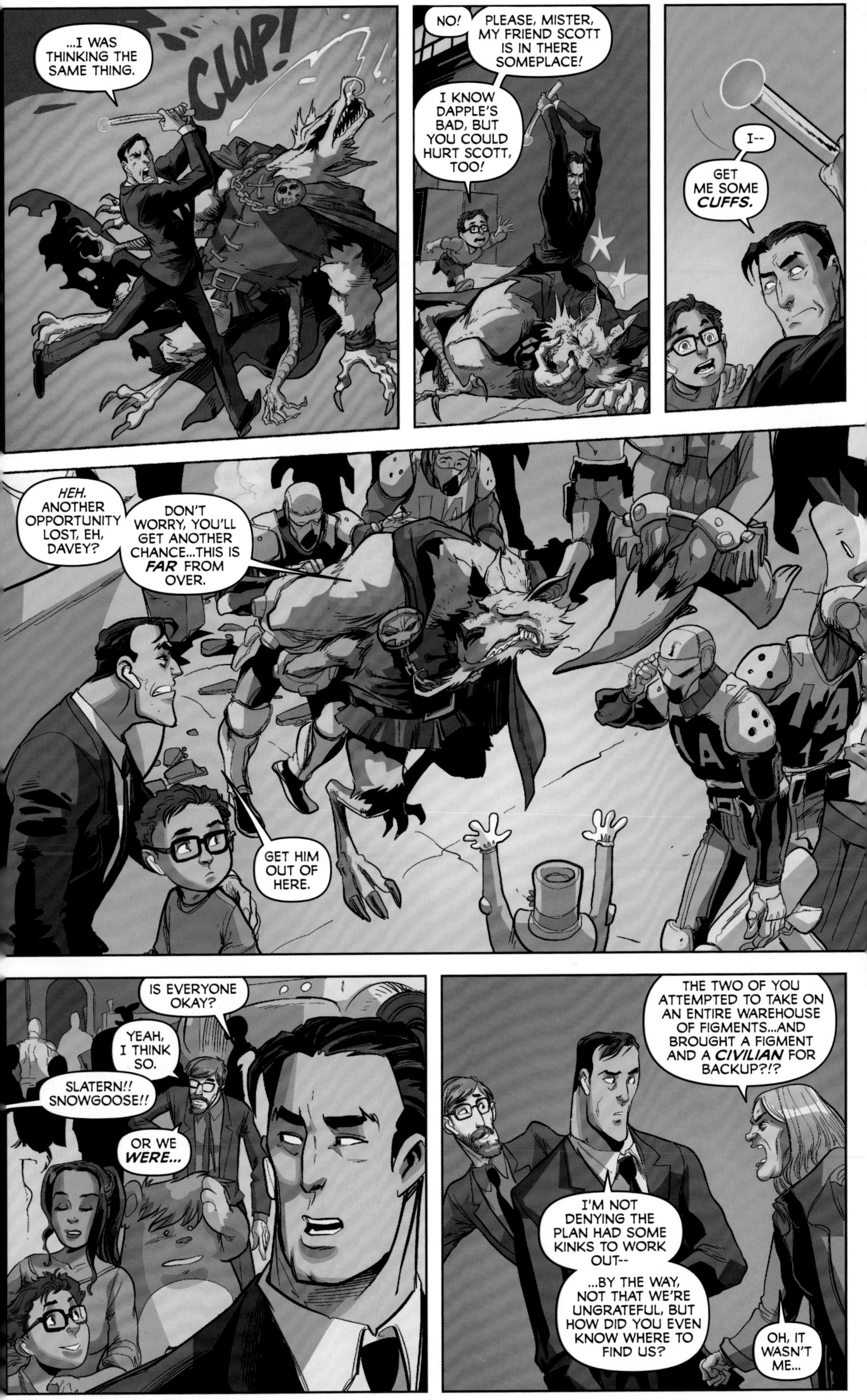
...I WAS THINKING THE SAME THING.
CLOP!
NO!
PLEASE, MISTER, MY FRIEND SCOTT IS IN THERE SOMEPLACE!
I KNOW DAPPLE'S BAD, BUT YOU COULD HURT SCOTT, TOO!
I--
GET ME SOME *CUFFS.*
HEH. ANOTHER OPPORTUNITY LOST, EH, DAVEY?
DON'T WORRY, YOU'LL GET ANOTHER CHANCE...THIS IS ***FAR*** FROM OVER.
GET HIM OUT OF HERE.
IS EVERYONE OKAY?
YEAH, I THINK SO.
SLATERN!! SNOWGOOSE!!
OR WE ***WERE...***
THE TWO OF YOU ATTEMPTED TO TAKE ON AN ENTIRE WAREHOUSE OF FIGMENTS...AND BROUGHT A FIGMENT AND A ***CIVILIAN*** FOR BACKUP?!?
I'M NOT DENYING THE PLAN HAD SOME KINKS TO WORK OUT--
...BY THE WAY, NOT THAT WE'RE UNGRATEFUL, BUT HOW DID YOU EVEN KNOW WHERE TO FIND US?
OH, IT WASN'T ME...

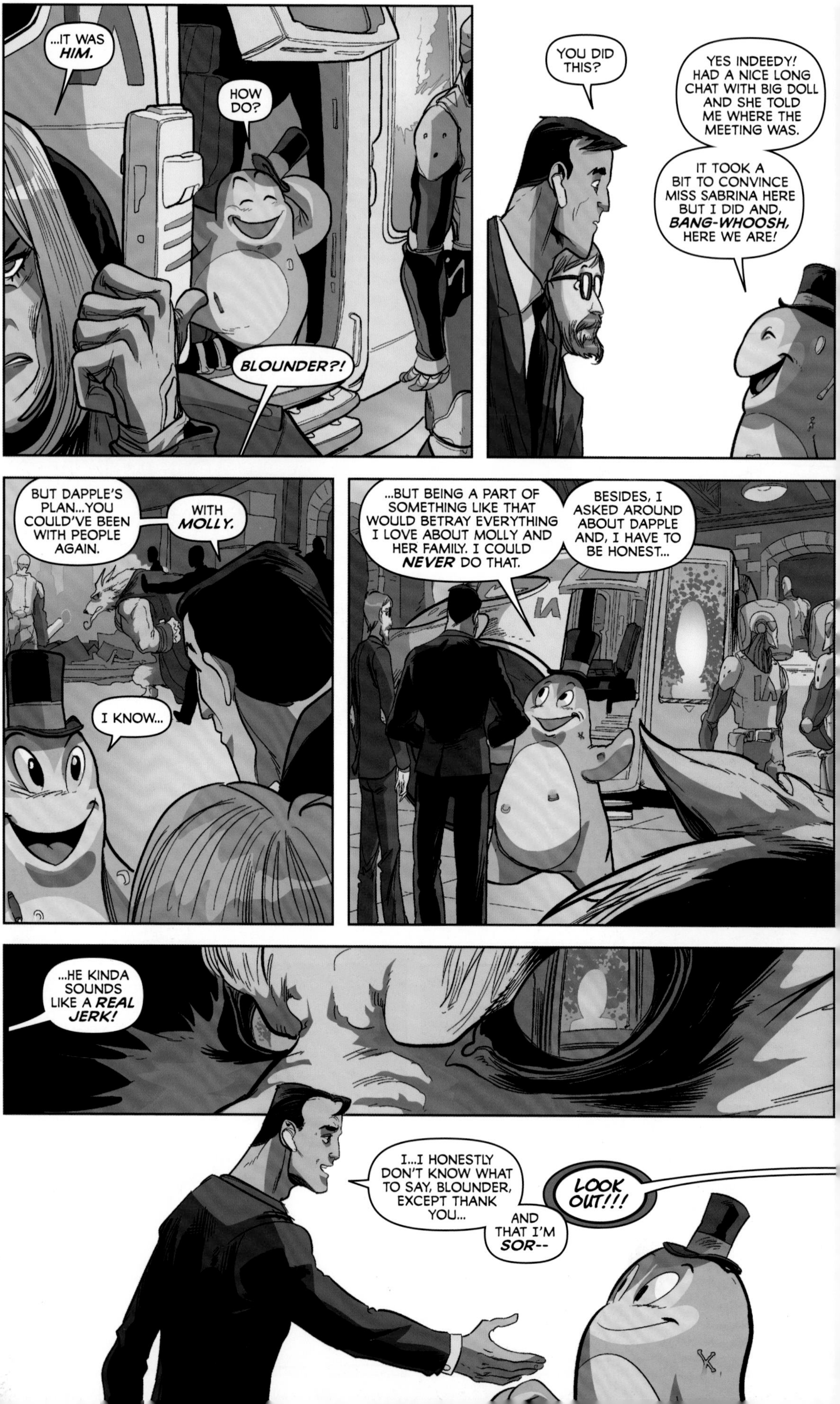
...IT WAS *HIM.*
HOW DO?
BLOUNDER?!
YOU DID THIS?
YES INDEEDY! HAD A NICE LONG CHAT WITH BIG DOLL AND SHE TOLD ME WHERE THE MEETING WAS.
IT TOOK A BIT TO CONVINCE MISS SABRINA HERE BUT I DID AND, *BANG-WHOOSH,* HERE WE ARE!
BUT DAPPLE'S PLAN...YOU COULD'VE BEEN WITH PEOPLE AGAIN.
WITH *MOLLY.*
I KNOW...
...BUT BEING A PART OF SOMETHING LIKE THAT WOULD BETRAY EVERYTHING I LOVE ABOUT MOLLY AND HER FAMILY. I COULD *NEVER* DO THAT.
BESIDES, I ASKED AROUND ABOUT DAPPLE AND, I HAVE TO BE HONEST...
...HE KINDA SOUNDS LIKE A *REAL JERK!*
I...I HONESTLY DON'T KNOW WHAT TO SAY, BLOUNDER, EXCEPT THANK YOU...
AND THAT I'M *SOR--*
LOOK OUT!!!

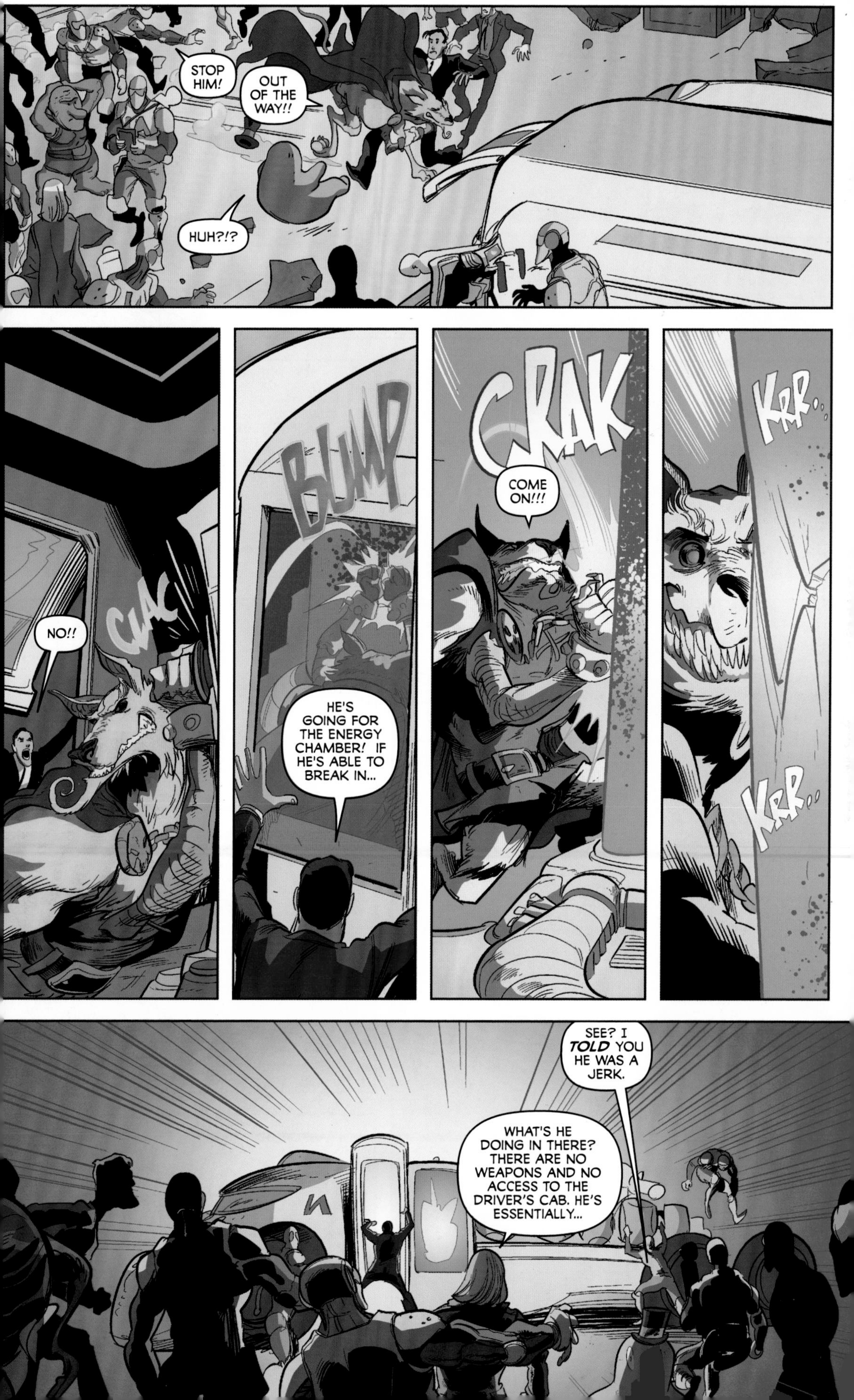
STOP HIM!
OUT OF THE WAY!!
HUH?!?
CLAC
NO!!
BUMP
HE'S GOING FOR THE ENERGY CHAMBER! IF HE'S ABLE TO BREAK IN...
CRAK
COME ON!!!
KRR...
KRR...
SEE? I TOLD YOU HE WAS A JERK.
WHAT'S HE DOING IN THERE? THERE ARE NO WEAPONS AND NO ACCESS TO THE DRIVER'S CAB. HE'S ESSENTIALLY...

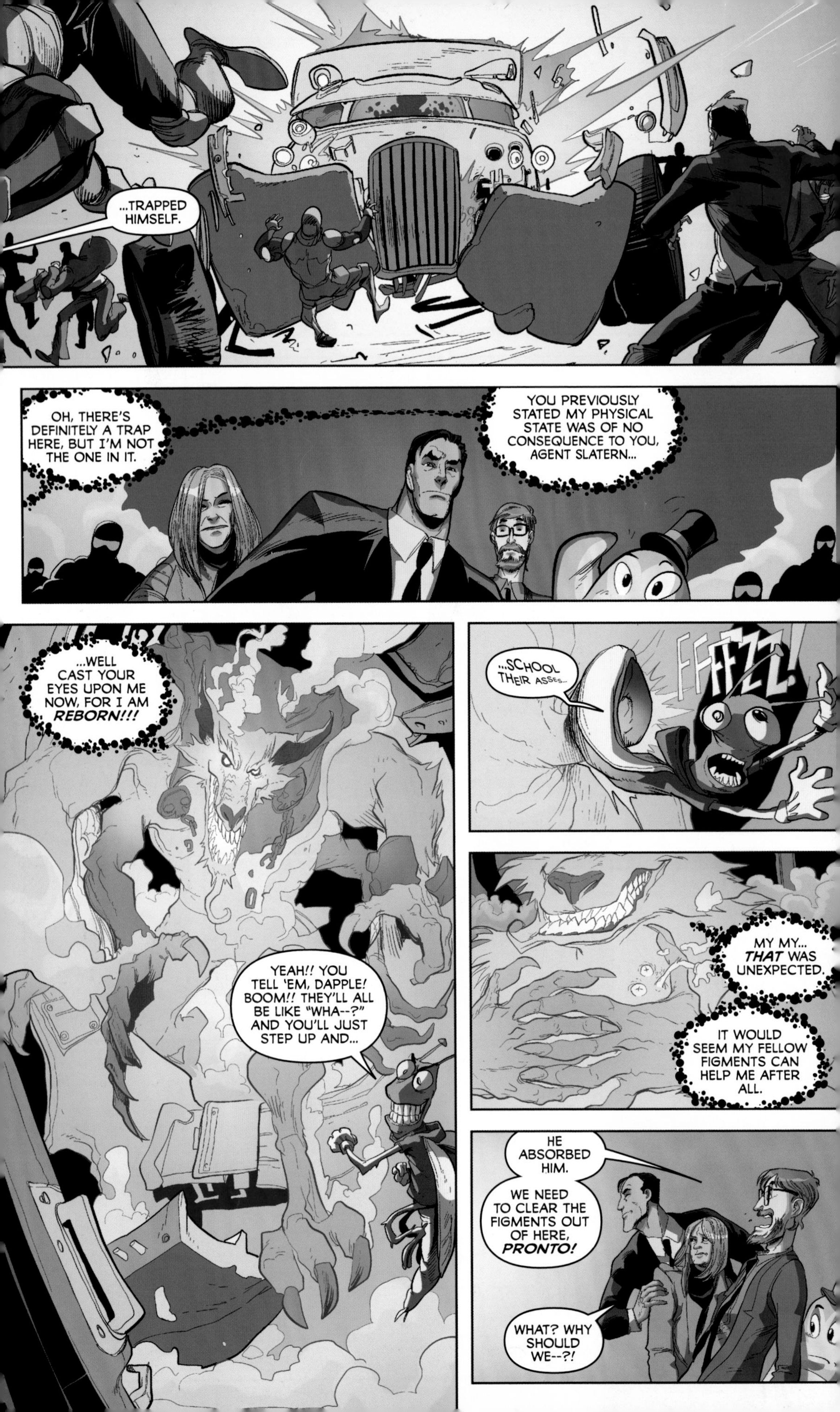
...TRAPPED HIMSELF.
OH, THERE'S DEFINITELY A TRAP HERE, BUT I'M NOT THE ONE IN IT.
YOU PREVIOUSLY STATED MY PHYSICAL STATE WAS OF NO CONSEQUENCE TO YOU, AGENT SLATERN...
...WELL CAST YOUR EYES UPON ME NOW, FOR I AM *REBORN!!!*
YEAH!! YOU TELL 'EM, DAPPLE! BOOM!! THEY'LL ALL BE LIKE "WHA--?" AND YOU'LL JUST STEP UP AND...
...SCHOOL THEIR ASSES...
FFFFZZ!
MY MY... *THAT* WAS UNEXPECTED.
IT WOULD SEEM MY FELLOW FIGMENTS CAN HELP ME AFTER ALL.
HE ABSORBED HIM.
WE NEED TO CLEAR THE FIGMENTS OUT OF HERE, *PRONTO!*
WHAT? WHY SHOULD WE--?!

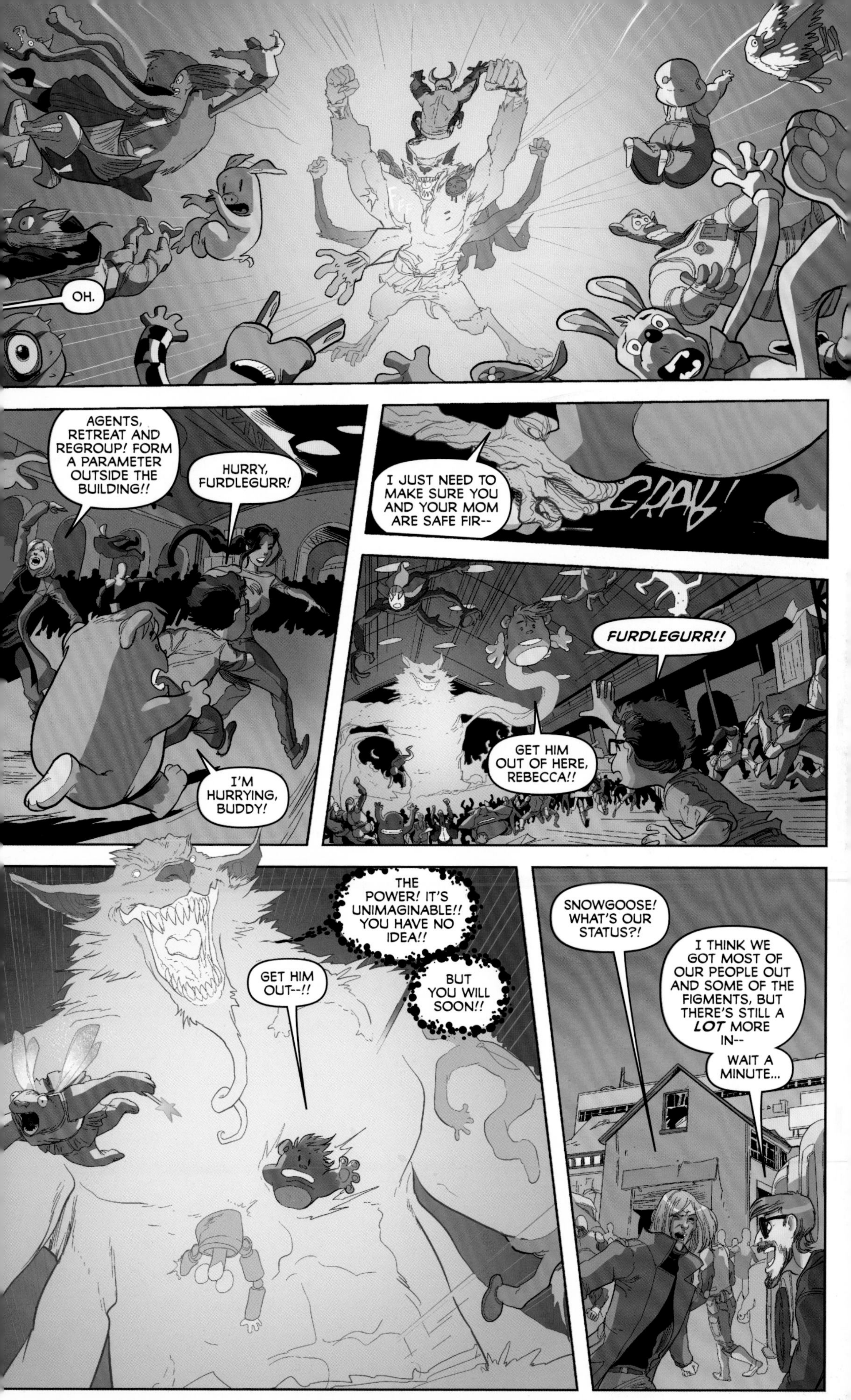

FFF
OH.
AGENTS, RETREAT AND REGROUP! FORM A PARAMETER OUTSIDE THE BUILDING!!
HURRY, FURDLEGURR!
I'M HURRYING, BUDDY!
I JUST NEED TO MAKE SURE YOU AND YOUR MOM ARE SAFE FIR--
GRAB!
FURDLEGURR!!
GET HIM OUT OF HERE, REBECCA!!
THE POWER! IT'S UNIMAGINABLE!! YOU HAVE NO IDEA!!
GET HIM OUT--!!
BUT YOU WILL SOON!!
SNOWGOOSE! WHAT'S OUR STATUS?!
I THINK WE GOT MOST OF OUR PEOPLE OUT AND SOME OF THE FIGMENTS, BUT THERE'S STILL A LOT MORE IN--
WAIT A MINUTE...

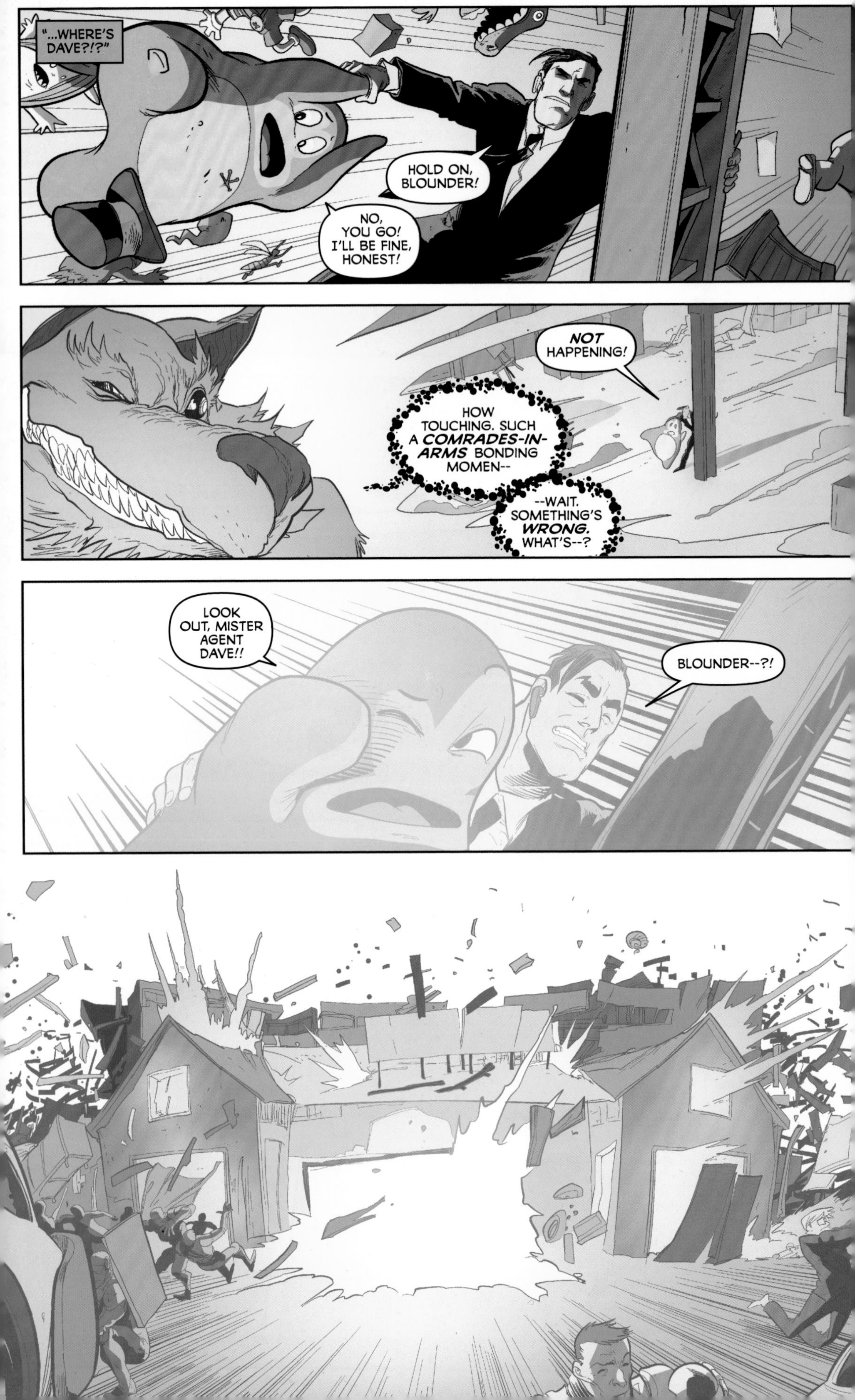
"...WHERE'S DAVE?!?"
HOLD ON, BLOUNDER!
NO, YOU GO! I'LL BE FINE, HONEST!
NOT HAPPENING!
HOW TOUCHING. SUCH A COMRADES-IN-ARMS BONDING MOMEN--
--WAIT. SOMETHING'S WRONG. WHAT'S--?
LOOK OUT, MISTER AGENT DAVE!!
BLOUNDER--?!

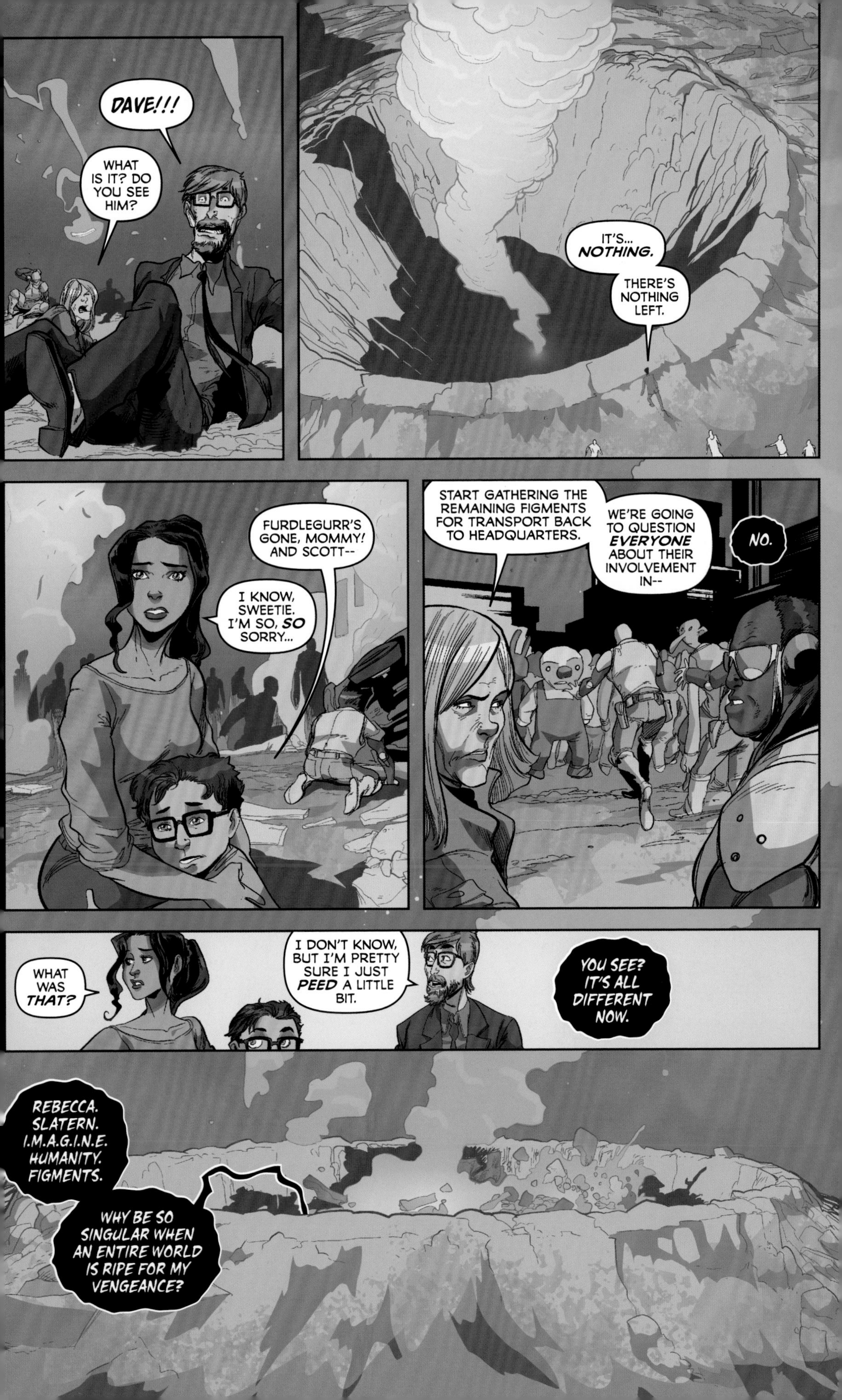
DAVE!!!
WHAT IS IT? DO YOU SEE HIM?
IT'S... NOTHING.
THERE'S NOTHING LEFT.
FURDLEGURR'S GONE, MOMMY! AND SCOTT--
I KNOW, SWEETIE. I'M SO, SO SORRY...
START GATHERING THE REMAINING FIGMENTS FOR TRANSPORT BACK TO HEADQUARTERS.
WE'RE GOING TO QUESTION EVERYONE ABOUT THEIR INVOLVEMENT IN--
NO.
WHAT WAS THAT?
I DON'T KNOW, BUT I'M PRETTY SURE I JUST PEED A LITTLE BIT.
YOU SEE? IT'S ALL DIFFERENT NOW.
REBECCA. SLATERN. I.M.A.G.I.N.E. HUMANITY. FIGMENTS.
WHY BE SO SINGULAR WHEN AN ENTIRE WORLD IS RIPE FOR MY VENGEANCE?

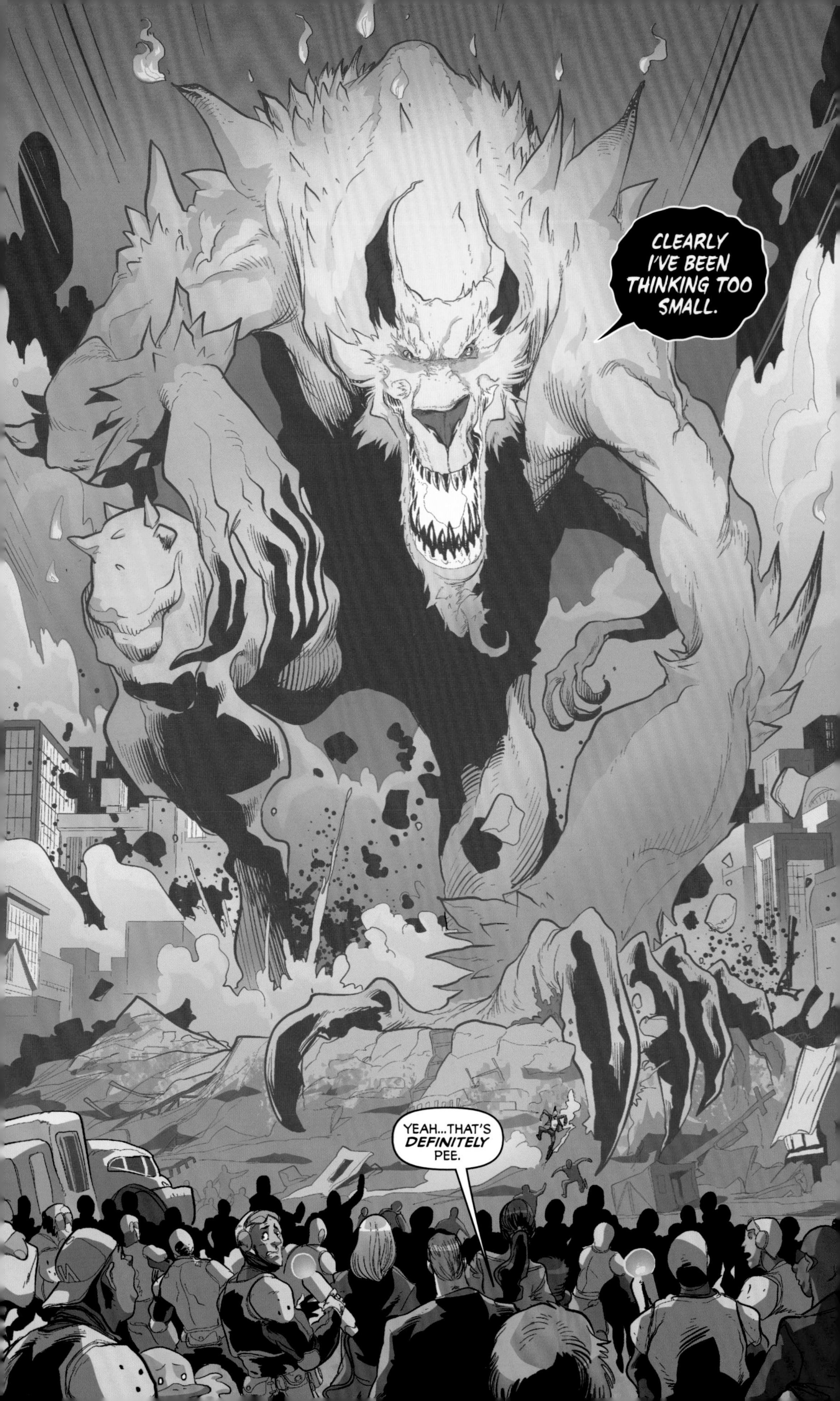
CLEARLY I'VE BEEN THINKING TOO SMALL.
YEAH...THAT'S *DEFINITELY* PEE.

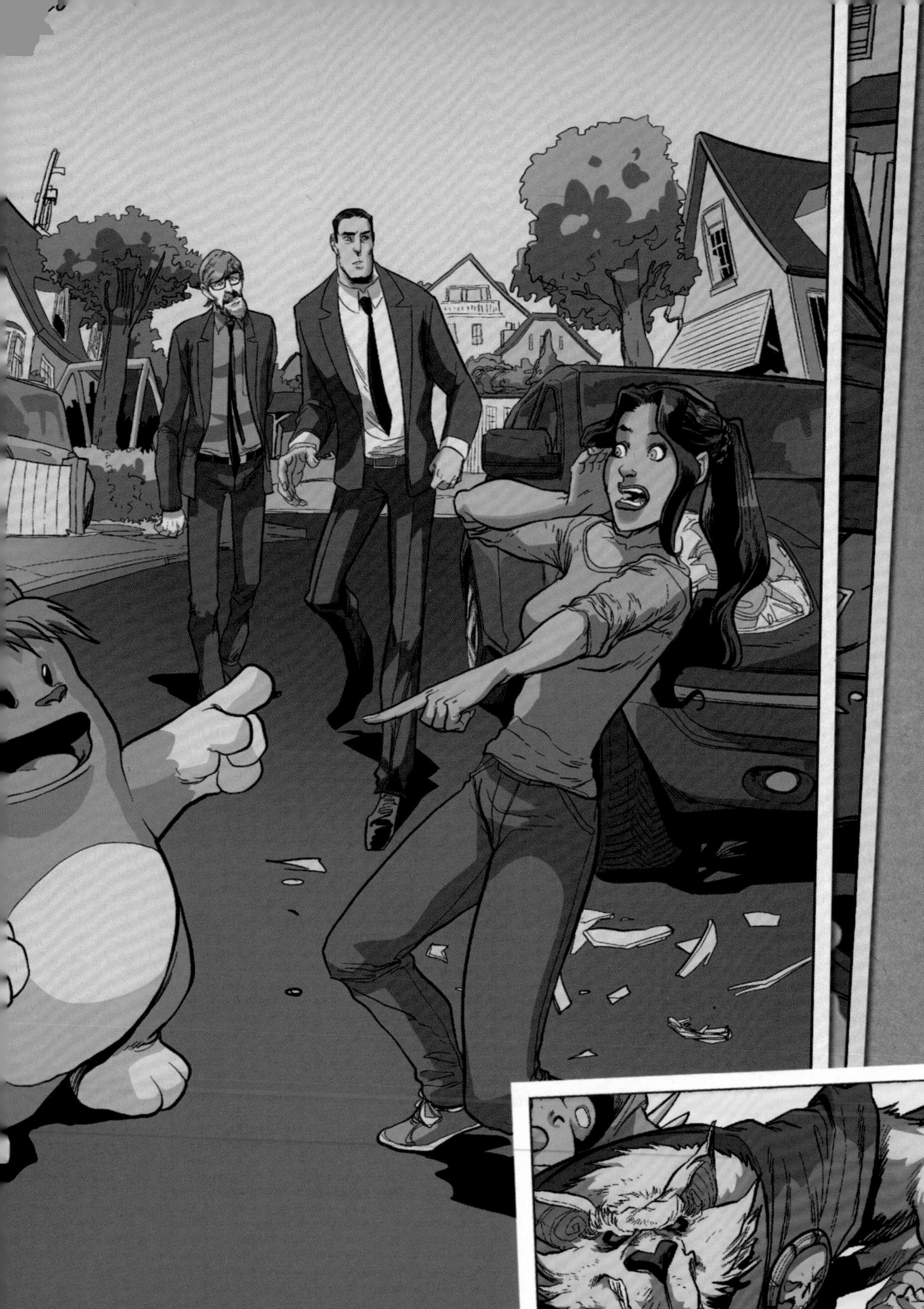

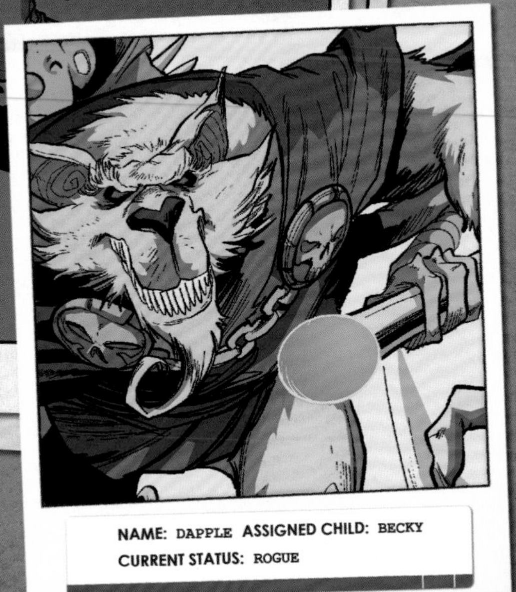
NAME: DAPPLE ASSIGNED CHILD: BECKY
CURRENT STATUS: ROGUE

ICIAL AGENT
ELD MANUAL

REVISED EDITION NO. 19-A

PROPERTY OF: DAVID SLATERN
AGENT NO.: ST-9870-146

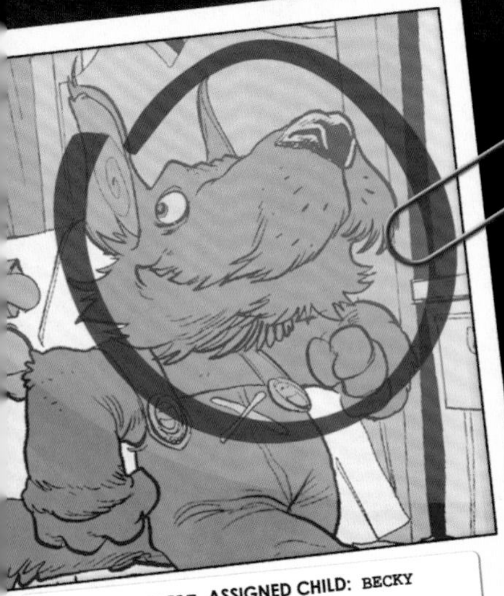

NAME: DAPPLE ASSIGNED CHILD: BECKY
CURRENT STATUS: UNKNOWN

QUIRED
Y WITH
EDURE
H ARE
OTECT
RMINE
SIBLE
ARIO.

IONAL
ERIFY
ERNAL
ENTS
SENT
RATE
MINE
DING
T OF
TING
ICE.

NED
RES
NAL
URE
F A
RNS
RED
ATA
BY
NTS
ING
ED
NS
T.

ED
ER
EY
LD
BE
ON
IC
ER
GE
CK
VE

POST-EVENT RECON:

- **DAPPLE** HOLDS A MEETING OF FIGMENTS FROM AROUND THE GLOBE. HE REVEALS HIS PLAN TO MERGE FIGMENTS WITH CHILDREN, MAKING THEM "AS REAL" AS HUMANS.
- DAPPLE REVEALS HIS PAST: BEING NEGLECTED BY YOUNG **REBECCA FAIRVIEW** AND BEING CAPTURED BY ROOKIE AGENT **DAVID SLATERN**. DURING HIS IMPRISONMENT, DAPPLE STUDIED THE HUMAN BRAIN AND, UPON HIS ESCAPE, USED THE ENERGY FUNNELED THROUGH I.M.A.G.I.N.E.'S EQUIPMENT TO MERGE WITH CHILDREN AND BECOME FULLY TANGIBLE.
- AGENTS SLATERN AND **TERRY SNOWGOOSE**, REBECCA AND FIGMENT **FURDLEGURR**, RUSH **ELLIOT**, ONLY TO FIND THEMSELVES SUR DAPPLE'S FOLLOWERS.
- **BLOUNDER**, HAVING LEARNED OF DAPPLE'S PL I.M.A.G.I.N.E. DIRECTOR **SABRINA QUIST**, THE MEETING, RESCUING THE OTHERS.
- DAPPLE BREAKS AN I.M.A.G.I.N.E. ENERGY ABSORB ITS POWER. HE TRANSFORMS INTO LIGHTNING ROD, DRAWING THEM INTO HIM EXPLODES INTO A GIGANTIC NEW FORM.
- IN THE AFTERMATH, DAVE AND BLOUNDER ARE M

REPORT CONTINUED IN CASE N

CASE FILE REFERENCE IMAGE: 9483

CHAPTER FOUR

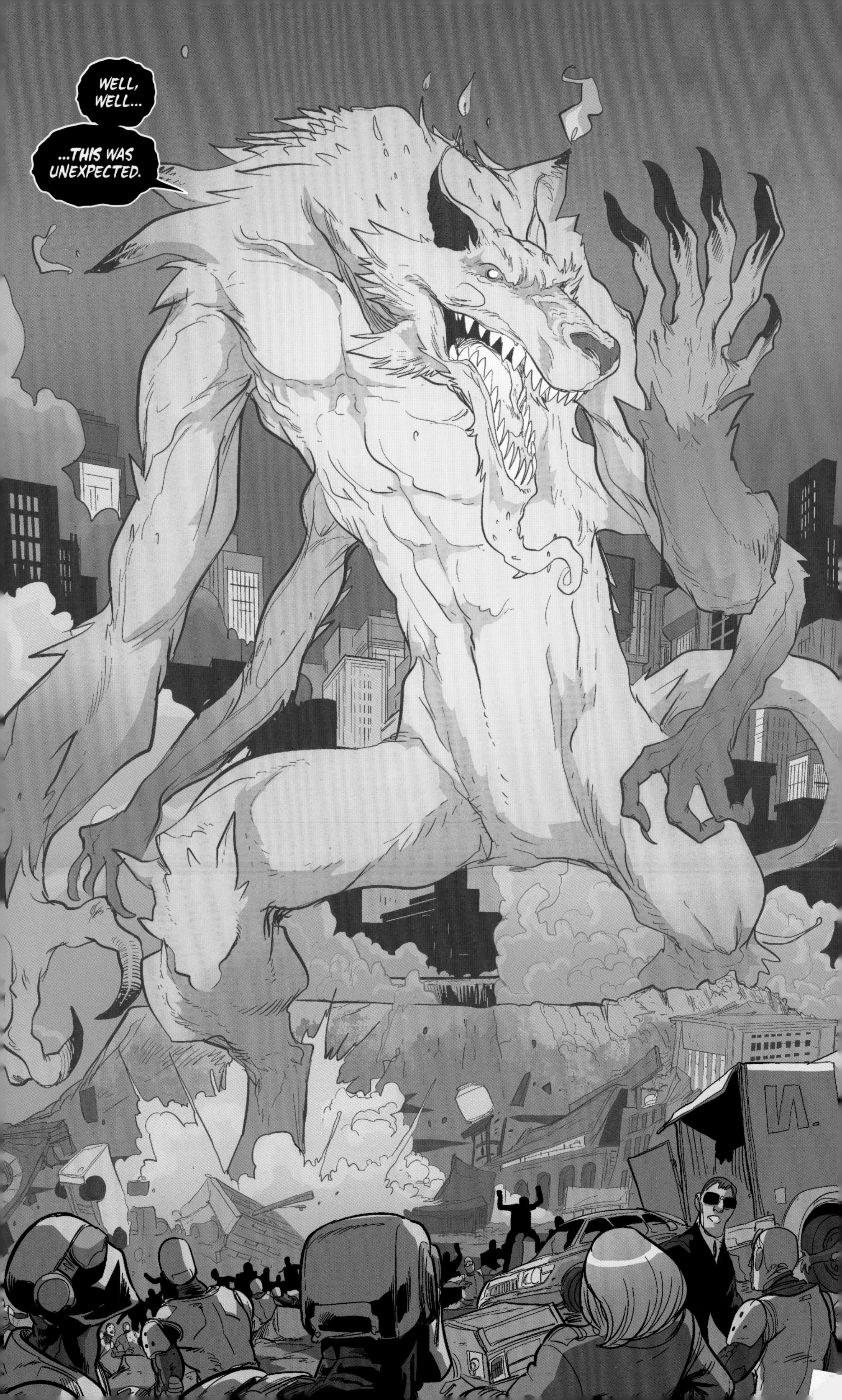
WELL, WELL...
...THIS WAS UNEXPECTED.

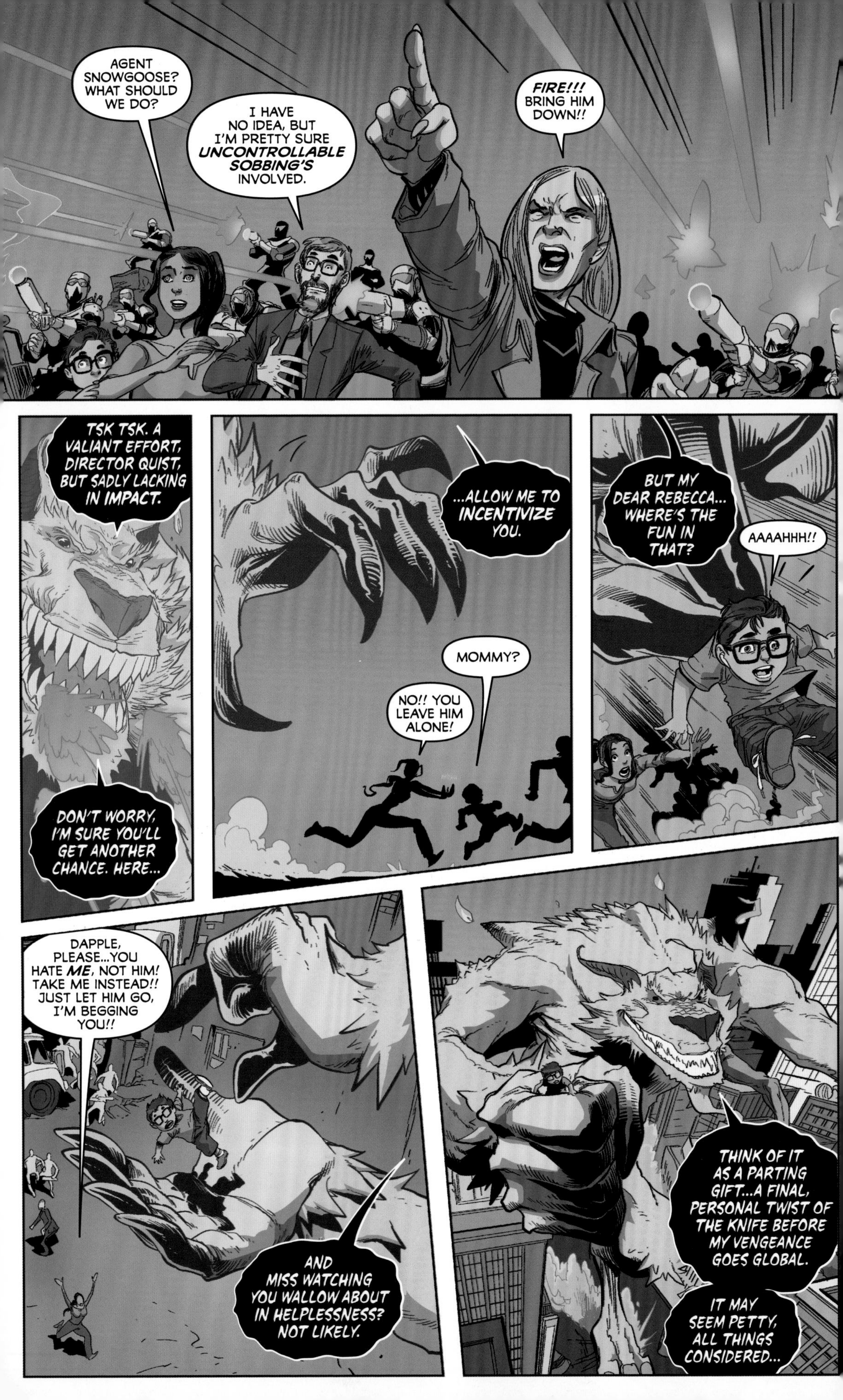
AGENT SNOWGOOSE? WHAT SHOULD WE DO?
I HAVE NO IDEA, BUT I'M PRETTY SURE UNCONTROLLABLE SOBBING'S INVOLVED.
FIRE!!! BRING HIM DOWN!!
TSK TSK. A VALIANT EFFORT, DIRECTOR QUIST, BUT SADLY LACKING IN IMPACT.
DON'T WORRY, I'M SURE YOU'LL GET ANOTHER CHANCE. HERE...
...ALLOW ME TO INCENTIVIZE YOU.
MOMMY?
NO!! YOU LEAVE HIM ALONE!
BUT MY DEAR REBECCA... WHERE'S THE FUN IN THAT?
AAAAHHH!!
DAPPLE, PLEASE...YOU HATE ME, NOT HIM! TAKE ME INSTEAD!! JUST LET HIM GO, I'M BEGGING YOU!!
AND MISS WATCHING YOU WALLOW ABOUT IN HELPLESSNESS? NOT LIKELY.
THINK OF IT AS A PARTING GIFT...A FINAL, PERSONAL TWIST OF THE KNIFE BEFORE MY VENGEANCE GOES GLOBAL.
IT MAY SEEM PETTY, ALL THINGS CONSIDERED...

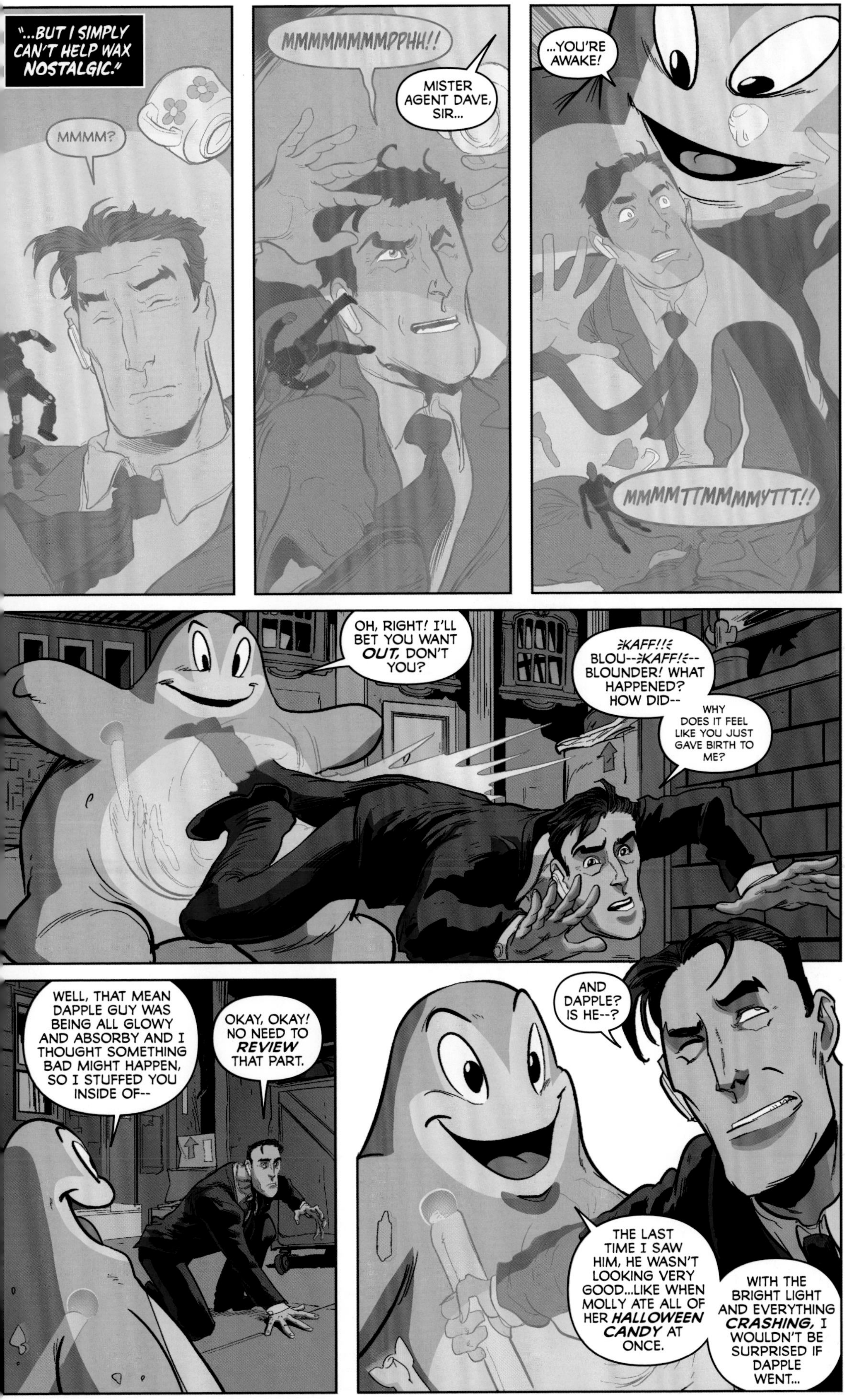
"...BUT I SIMPLY CAN'T HELP WAX NOSTALGIC."
MMMM?
MMMMMMMMDPHH!!
MISTER AGENT DAVE, SIR...
...YOU'RE AWAKE!
MMMMTTMMMMYTTT!!
OH, RIGHT! I'LL BET YOU WANT *OUT,* DON'T YOU?
KAFF!! BLOU--*KAFF!*-- BLOUNDER! WHAT HAPPENED? HOW DID--
WHY DOES IT FEEL LIKE YOU JUST GAVE BIRTH TO ME?
WELL, THAT MEAN DAPPLE GUY WAS BEING ALL GLOWY AND ABSORBY AND I THOUGHT SOMETHING BAD MIGHT HAPPEN, SO I STUFFED YOU INSIDE OF--
OKAY, OKAY! NO NEED TO *REVIEW* THAT PART.
AND DAPPLE? IS HE--?
THE LAST TIME I SAW HIM, HE WASN'T LOOKING VERY GOOD...LIKE WHEN MOLLY ATE ALL OF HER *HALLOWEEN CANDY* AT ONCE.
WITH THE BRIGHT LIGHT AND EVERYTHING *CRASHING,* I WOULDN'T BE SURPRISED IF DAPPLE WENT...

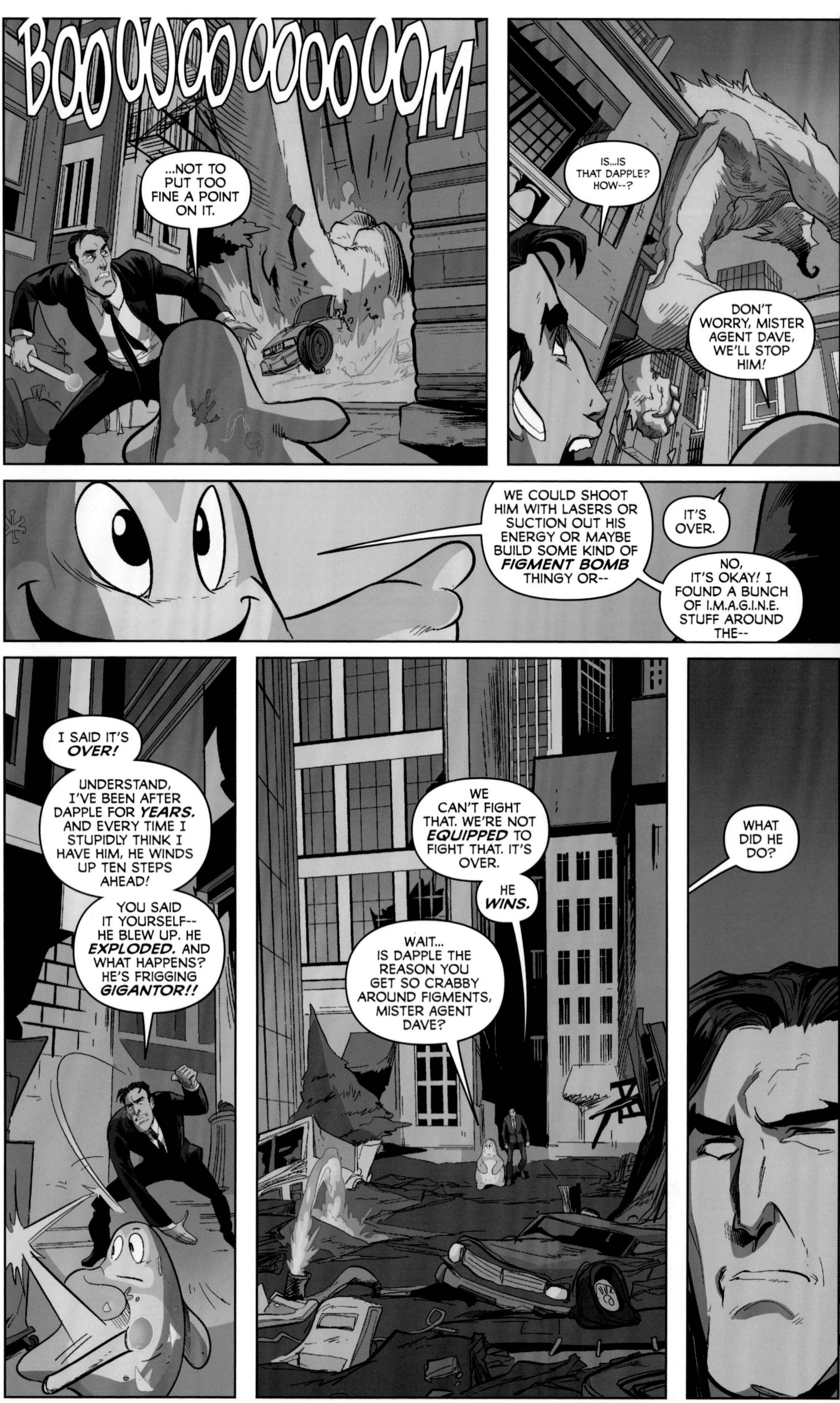

BOOOOOOOOOOOOM
...NOT TO PUT TOO FINE A POINT ON IT.
IS...IS THAT DAPPLE? HOW--?
DON'T WORRY, MISTER AGENT DAVE, WE'LL STOP HIM!
WE COULD SHOOT HIM WITH LASERS OR SUCTION OUT HIS ENERGY OR MAYBE BUILD SOME KIND OF FIGMENT BOMB THINGY OR--
IT'S OVER.
NO, IT'S OKAY! I FOUND A BUNCH OF I.M.A.G.I.N.E. STUFF AROUND THE--
I SAID IT'S OVER!
UNDERSTAND, I'VE BEEN AFTER DAPPLE FOR YEARS. AND EVERY TIME I STUPIDLY THINK I HAVE HIM, HE WINDS UP TEN STEPS AHEAD!
YOU SAID IT YOURSELF-- HE BLEW UP. HE EXPLODED. AND WHAT HAPPENS? HE'S FRIGGING GIGANTOR!!
WE CAN'T FIGHT THAT. WE'RE NOT EQUIPPED TO FIGHT THAT. IT'S OVER.
HE WINS.
WAIT... IS DAPPLE THE REASON YOU GET SO CRABBY AROUND FIGMENTS, MISTER AGENT DAVE?
WHAT DID HE DO?

YOU HAVE TO **DO** SOMETHING!!

MS. FAIRVIEW, I KNOW YOU'RE, LIKE, **TOTALLY** STRESSED AND EVERYTHING BUT WE'RE WORKING ON IT!

DIRECTOR QUIST IS GETTING A HOLD OF THE **TOKYO** BRANCH. WE'RE PRETTY SURE THEY KNOW HOW TO HANDLE **GINORMOUS** FIGMENTS OVER THERE.

I DON'T WANT THE TOKYO BRANCH, I DON'T WANT DIRECTOR QUIST. YOU ZAPPED ME AT MY HOUSE, YOU WATCHED DAPPLE TAKE MY SON...YOU **OWE** ME.

I WANT **YOU.**

ME?

YOU DON'T WANT ME! I'M A **TERRIBLE** AGENT!

IN ONE WEEK I LOST MY WEAPON, ALMOST GOT DAVE KILLED, GOT KNOCKED OUT **EIGHT** TIMES, TOTALED AN SUV, FORGOT MY EARPIECE, SHOT--

THE EARPIECE.

DIRECTOR QUIST! I HAVE AN IDEA!

ELLIOT WAS ABLE TO SEE **ALL** THE FIGMENTS, RIGHT? SO DAPPLE MUST'VE GOTTEN HIS HANDS ON A--

HQ'S SCRAMBLED THREE CHOPPERS, MA'AM. ETA THIRTY-FIVE MINUTES.

DIRECTOR QUI--

I HEARD YOU. REMOVING THE EARPIECE **COULD** MAKE THE BOY IMMUNE TO DAPPLE'S ATTACKS, BUT HOW DO YOU PROPOSE REACHING HIM WITHOUT AIR SUPPORT? GROWING A PAIR OF WINGS?

I APPRECIATE YOUR ENTHUSIASM, TERRY, BUT I NEED YOU TO ASSIST WITH CROWD CONTROL...

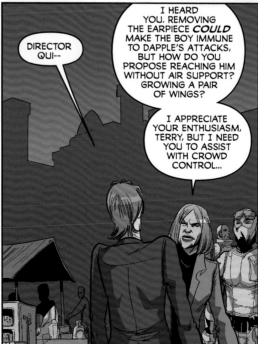

...AND LET THE **REAL** AGENTS DO THEIR JOBS.

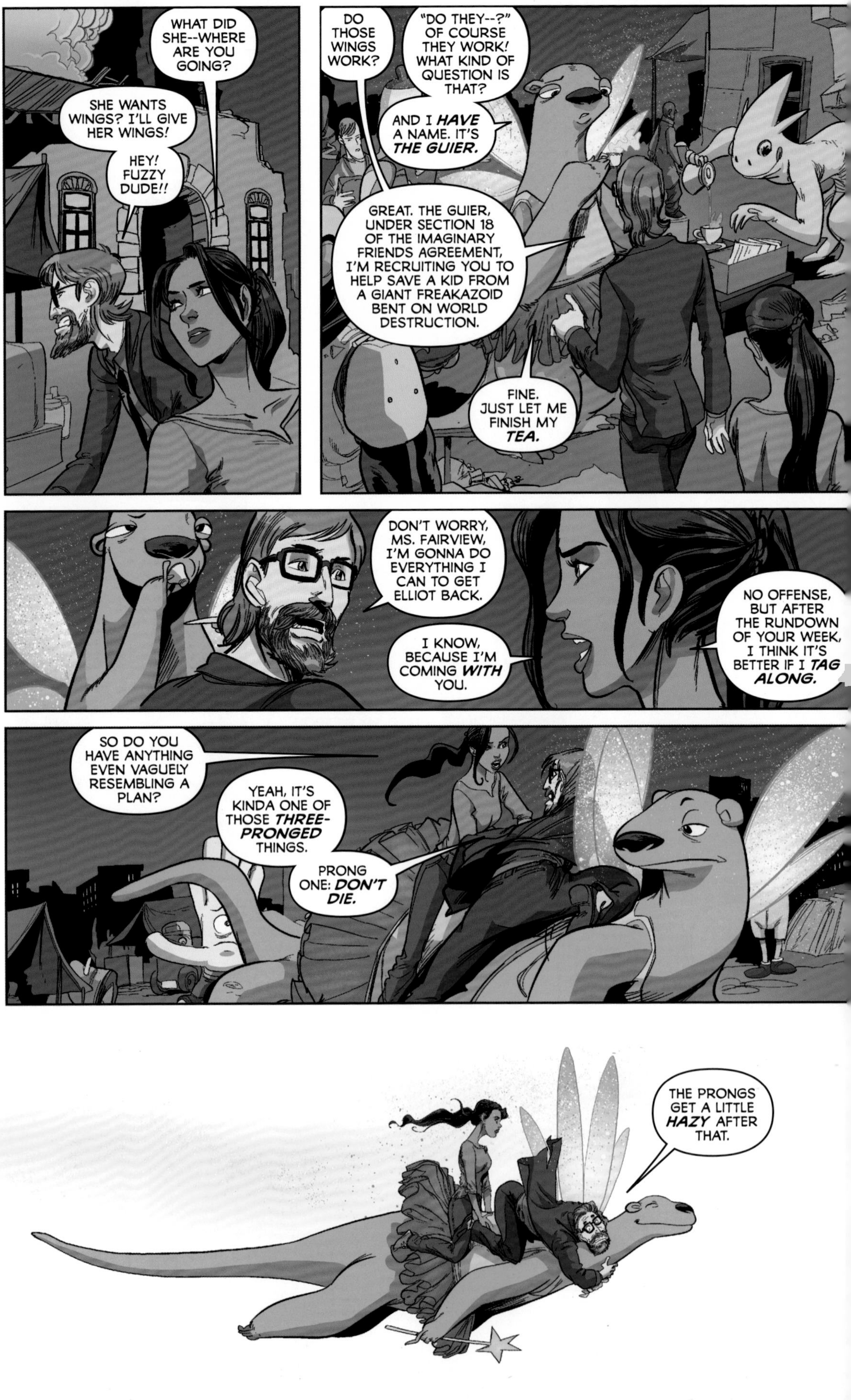
WHAT DID SHE--WHERE ARE YOU GOING?
SHE WANTS WINGS? I'LL GIVE HER WINGS!
HEY! FUZZY DUDE!!
DO THOSE WINGS WORK?
"DO THEY--?" OF COURSE THEY WORK! WHAT KIND OF QUESTION IS THAT?
AND I *HAVE* A NAME. IT'S ***THE GUIER.***
GREAT. THE GUIER, UNDER SECTION 18 OF THE IMAGINARY FRIENDS AGREEMENT, I'M RECRUITING YOU TO HELP SAVE A KID FROM A GIANT FREAKAZOID BENT ON WORLD DESTRUCTION.
FINE. JUST LET ME FINISH MY ***TEA.***
DON'T WORRY, MS. FAIRVIEW, I'M GONNA DO EVERYTHING I CAN TO GET ELLIOT BACK.
I KNOW, BECAUSE I'M COMING ***WITH*** YOU.
NO OFFENSE, BUT AFTER THE RUNDOWN OF YOUR WEEK, I THINK IT'S BETTER IF I ***TAG ALONG.***
SO DO YOU HAVE ANYTHING EVEN VAGUELY RESEMBLING A PLAN?
YEAH, IT'S KINDA ONE OF THOSE ***THREE-PRONGED*** THINGS.
PRONG ONE: ***DON'T DIE.***
THE PRONGS GET A LITTLE ***HAZY*** AFTER THAT.

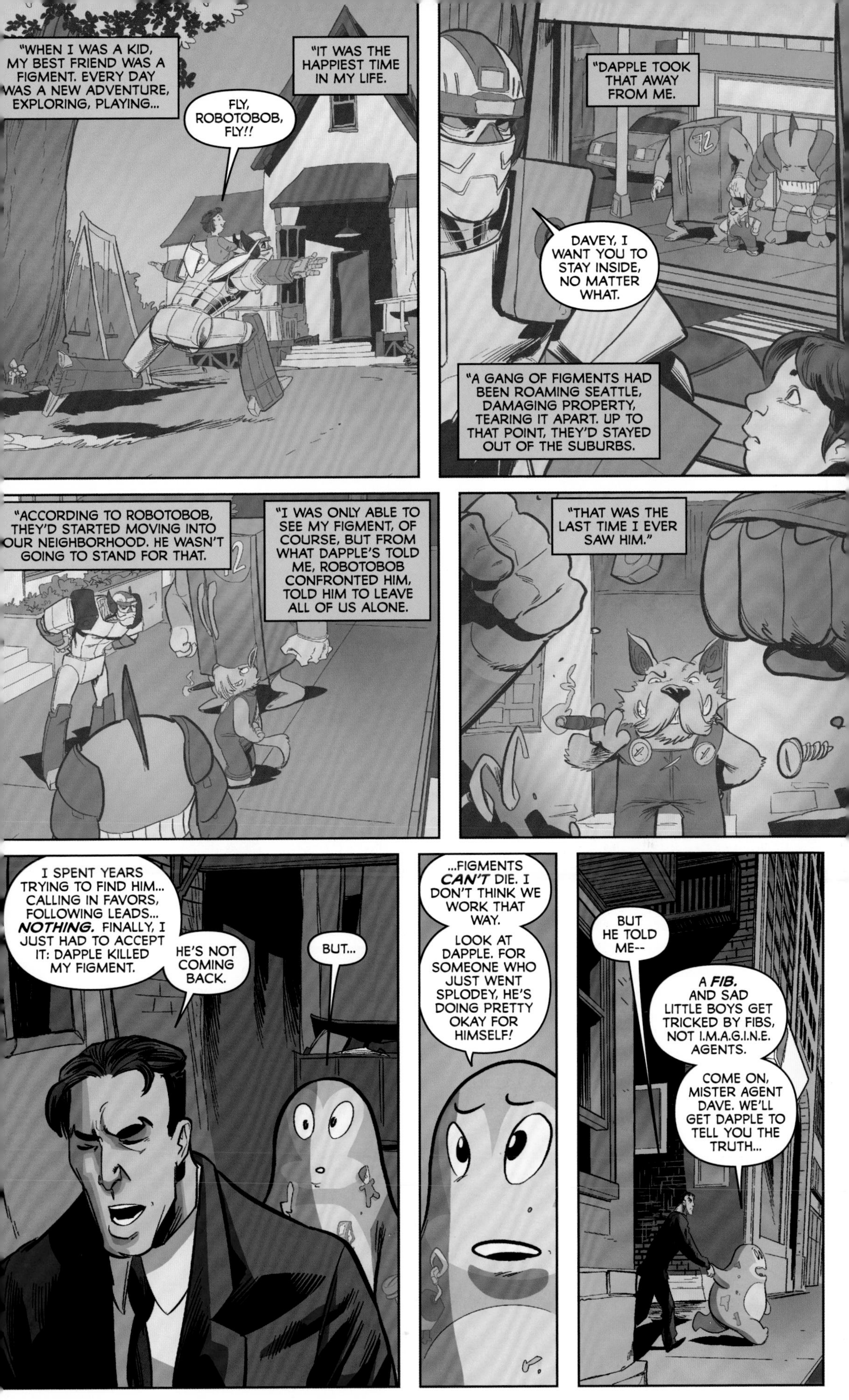
"WHEN I WAS A KID, MY BEST FRIEND WAS A FIGMENT. EVERY DAY WAS A NEW ADVENTURE, EXPLORING, PLAYING...
"IT WAS THE HAPPIEST TIME IN MY LIFE.
FLY, ROBOTOBOB, FLY!!
"DAPPLE TOOK THAT AWAY FROM ME.
DAVEY, I WANT YOU TO STAY INSIDE, NO MATTER WHAT.
"A GANG OF FIGMENTS HAD BEEN ROAMING SEATTLE, DAMAGING PROPERTY, TEARING IT APART. UP TO THAT POINT, THEY'D STAYED OUT OF THE SUBURBS.
"ACCORDING TO ROBOTOBOB, THEY'D STARTED MOVING INTO OUR NEIGHBORHOOD. HE WASN'T GOING TO STAND FOR THAT.
"I WAS ONLY ABLE TO SEE MY FIGMENT, OF COURSE, BUT FROM WHAT DAPPLE'S TOLD ME, ROBOTOBOB CONFRONTED HIM, TOLD HIM TO LEAVE ALL OF US ALONE.
"THAT WAS THE LAST TIME I EVER SAW HIM."
I SPENT YEARS TRYING TO FIND HIM... CALLING IN FAVORS, FOLLOWING LEADS... NOTHING. FINALLY, I JUST HAD TO ACCEPT IT: DAPPLE KILLED MY FIGMENT.
HE'S NOT COMING BACK.
BUT...
...FIGMENTS CAN'T DIE. I DON'T THINK WE WORK THAT WAY.
LOOK AT DAPPLE. FOR SOMEONE WHO JUST WENT SPLODEY, HE'S DOING PRETTY OKAY FOR HIMSELF!
BUT HE TOLD ME--
A FIB. AND SAD LITTLE BOYS GET TRICKED BY FIBS, NOT I.M.A.G.I.N.E. AGENTS.
COME ON, MISTER AGENT DAVE. WE'LL GET DAPPLE TO TELL YOU THE TRUTH...

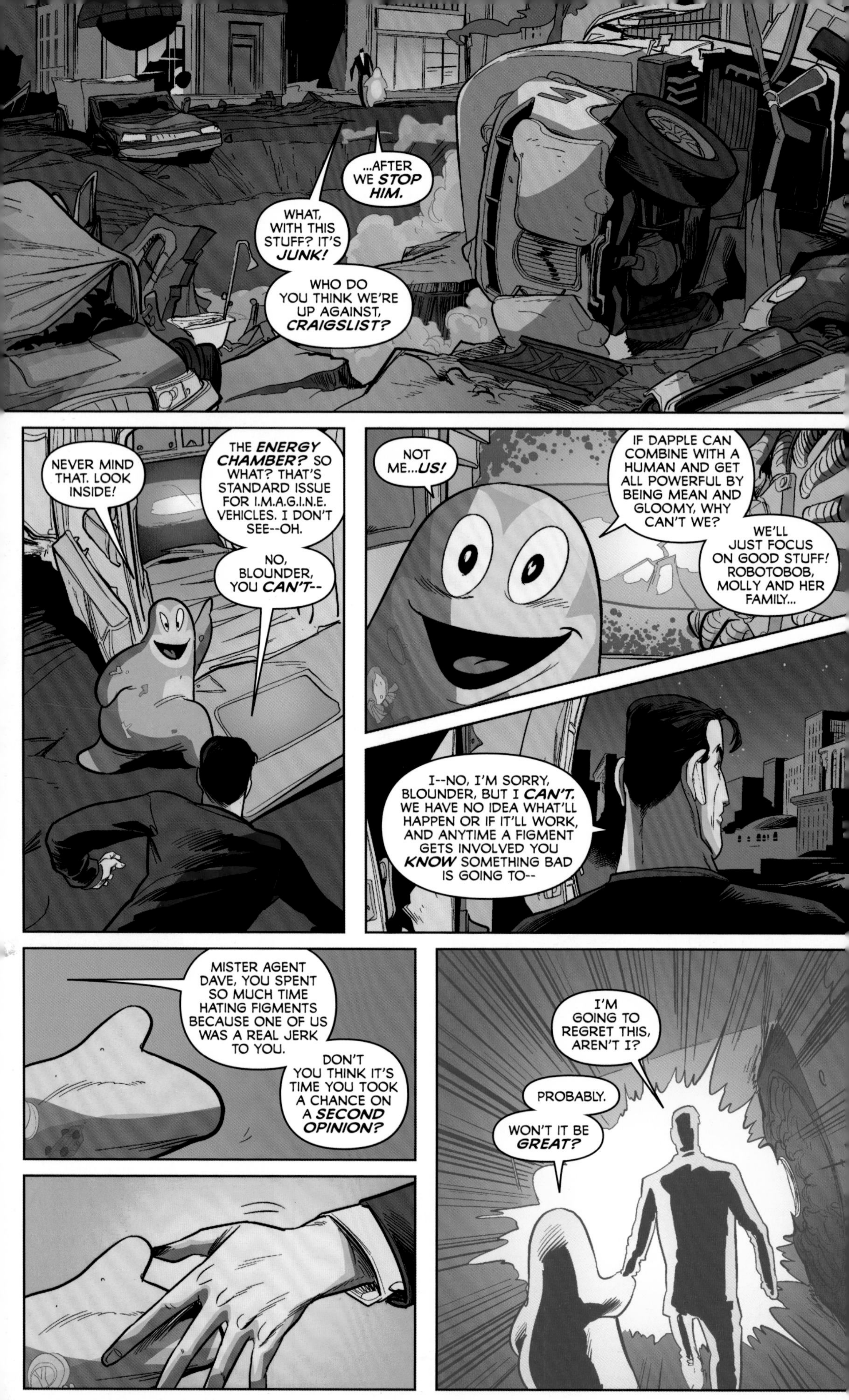

...AFTER WE *STOP* *HIM.*
WHAT, WITH THIS STUFF? IT'S *JUNK!*
WHO DO YOU THINK WE'RE UP AGAINST, *CRAIGSLIST?*
NEVER MIND THAT. LOOK INSIDE!
THE *ENERGY CHAMBER?* SO WHAT? THAT'S STANDARD ISSUE FOR I.M.A.G.I.N.E. VEHICLES. I DON'T SEE--OH.
NO, BLOUNDER, YOU *CAN'T*--
NOT ME...*US!*
IF DAPPLE CAN COMBINE WITH A HUMAN AND GET ALL POWERFUL BY BEING MEAN AND GLOOMY, WHY CAN'T WE?
WE'LL JUST FOCUS ON GOOD STUFF! ROBOTOBOB, MOLLY AND HER FAMILY...
I--NO, I'M SORRY, BLOUNDER, BUT I *CAN'T.* WE HAVE NO IDEA WHAT'LL HAPPEN OR IF IT'LL WORK, AND ANYTIME A FIGMENT GETS INVOLVED YOU *KNOW* SOMETHING BAD IS GOING TO--
MISTER AGENT DAVE, YOU SPENT SO MUCH TIME HATING FIGMENTS BECAUSE ONE OF US WAS A REAL JERK TO YOU.
DON'T YOU THINK IT'S TIME YOU TOOK A CHANCE ON A *SECOND OPINION?*
I'M GOING TO REGRET THIS, AREN'T I?
PROBABLY.
WON'T IT BE *GREAT?*

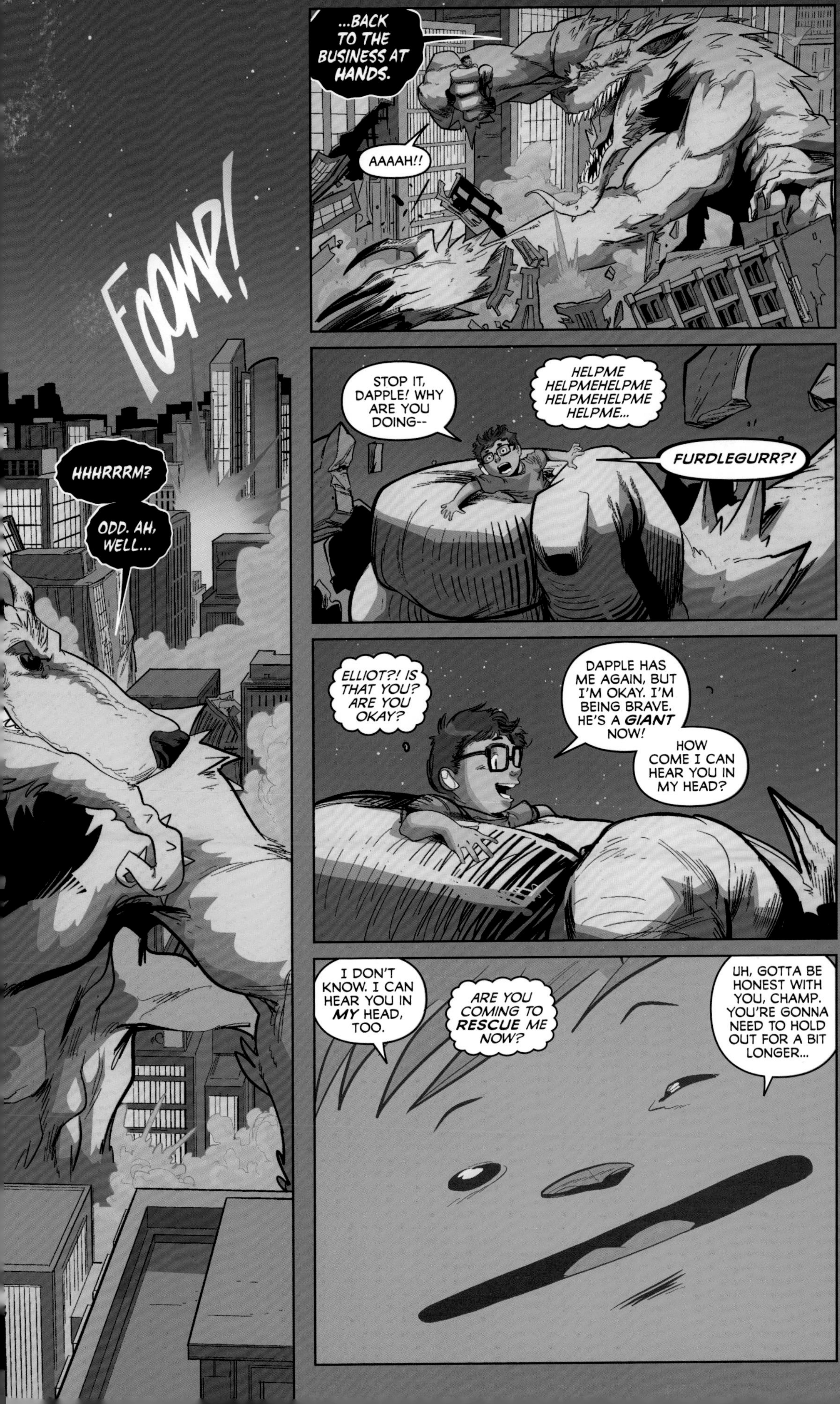
FOOMP!
HHHRRRM?
ODD. AH, WELL...
...BACK TO THE BUSINESS AT HANDS.
AAAAH!!
STOP IT, DAPPLE! WHY ARE YOU DOING--
HELPME HELPMEHELPME HELPMEHELPME HELPME...
FURDLEGURR?!
ELLIOT?! IS THAT YOU? ARE YOU OKAY?
DAPPLE HAS ME AGAIN, BUT I'M OKAY. I'M BEING BRAVE. HE'S A GIANT NOW!
HOW COME I CAN HEAR YOU IN MY HEAD?
I DON'T KNOW. I CAN HEAR YOU IN MY HEAD, TOO.
ARE YOU COMING TO RESCUE ME NOW?
UH, GOTTA BE HONEST WITH YOU, CHAMP. YOU'RE GONNA NEED TO HOLD OUT FOR A BIT LONGER...

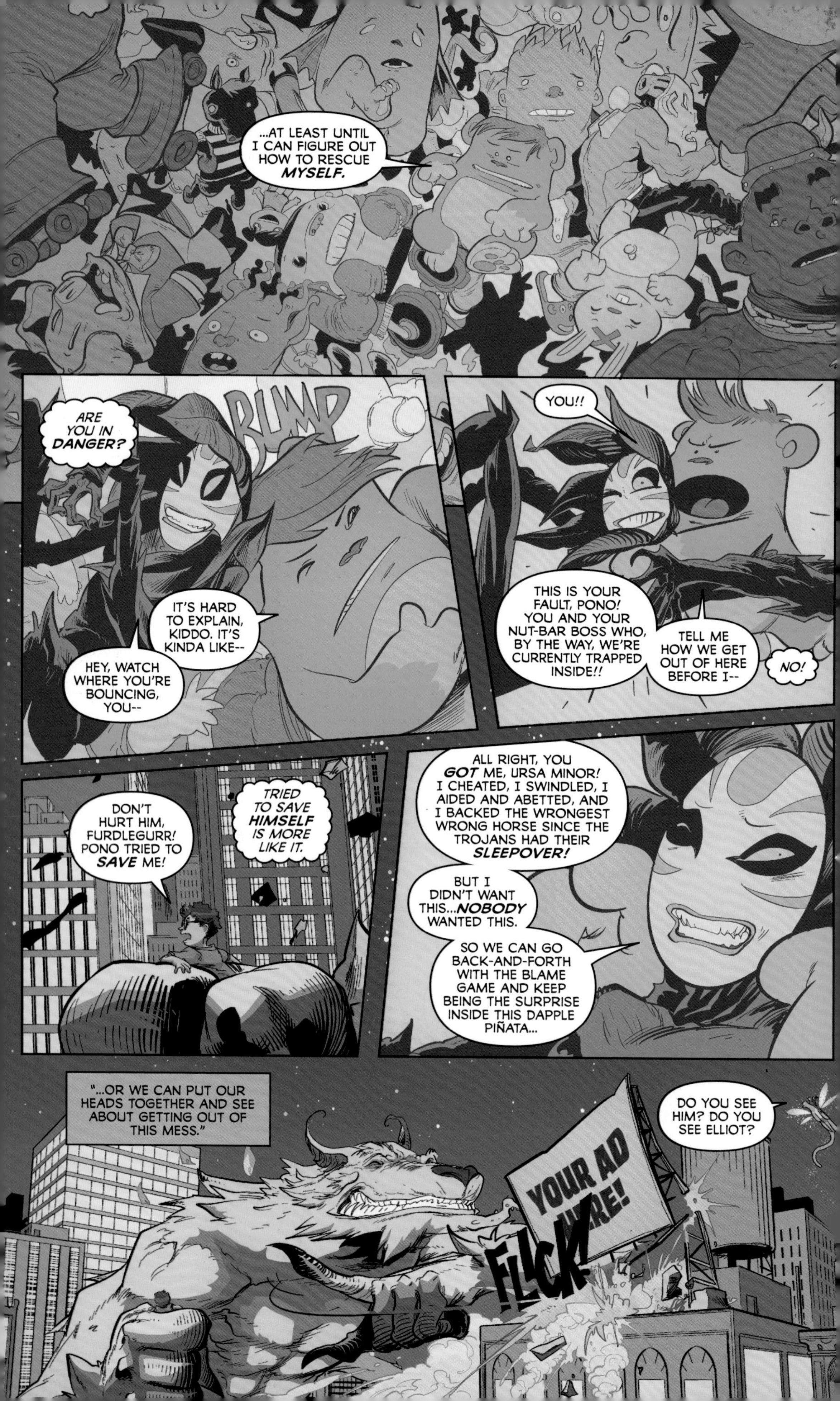

...AT LEAST UNTIL I CAN FIGURE OUT HOW TO RESCUE ***MYSELF.***
*ARE YOU IN **DANGER?***
BUMP
IT'S HARD TO EXPLAIN, KIDDO. IT'S KINDA LIKE--
HEY, WATCH WHERE YOU'RE BOUNCING, YOU--
YOU*!!*
THIS IS YOUR FAULT, PONO*!* YOU AND YOUR NUT-BAR BOSS WHO, BY THE WAY, WE'RE CURRENTLY TRAPPED INSIDE*!!*
TELL ME HOW WE GET OUT OF HERE BEFORE I--
NO!
DON'T HURT HIM, FURDLEGURR! PONO TRIED TO ***SAVE*** ME!
*TRIED TO SAVE **HIMSELF** IS MORE LIKE IT.*
ALL RIGHT, YOU ***GOT*** ME, URSA MINOR*!* I CHEATED, I SWINDLED, I AIDED AND ABETTED, AND I BACKED THE WRONGEST WRONG HORSE SINCE THE TROJANS HAD THEIR ***SLEEPOVER!***
BUT I DIDN'T WANT THIS...***NOBODY*** WANTED THIS.
SO WE CAN GO BACK-AND-FORTH WITH THE BLAME GAME AND KEEP BEING THE SURPRISE INSIDE THIS DAPPLE PIÑATA...
"...OR WE CAN PUT OUR HEADS TOGETHER AND SEE ABOUT GETTING OUT OF THIS MESS."
DO YOU SEE HIM? DO YOU SEE ELLIOT?
YOUR AD HERE!
FLICK!

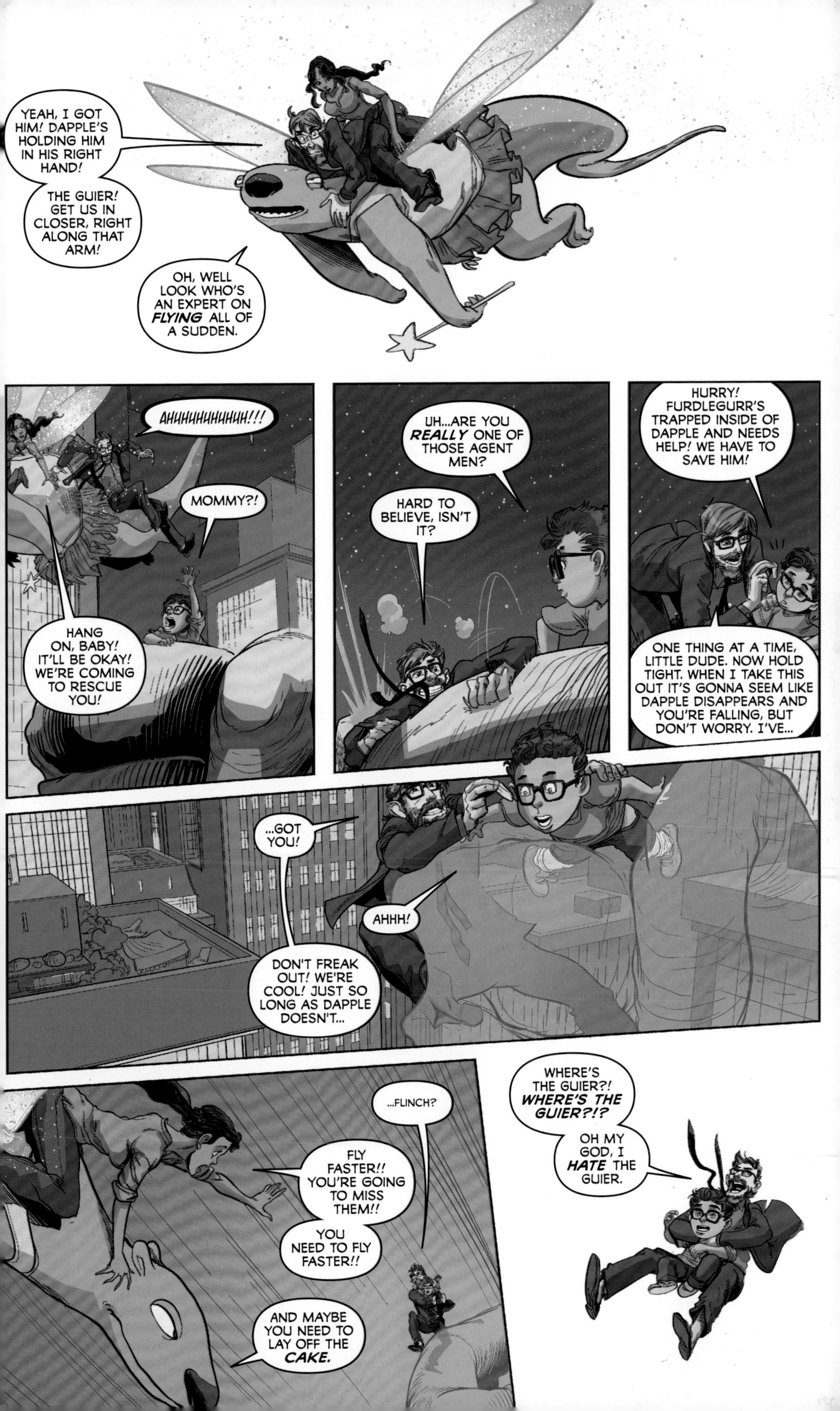

YEAH, I GOT HIM! DAPPLE'S HOLDING HIM IN HIS RIGHT HAND!
THE GUIER! GET US IN CLOSER, RIGHT ALONG THAT ARM!
OH, WELL LOOK WHO'S AN EXPERT ON *FLYING* ALL OF A SUDDEN.
AHHHHHHHHHHH!!!
MOMMY?!
HANG ON, BABY! IT'LL BE OKAY! WE'RE COMING TO RESCUE YOU!
UH...ARE YOU *REALLY* ONE OF THOSE AGENT MEN?
HARD TO BELIEVE, ISN'T IT?
HURRY! FURDLEGURR'S TRAPPED INSIDE OF DAPPLE AND NEEDS HELP! WE HAVE TO SAVE HIM!
ONE THING AT A TIME, LITTLE DUDE. NOW HOLD TIGHT. WHEN I TAKE THIS OUT IT'S GONNA SEEM LIKE DAPPLE DISAPPEARS AND YOU'RE FALLING, BUT DON'T WORRY. I'VE...
...GOT YOU!
AHHH!
DON'T FREAK OUT! WE'RE COOL! JUST SO LONG AS DAPPLE DOESN'T...
...FLINCH?
FLY FASTER!! YOU'RE GOING TO MISS THEM!!
YOU NEED TO FLY FASTER!!
AND MAYBE YOU NEED TO LAY OFF THE *CAKE.*
WHERE'S THE GUIER?! *WHERE'S THE GUIER?!?*
OH MY GOD, I *HATE* THE GUIER.

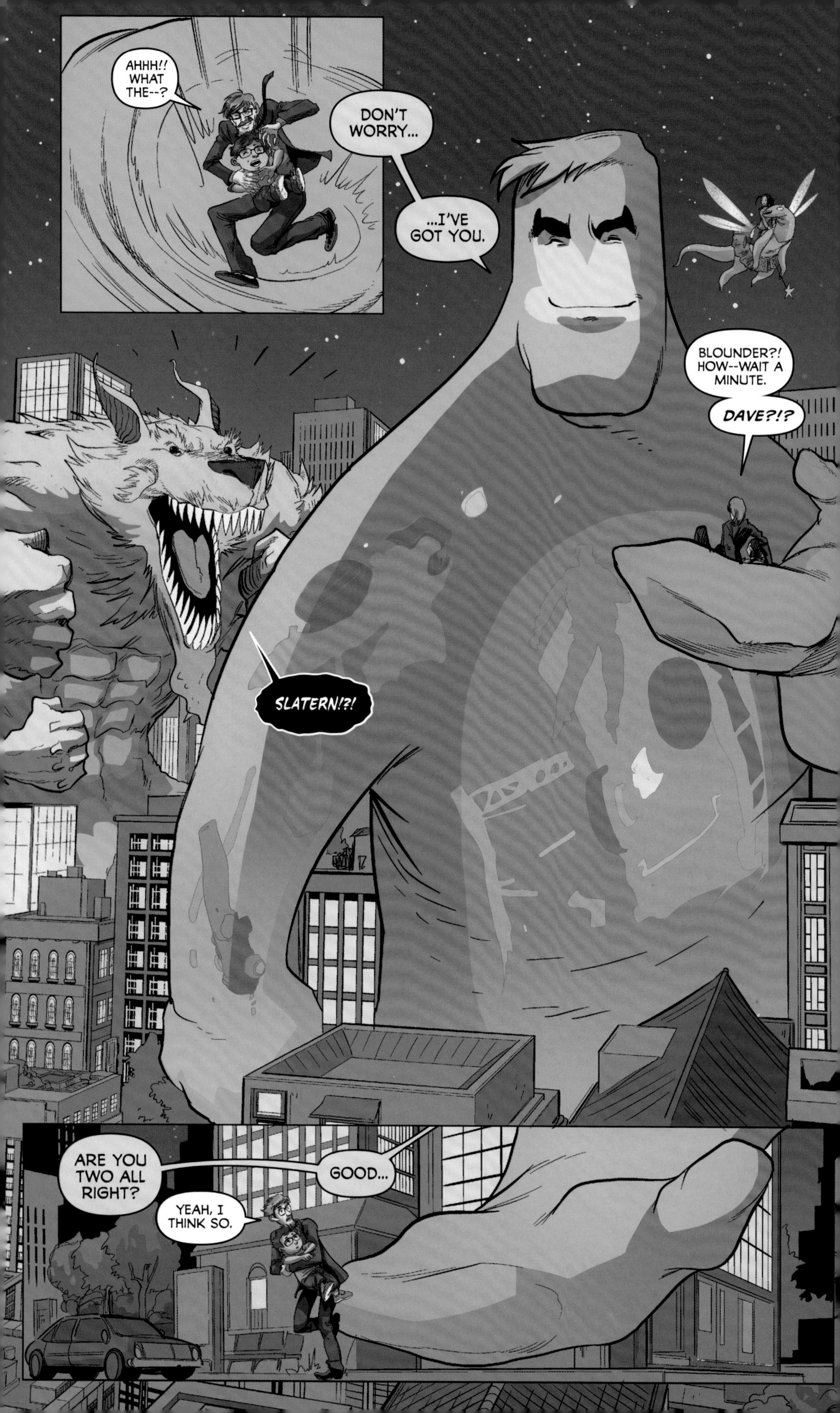
AHHH!! WHAT THE--?
DON'T WORRY...
...I'VE GOT YOU.
BLOUNDER?! HOW--WAIT A MINUTE.
DAVE?!?
SLATERN!?!
ARE YOU TWO ALL RIGHT?
YEAH, I THINK SO.
GOOD...

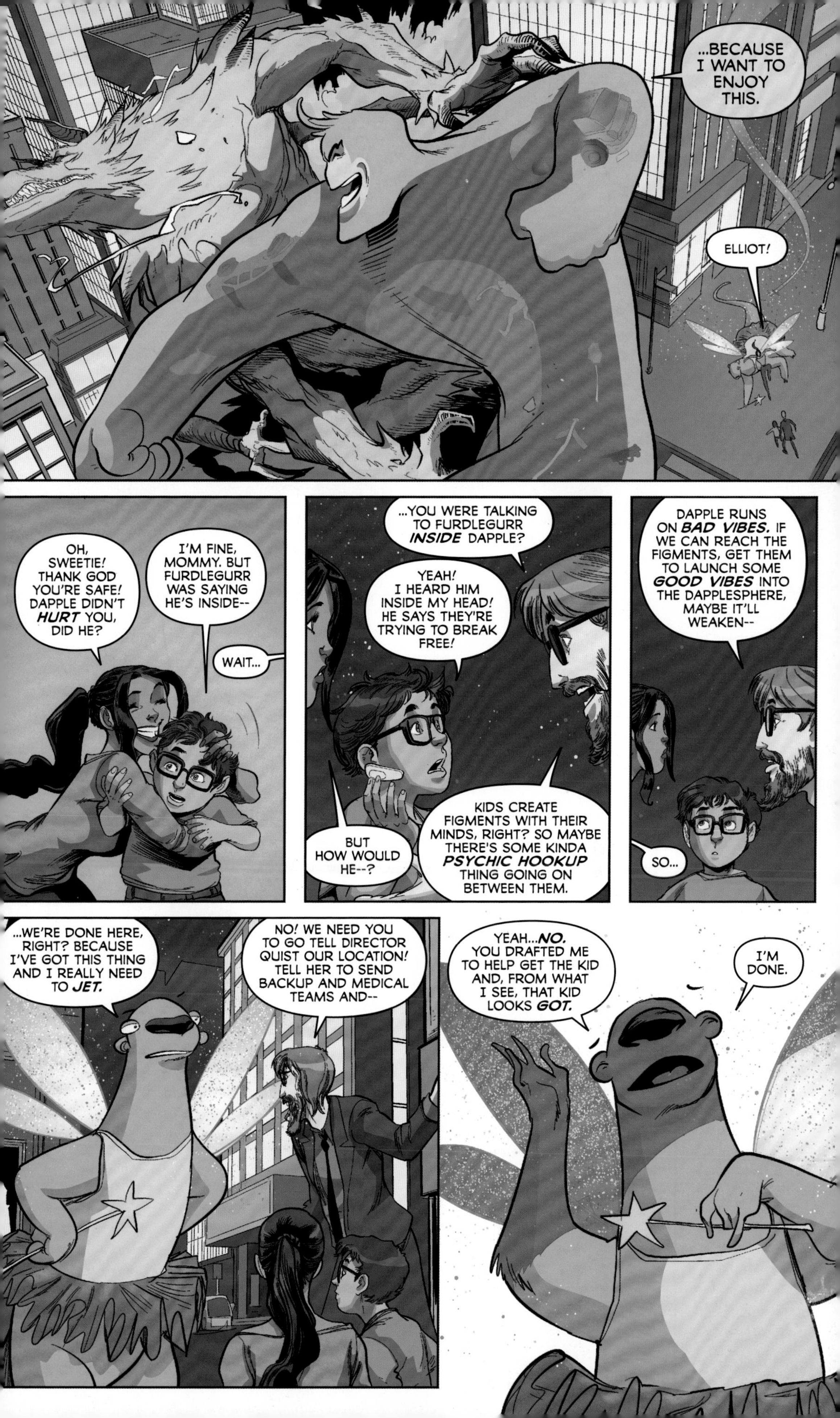

...BECAUSE I WANT TO ENJOY THIS.
ELLIOT!
OH, SWEETIE! THANK GOD YOU'RE SAFE! DAPPLE DIDN'T *HURT* YOU, DID HE?
I'M FINE, MOMMY. BUT FURDLEGURR WAS SAYING HE'S INSIDE--
WAIT...
...YOU WERE TALKING TO FURDLEGURR *INSIDE* DAPPLE?
YEAH! I HEARD HIM INSIDE MY HEAD! HE SAYS THEY'RE TRYING TO BREAK FREE!
BUT HOW WOULD HE--?
KIDS CREATE FIGMENTS WITH THEIR MINDS, RIGHT? SO MAYBE THERE'S SOME KINDA *PSYCHIC HOOKUP* THING GOING ON BETWEEN THEM.
DAPPLE RUNS ON *BAD VIBES.* IF WE CAN REACH THE FIGMENTS, GET THEM TO LAUNCH SOME *GOOD VIBES* INTO THE DAPPLESPHERE, MAYBE IT'LL WEAKEN--
SO...
...WE'RE DONE HERE, RIGHT? BECAUSE I'VE GOT THIS THING AND I REALLY NEED TO *JET.*
NO! WE NEED YOU TO GO TELL DIRECTOR QUIST OUR LOCATION! TELL HER TO SEND BACKUP AND MEDICAL TEAMS AND--
YEAH...*NO.* YOU DRAFTED ME TO HELP GET THE KID AND, FROM WHAT I SEE, THAT KID LOOKS *GOT.*
I'M DONE.

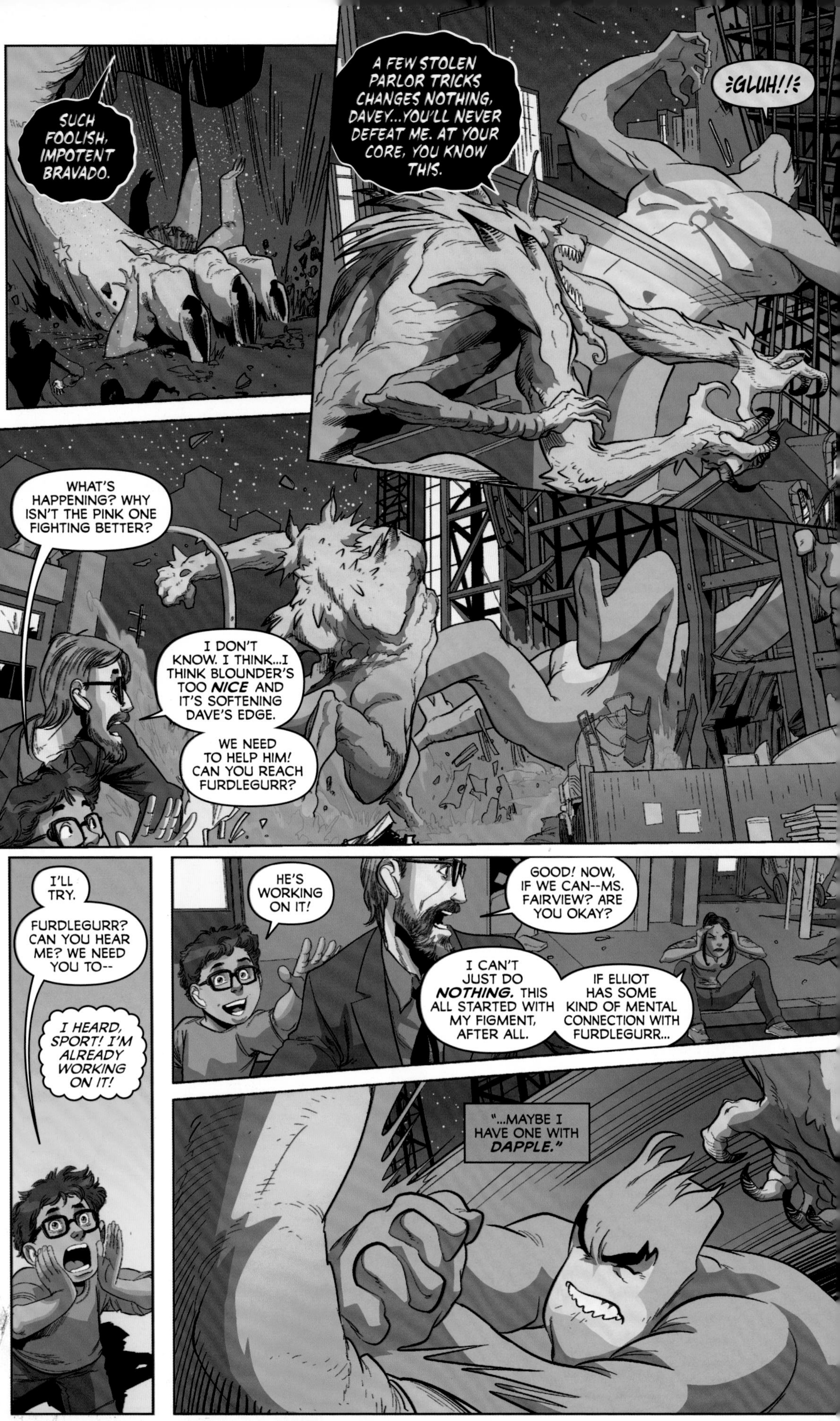
SUCH FOOLISH, IMPOTENT BRAVADO.
A FEW STOLEN PARLOR TRICKS CHANGES NOTHING, DAVEY...YOU'LL NEVER DEFEAT ME. AT YOUR CORE, YOU KNOW THIS.
GLUH!!
WHAT'S HAPPENING? WHY ISN'T THE PINK ONE FIGHTING BETTER?
I DON'T KNOW. I THINK...I THINK BLOUNDER'S TOO NICE AND IT'S SOFTENING DAVE'S EDGE.
WE NEED TO HELP HIM! CAN YOU REACH FURDLEGURR?
I'LL TRY.
FURDLEGURR? CAN YOU HEAR ME? WE NEED YOU TO--
I HEARD, SPORT! I'M ALREADY WORKING ON IT!
HE'S WORKING ON IT!
GOOD! NOW, IF WE CAN--MS. FAIRVIEW? ARE YOU OKAY?
I CAN'T JUST DO NOTHING. THIS ALL STARTED WITH MY FIGMENT, AFTER ALL.
IF ELLIOT HAS SOME KIND OF MENTAL CONNECTION WITH FURDLEGURR...
"...MAYBE I HAVE ONE WITH DAPPLE."

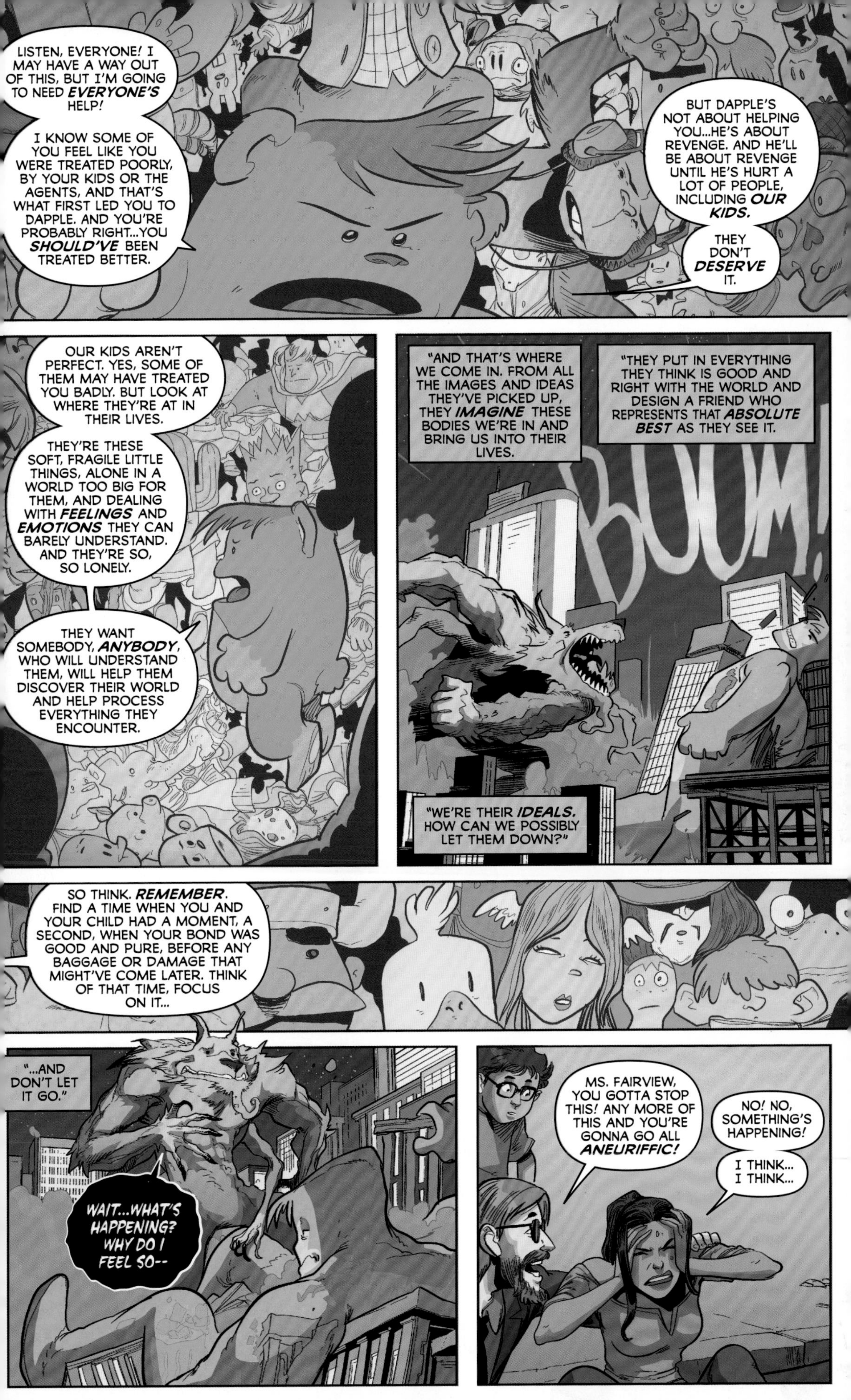
LISTEN, EVERYONE! I MAY HAVE A WAY OUT OF THIS, BUT I'M GOING TO NEED *EVERYONE'S* HELP!
I KNOW SOME OF YOU FEEL LIKE YOU WERE TREATED POORLY, BY YOUR KIDS OR THE AGENTS, AND THAT'S WHAT FIRST LED YOU TO DAPPLE. AND YOU'RE PROBABLY RIGHT...YOU *SHOULD'VE* BEEN TREATED BETTER.
BUT DAPPLE'S NOT ABOUT HELPING YOU...HE'S ABOUT REVENGE. AND HE'LL BE ABOUT REVENGE UNTIL HE'S HURT A LOT OF PEOPLE, INCLUDING *OUR KIDS.*
THEY DON'T *DESERVE* IT.
OUR KIDS AREN'T PERFECT. YES, SOME OF THEM MAY HAVE TREATED YOU BADLY. BUT LOOK AT WHERE THEY'RE AT IN THEIR LIVES.
THEY'RE THESE SOFT, FRAGILE LITTLE THINGS, ALONE IN A WORLD TOO BIG FOR THEM, AND DEALING WITH *FEELINGS* AND *EMOTIONS* THEY CAN BARELY UNDERSTAND. AND THEY'RE SO, SO LONELY.
THEY WANT SOMEBODY, *ANYBODY*, WHO WILL UNDERSTAND THEM, WILL HELP THEM DISCOVER THEIR WORLD AND HELP PROCESS EVERYTHING THEY ENCOUNTER.
"AND THAT'S WHERE WE COME IN. FROM ALL THE IMAGES AND IDEAS THEY'VE PICKED UP, THEY *IMAGINE* THESE BODIES WE'RE IN AND BRING US INTO THEIR LIVES.
"THEY PUT IN EVERYTHING THEY THINK IS GOOD AND RIGHT WITH THE WORLD AND DESIGN A FRIEND WHO REPRESENTS THAT *ABSOLUTE BEST* AS THEY SEE IT.
BOOM!
"WE'RE THEIR *IDEALS.* HOW CAN WE POSSIBLY LET THEM DOWN?"
SO THINK. *REMEMBER*. FIND A TIME WHEN YOU AND YOUR CHILD HAD A MOMENT, A SECOND, WHEN YOUR BOND WAS GOOD AND PURE, BEFORE ANY BAGGAGE OR DAMAGE THAT MIGHT'VE COME LATER. THINK OF THAT TIME, FOCUS ON IT...
"...AND DON'T LET IT GO."
WAIT...WHAT'S HAPPENING? WHY DO I FEEL SO--
MS. FAIRVIEW, YOU GOTTA STOP THIS! ANY MORE OF THIS AND YOU'RE GONNA GO ALL *ANEURIFFIC!*
NO! NO, SOMETHING'S HAPPENING!
I THINK... I THINK...

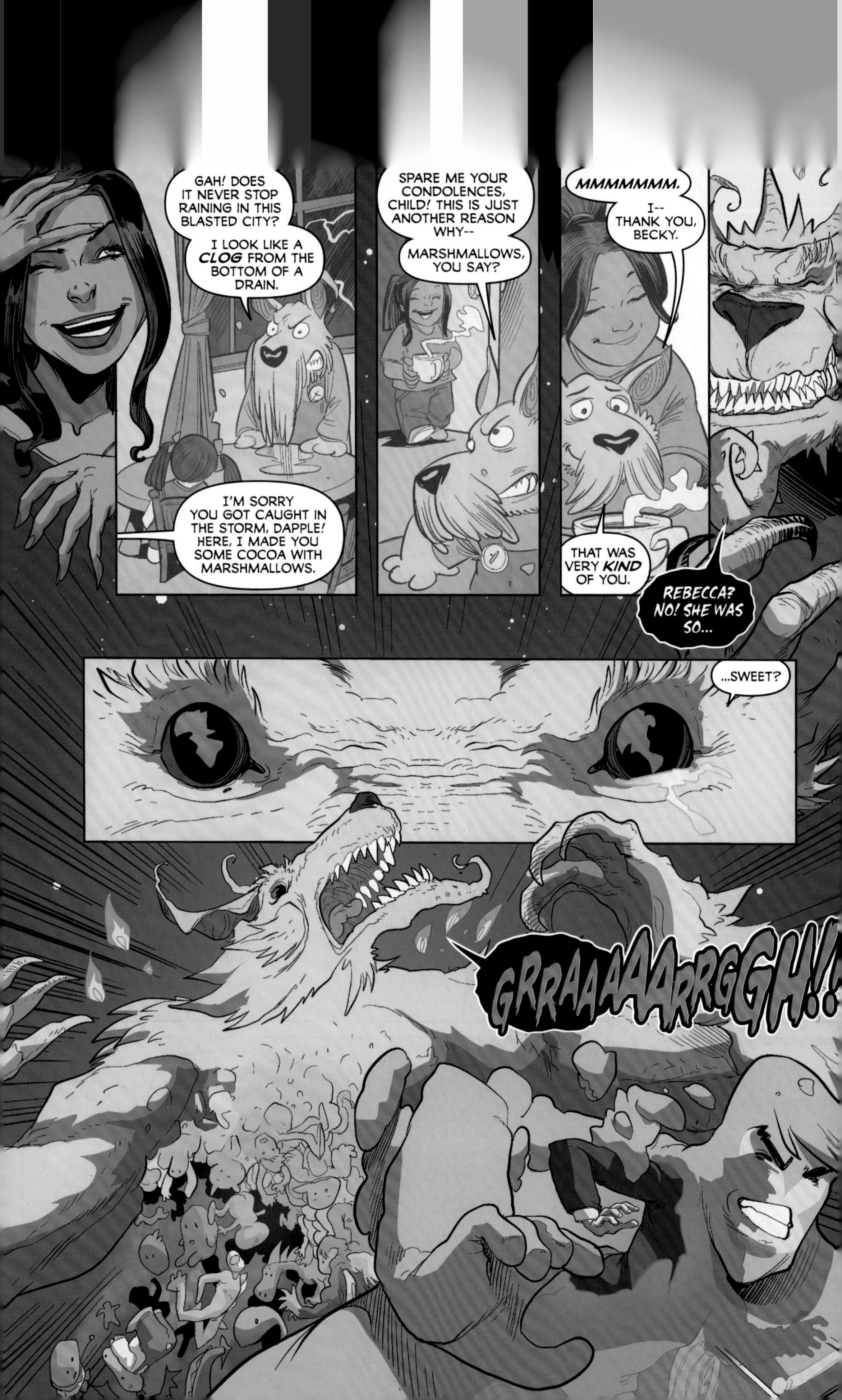

GAH! DOES IT NEVER STOP RAINING IN THIS BLASTED CITY?
I LOOK LIKE A *CLOG* FROM THE BOTTOM OF A DRAIN.
I'M SORRY YOU GOT CAUGHT IN THE STORM, DAPPLE! HERE, I MADE YOU SOME COCOA WITH MARSHMALLOWS.
SPARE ME YOUR CONDOLENCES, CHILD! THIS IS JUST ANOTHER REASON WHY--
MARSHMALLOWS, YOU SAY?
MMMMMMM.
I-- THANK YOU, BECKY.
THAT WAS VERY *KIND* OF YOU.
REBECCA? NO! SHE WAS SO...
...SWEET?
GRRAAAAARRGGH!!

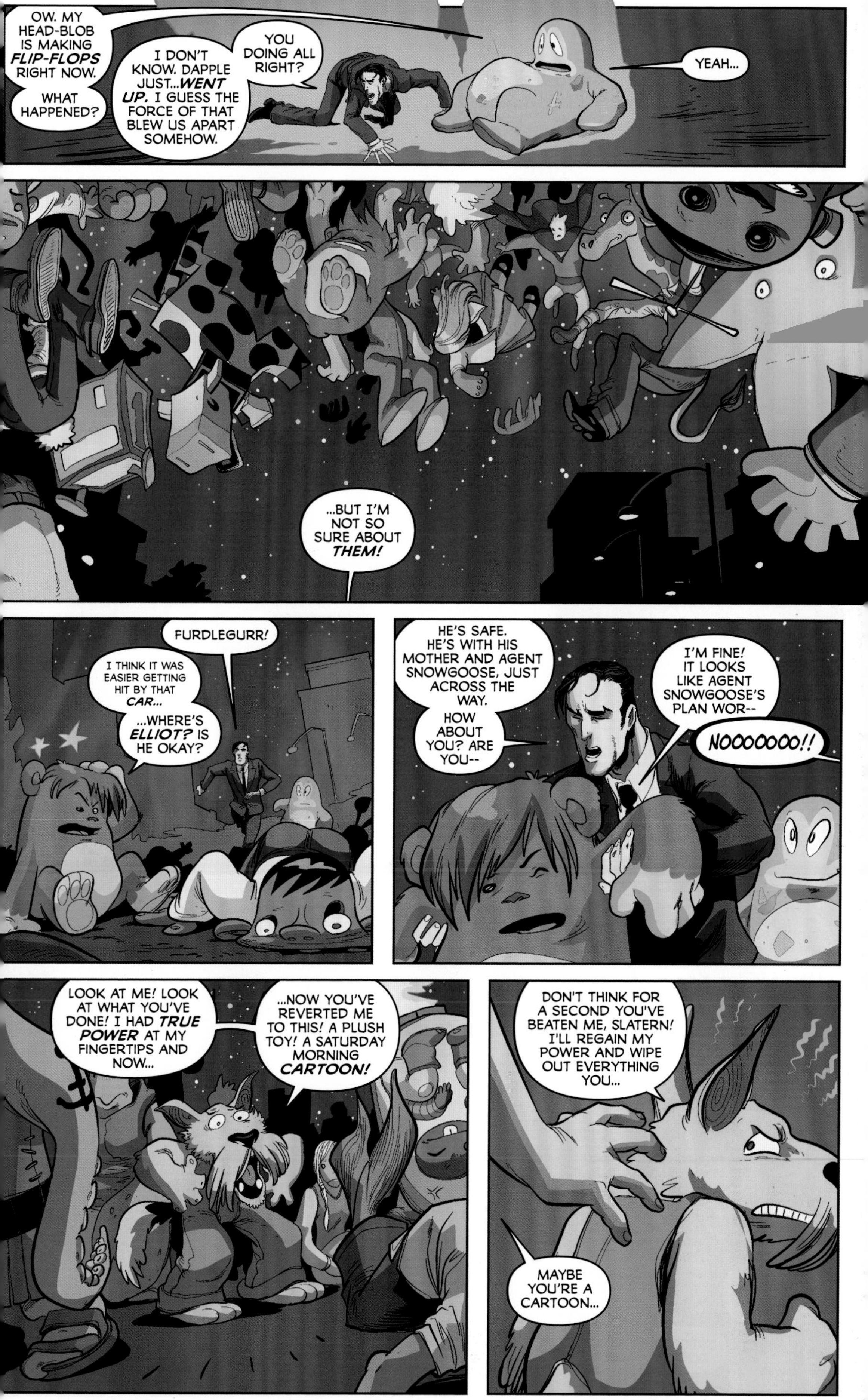
OW. MY HEAD-BLOB IS MAKING *FLIP-FLOPS* RIGHT NOW.
WHAT HAPPENED?
YOU DOING ALL RIGHT?
I DON'T KNOW. DAPPLE JUST...*WENT UP.* I GUESS THE FORCE OF THAT BLEW US APART SOMEHOW.
YEAH...
...BUT I'M NOT SO SURE ABOUT *THEM!*
FURDLEGURR!
I THINK IT WAS EASIER GETTING HIT BY THAT *CAR...*
...WHERE'S *ELLIOT?* IS HE OKAY?
HE'S SAFE. HE'S WITH HIS MOTHER AND AGENT SNOWGOOSE, JUST ACROSS THE WAY.
HOW ABOUT YOU? ARE YOU--
I'M FINE! IT LOOKS LIKE AGENT SNOWGOOSE'S PLAN WOR--
NOOOOOOO!!
LOOK AT ME! LOOK AT WHAT YOU'VE DONE! I HAD *TRUE POWER* AT MY FINGERTIPS AND NOW...
...NOW YOU'VE REVERTED ME TO THIS! A PLUSH TOY! A SATURDAY MORNING *CARTOON!*
DON'T THINK FOR A SECOND YOU'VE BEATEN ME, SLATERN! I'LL REGAIN MY POWER AND WIPE OUT EVERYTHING YOU...
MAYBE YOU'RE A CARTOON...

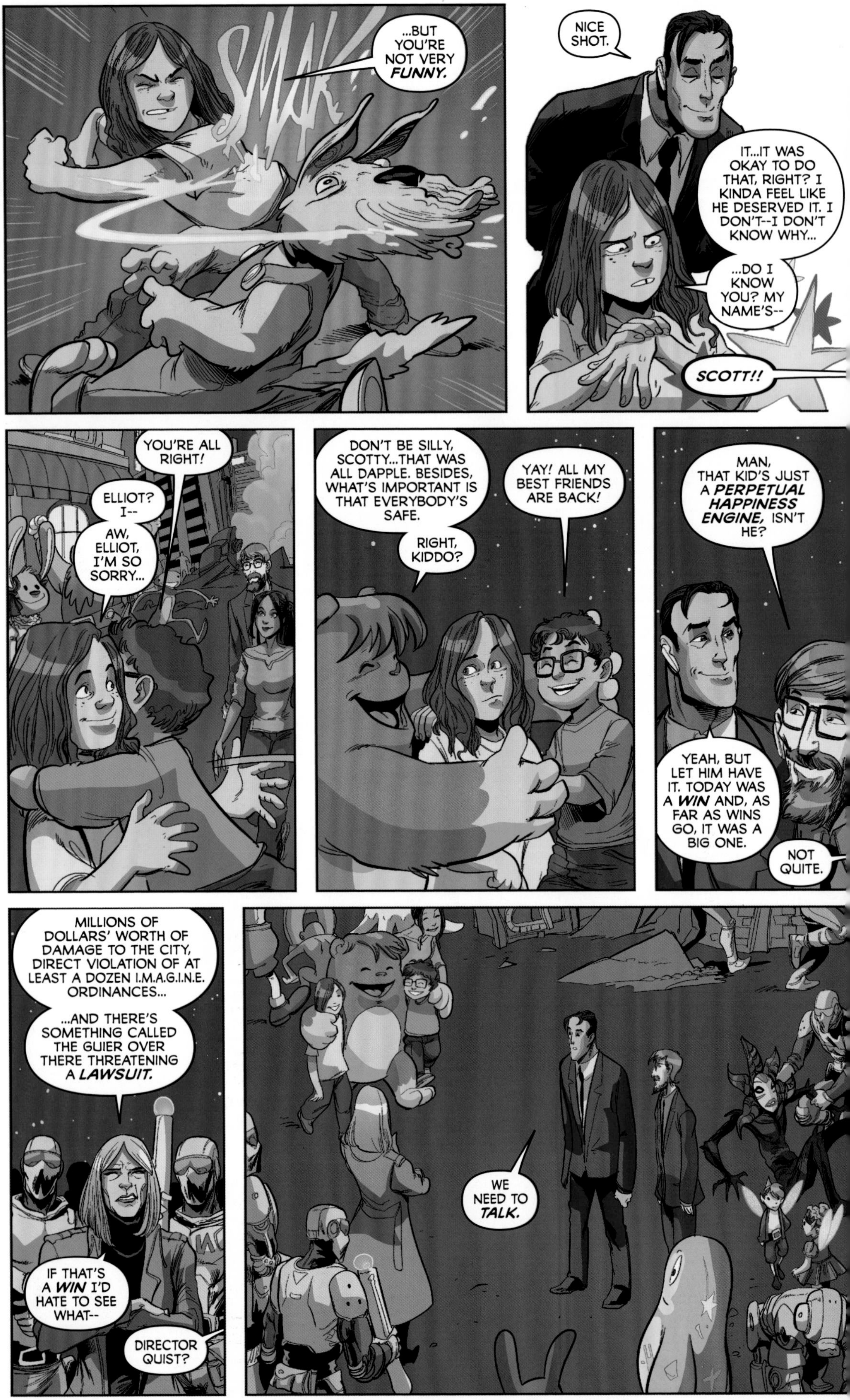
SMAK!
...BUT YOU'RE NOT VERY FUNNY.
NICE SHOT.
IT...IT WAS OKAY TO DO THAT, RIGHT? I KINDA FEEL LIKE HE DESERVED IT. I DON'T--I DON'T KNOW WHY...
...DO I KNOW YOU? MY NAME'S--
SCOTT!!
YOU'RE ALL RIGHT!
ELLIOT? I--
AW, ELLIOT, I'M SO SORRY...
DON'T BE SILLY, SCOTTY...THAT WAS ALL DAPPLE. BESIDES, WHAT'S IMPORTANT IS THAT EVERYBODY'S SAFE.
RIGHT, KIDDO?
YAY! ALL MY BEST FRIENDS ARE BACK!
MAN, THAT KID'S JUST A PERPETUAL HAPPINESS ENGINE, ISN'T HE?
YEAH, BUT LET HIM HAVE IT. TODAY WAS A WIN AND, AS FAR AS WINS GO, IT WAS A BIG ONE.
NOT QUITE.
MILLIONS OF DOLLARS' WORTH OF DAMAGE TO THE CITY, DIRECT VIOLATION OF AT LEAST A DOZEN I.M.A.G.I.N.E. ORDINANCES...
...AND THERE'S SOMETHING CALLED THE GUIER OVER THERE THREATENING A LAWSUIT.
IF THAT'S A WIN I'D HATE TO SEE WHAT--
DIRECTOR QUIST?
WE NEED TO TALK.

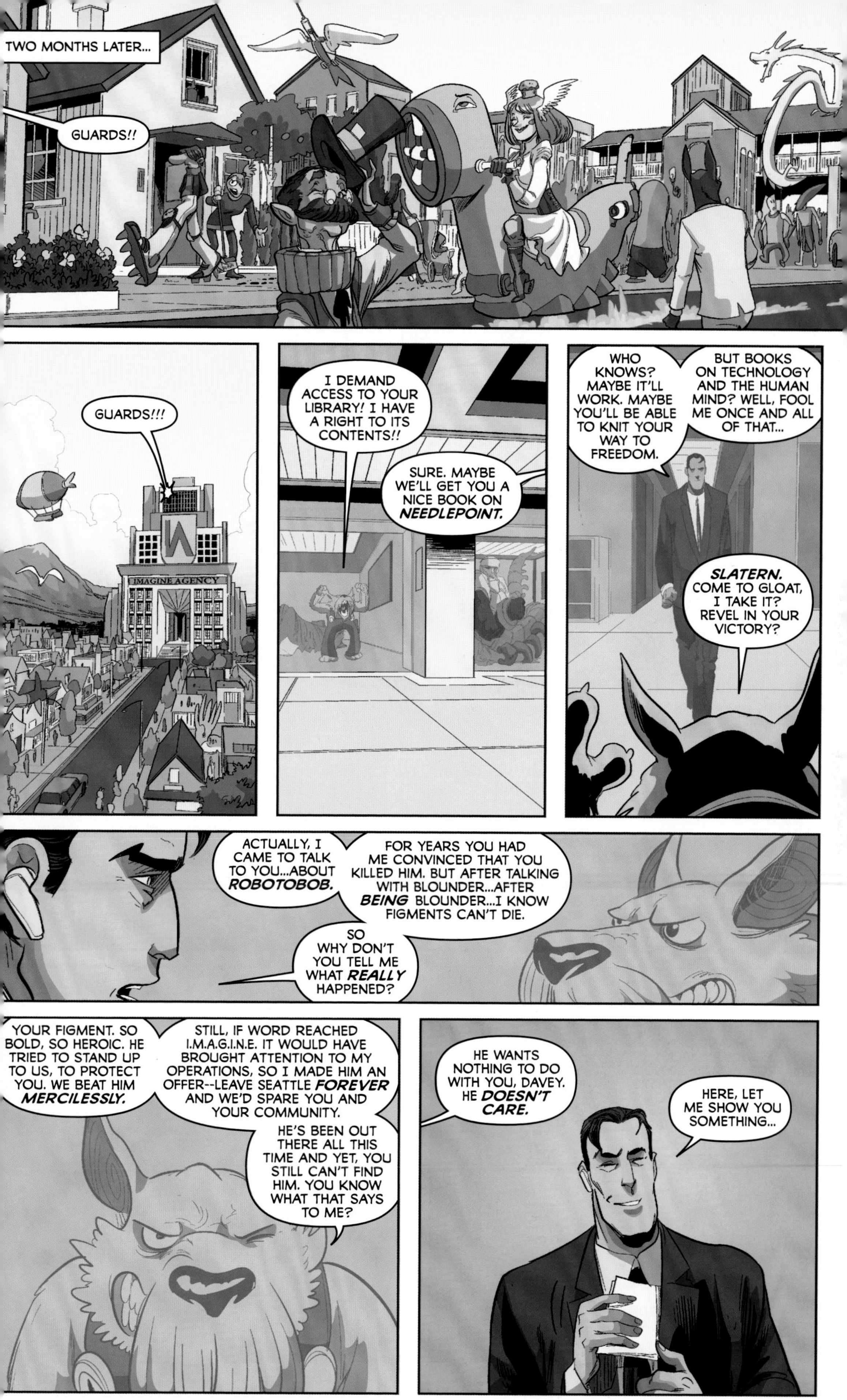

TWO MONTHS LATER...
GUARDS!!
GUARDS!!!
IMAGINE AGENCY
I DEMAND ACCESS TO YOUR LIBRARY! I HAVE A RIGHT TO ITS CONTENTS!!
SURE. MAYBE WE'LL GET YOU A NICE BOOK ON NEEDLEPOINT.
WHO KNOWS? MAYBE IT'LL WORK. MAYBE YOU'LL BE ABLE TO KNIT YOUR WAY TO FREEDOM.
BUT BOOKS ON TECHNOLOGY AND THE HUMAN MIND? WELL, FOOL ME ONCE AND ALL OF THAT...
SLATERN. COME TO GLOAT, I TAKE IT? REVEL IN YOUR VICTORY?
ACTUALLY, I CAME TO TALK TO YOU...ABOUT ROBOTOBOB.
FOR YEARS YOU HAD ME CONVINCED THAT YOU KILLED HIM. BUT AFTER TALKING WITH BLOUNDER...AFTER BEING BLOUNDER...I KNOW FIGMENTS CAN'T DIE.
SO WHY DON'T YOU TELL ME WHAT REALLY HAPPENED?
YOUR FIGMENT. SO BOLD, SO HEROIC. HE TRIED TO STAND UP TO US, TO PROTECT YOU. WE BEAT HIM MERCILESSLY.
STILL, IF WORD REACHED I.M.A.G.I.N.E. IT WOULD HAVE BROUGHT ATTENTION TO MY OPERATIONS, SO I MADE HIM AN OFFER--LEAVE SEATTLE FOREVER AND WE'D SPARE YOU AND YOUR COMMUNITY.
HE'S BEEN OUT THERE ALL THIS TIME AND YET, YOU STILL CAN'T FIND HIM. YOU KNOW WHAT THAT SAYS TO ME?
HE WANTS NOTHING TO DO WITH YOU, DAVEY. HE DOESN'T CARE.
HERE, LET ME SHOW YOU SOMETHING...

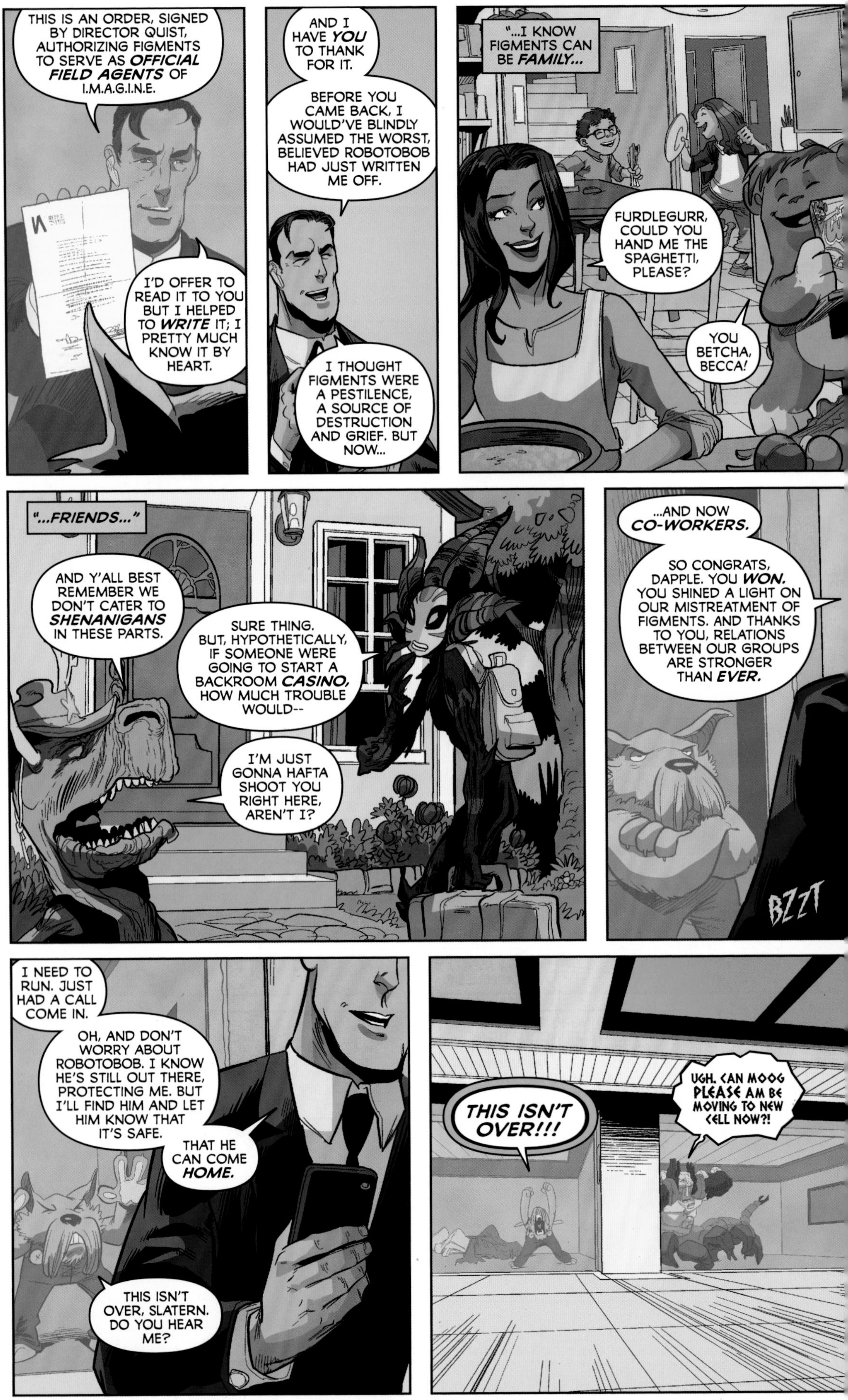
THIS IS AN ORDER, SIGNED BY DIRECTOR QUIST, AUTHORIZING FIGMENTS TO SERVE AS OFFICIAL FIELD AGENTS OF I.M.A.G.I.N.E.
I'D OFFER TO READ IT TO YOU BUT I HELPED TO WRITE IT; I PRETTY MUCH KNOW IT BY HEART.
AND I HAVE YOU TO THANK FOR IT.
BEFORE YOU CAME BACK, I WOULD'VE BLINDLY ASSUMED THE WORST, BELIEVED ROBOTOBOB HAD JUST WRITTEN ME OFF.
I THOUGHT FIGMENTS WERE A PESTILENCE, A SOURCE OF DESTRUCTION AND GRIEF. BUT NOW...
"...I KNOW FIGMENTS CAN BE FAMILY...
FURDLEGURR, COULD YOU HAND ME THE SPAGHETTI, PLEASE?
YOU BETCHA, BECCA!
"...FRIENDS..."
AND Y'ALL BEST REMEMBER WE DON'T CATER TO SHENANIGANS IN THESE PARTS.
SURE THING. BUT, HYPOTHETICALLY, IF SOMEONE WERE GOING TO START A BACKROOM CASINO, HOW MUCH TROUBLE WOULD--
I'M JUST GONNA HAFTA SHOOT YOU RIGHT HERE, AREN'T I?
...AND NOW CO-WORKERS.
SO CONGRATS, DAPPLE. YOU WON. YOU SHINED A LIGHT ON OUR MISTREATMENT OF FIGMENTS. AND THANKS TO YOU, RELATIONS BETWEEN OUR GROUPS ARE STRONGER THAN EVER.
BZZT
I NEED TO RUN. JUST HAD A CALL COME IN.
OH, AND DON'T WORRY ABOUT ROBOTOBOB. I KNOW HE'S STILL OUT THERE, PROTECTING ME. BUT I'LL FIND HIM AND LET HIM KNOW THAT IT'S SAFE.
THAT HE CAN COME HOME.
THIS ISN'T OVER, SLATERN. DO YOU HEAR ME?
THIS ISN'T OVER!!!
UGH. CAN MOOG PLEASE AM BE MOVING TO NEW CELL NOW?!

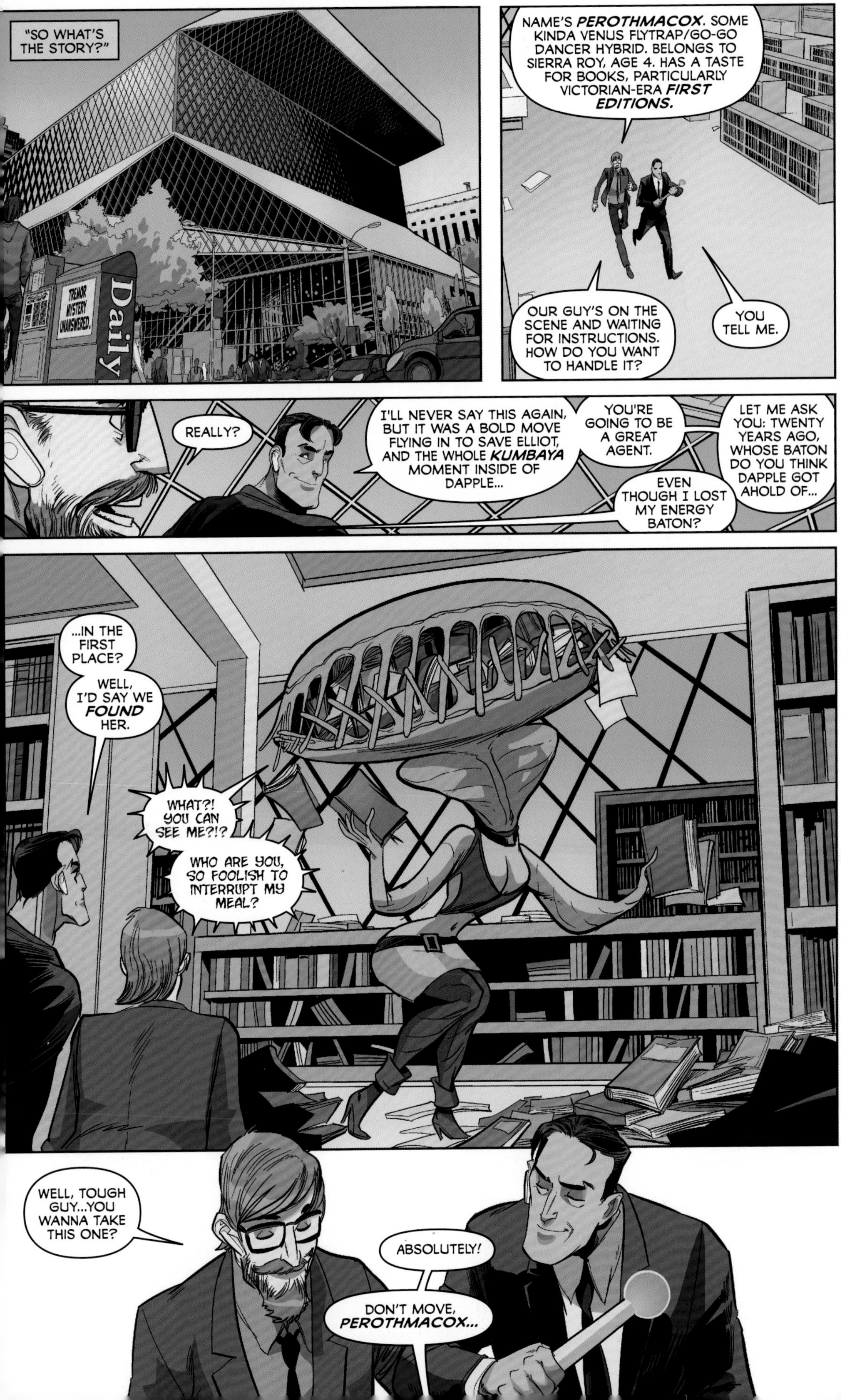

"SO WHAT'S THE STORY?"
TREMOR MYSTERY UNANSWERED.
Daily
NAME'S PEROTHMACOX. SOME KINDA VENUS FLYTRAP/GO-GO DANCER HYBRID. BELONGS TO SIERRA ROY, AGE 4. HAS A TASTE FOR BOOKS, PARTICULARLY VICTORIAN-ERA FIRST EDITIONS.
OUR GUY'S ON THE SCENE AND WAITING FOR INSTRUCTIONS. HOW DO YOU WANT TO HANDLE IT?
YOU TELL ME.
REALLY?
I'LL NEVER SAY THIS AGAIN, BUT IT WAS A BOLD MOVE FLYING IN TO SAVE ELLIOT, AND THE WHOLE KUMBAYA MOMENT INSIDE OF DAPPLE...
YOU'RE GOING TO BE A GREAT AGENT.
EVEN THOUGH I LOST MY ENERGY BATON?
LET ME ASK YOU: TWENTY YEARS AGO, WHOSE BATON DO YOU THINK DAPPLE GOT AHOLD OF...
...IN THE FIRST PLACE?
WELL, I'D SAY WE FOUND HER.
WHAT?! YOU CAN SEE ME?!?
WHO ARE YOU, SO FOOLISH TO INTERRUPT MY MEAL?
WELL, TOUGH GUY...YOU WANNA TAKE THIS ONE?
ABSOLUTELY!
DON'T MOVE, PEROTHMACOX...

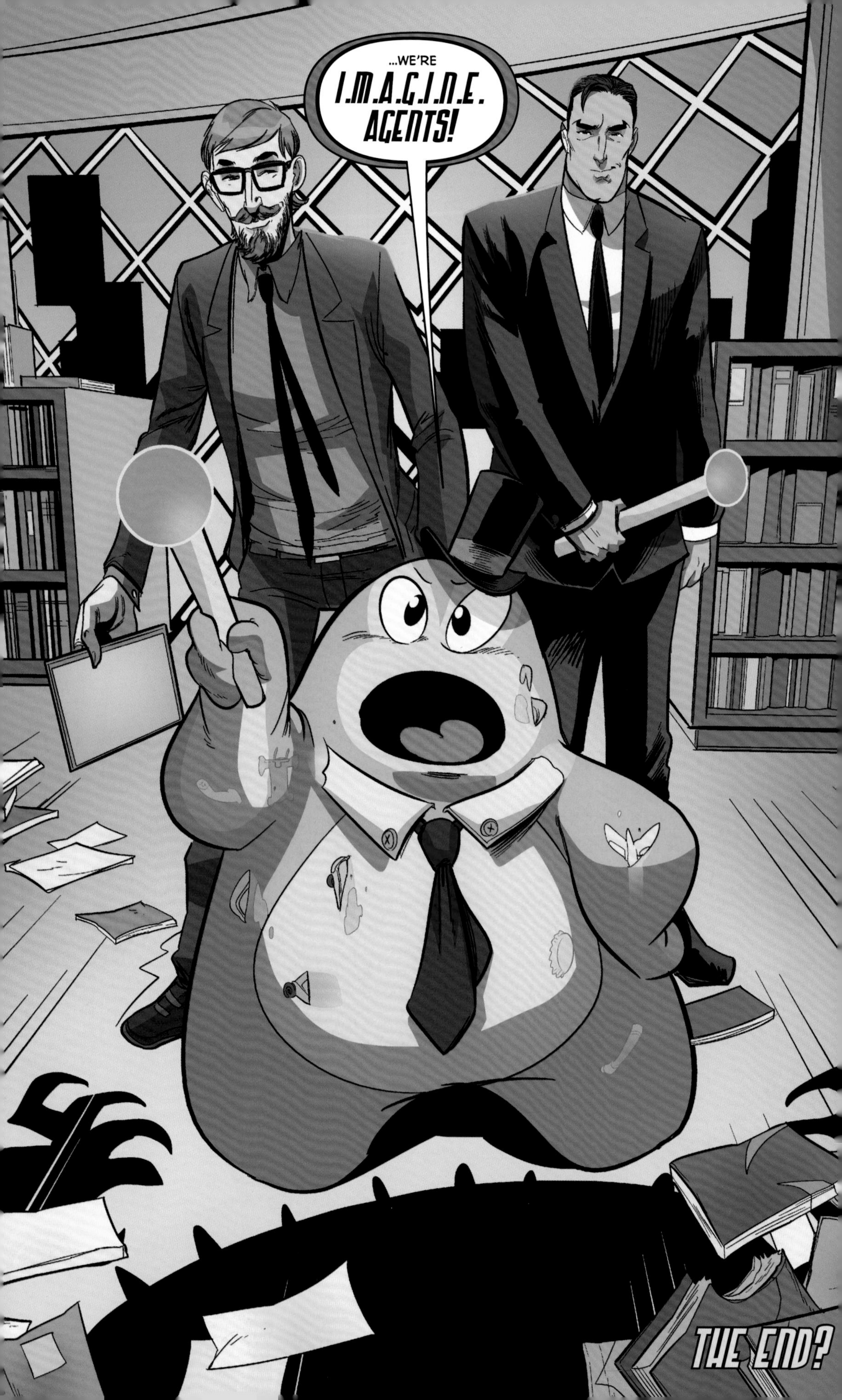
...WE'RE
I.M.A.G.I.N.E. AGENTS!
THE END?

IMAGINE AGENTS™

COVER GALLERY

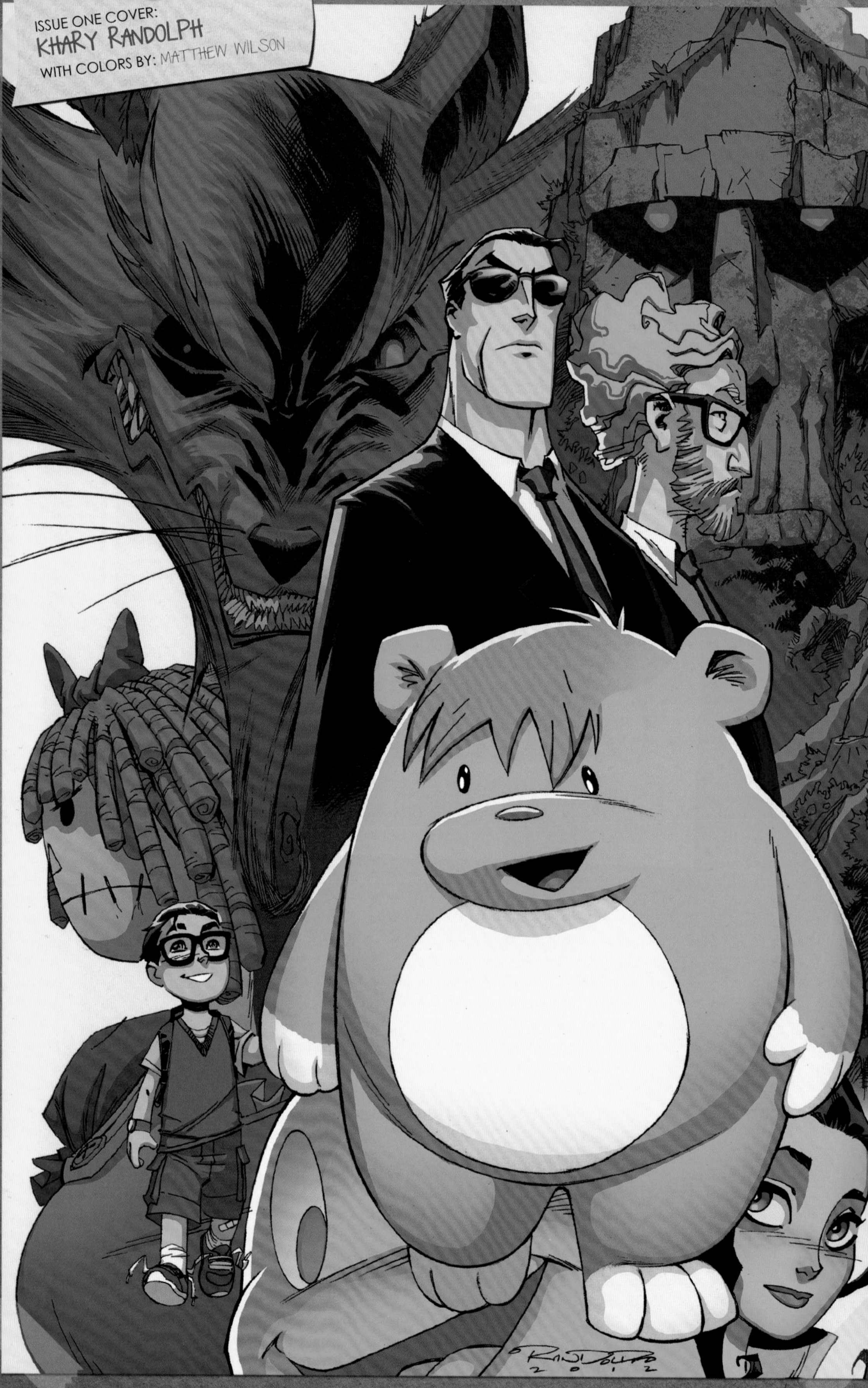

ISSUE ONE COVER:
KHARY RANDOLPH
WITH COLORS BY: MATTHEW WILSON

ISSUE TWO COVER:
KHARY RANDOLPH
WITH COLORS BY: MATTHEW WILSON

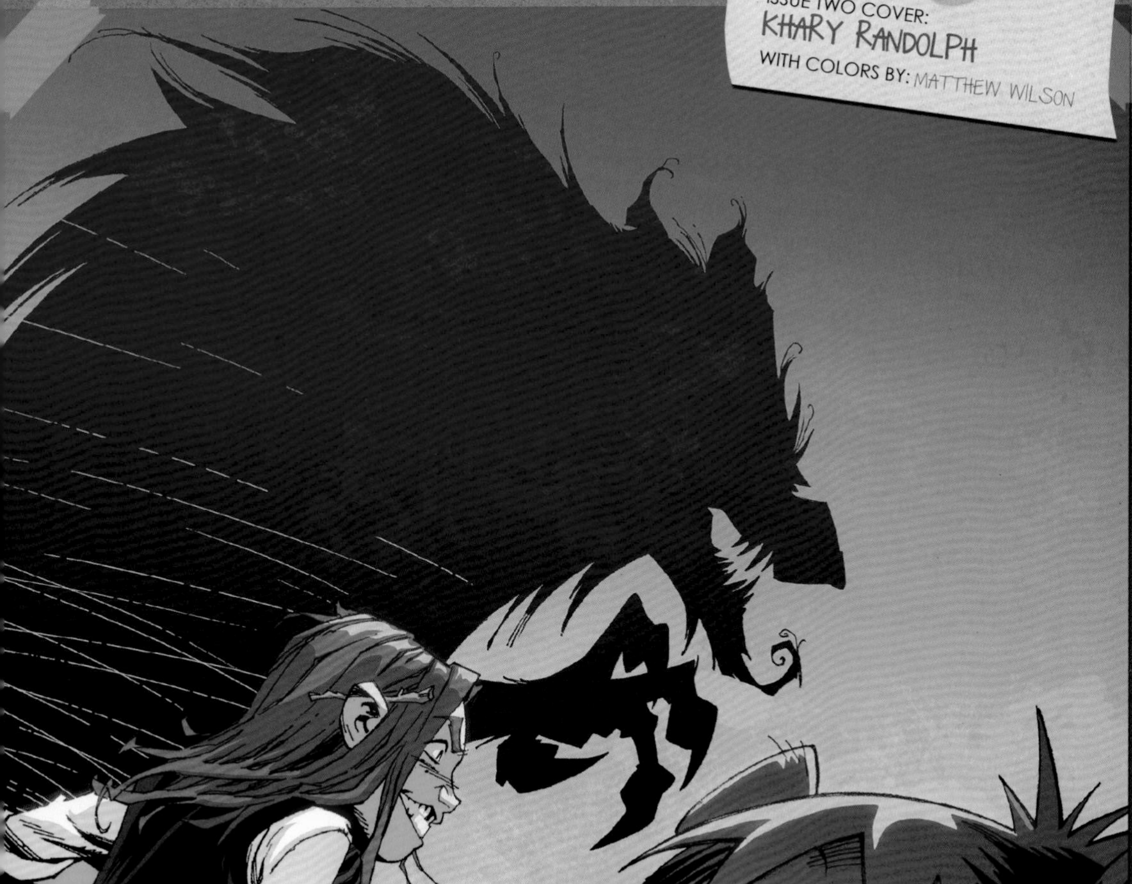

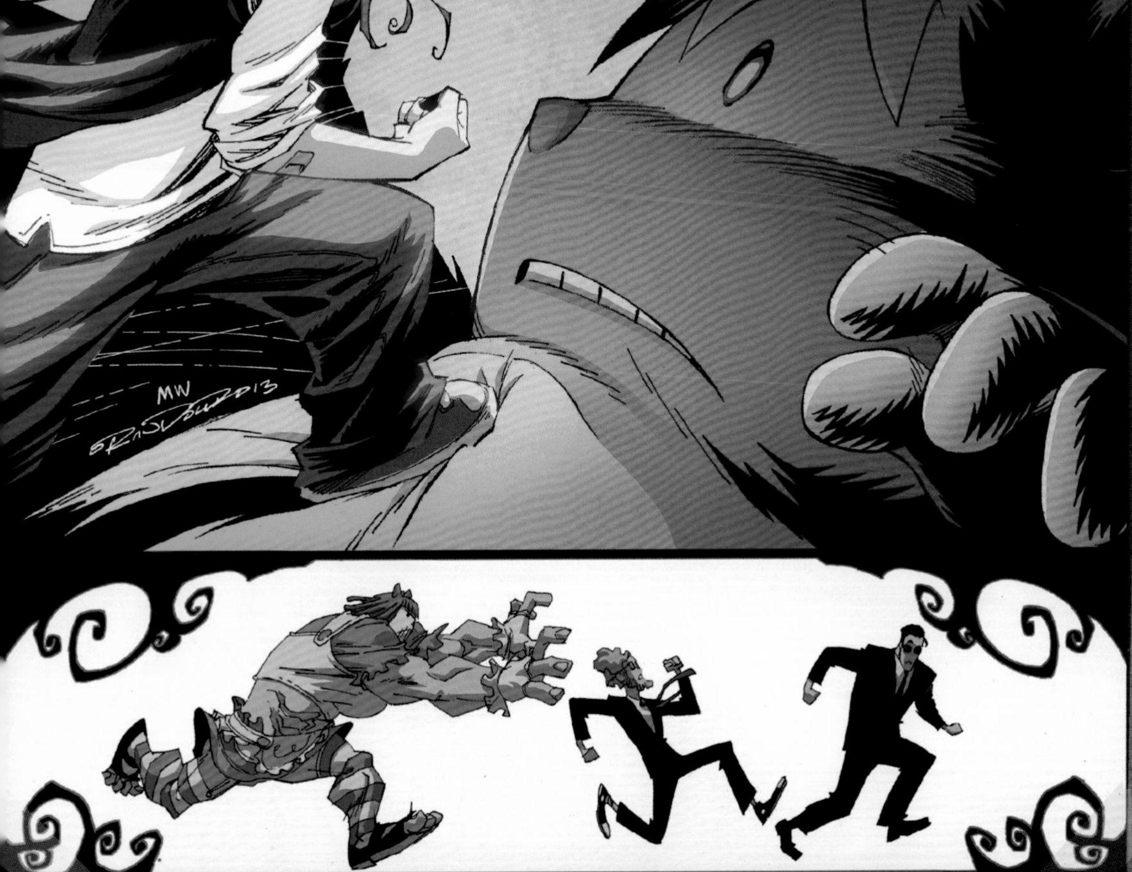

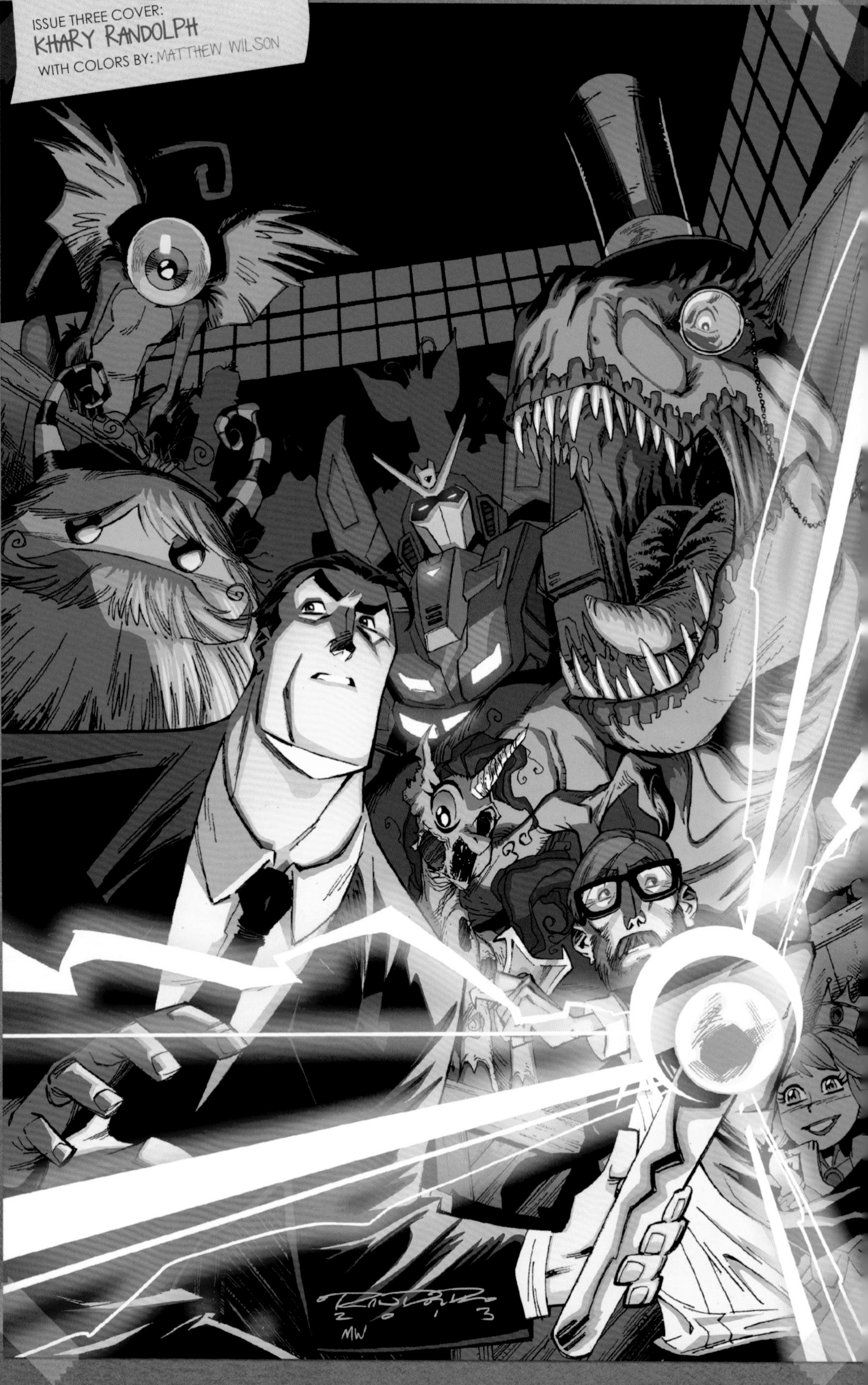

ISSUE THREE COVER:
KHARY RANDOLPH
WITH COLORS BY: MATTHEW WILSON

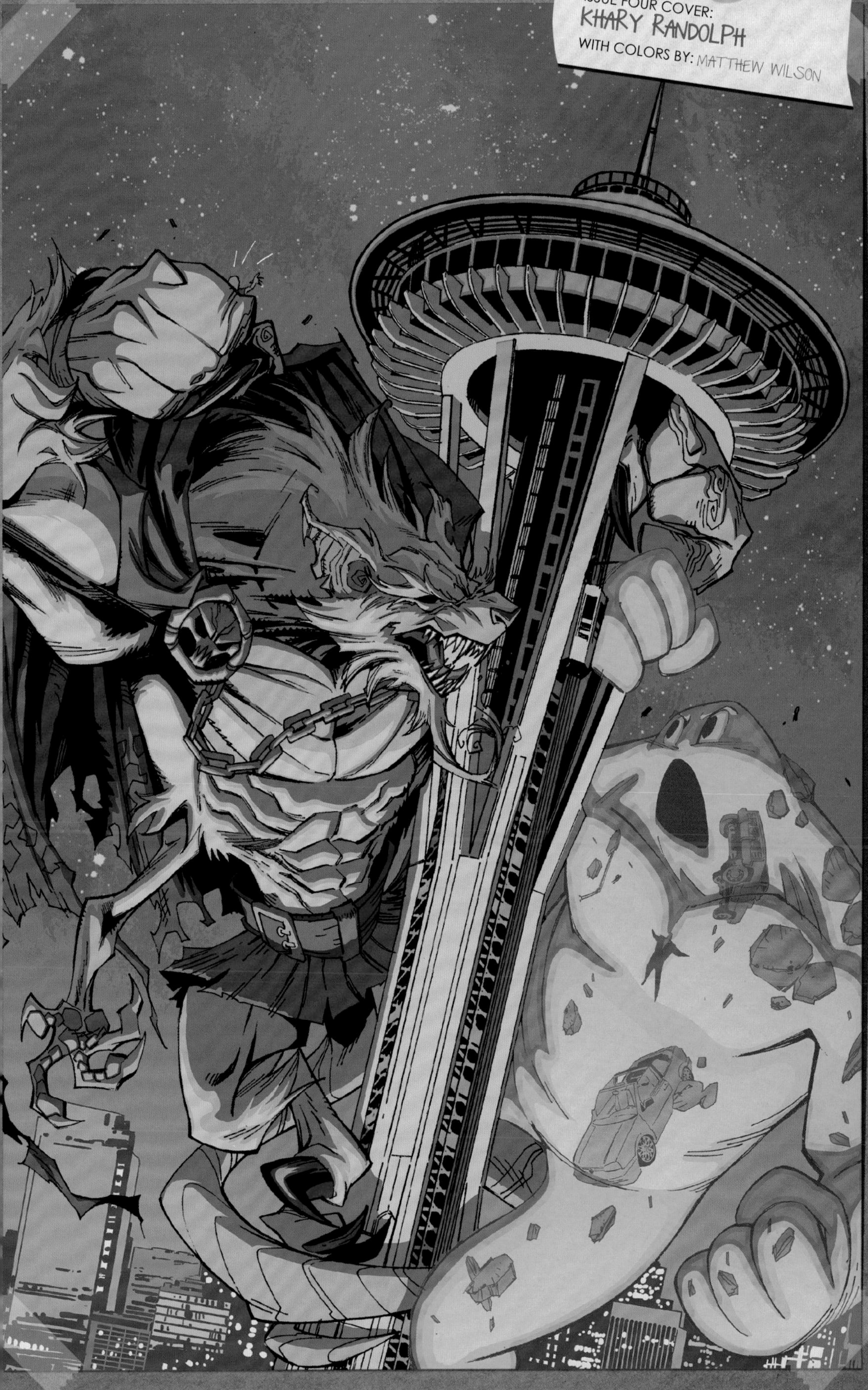

ISSUE FOUR COVER:
KHARY RANDOLPH
WITH COLORS BY: MATTHEW WILSON

ISSUE ONE THROUGH FOUR
CONNECTING COVERS:
FELIPE SMITH

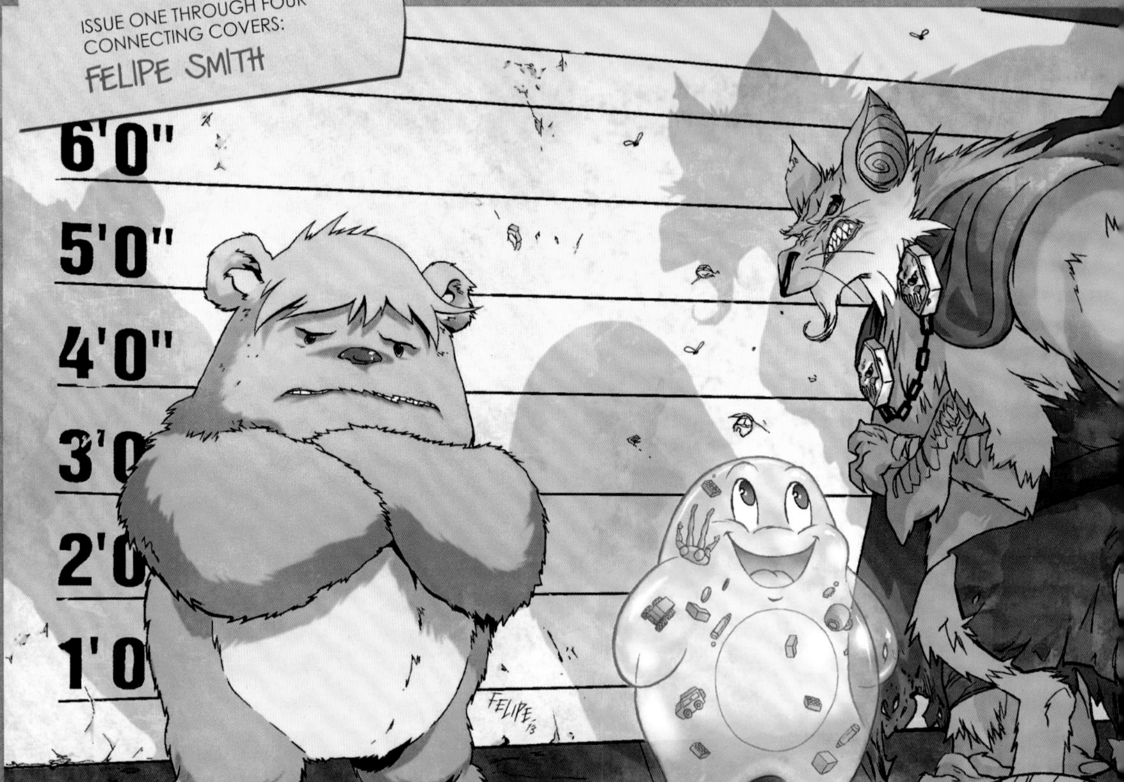
6'0"
5'0"
4'0"
3'0
2'0
1'0
FELIPE '13
FELIPE '13

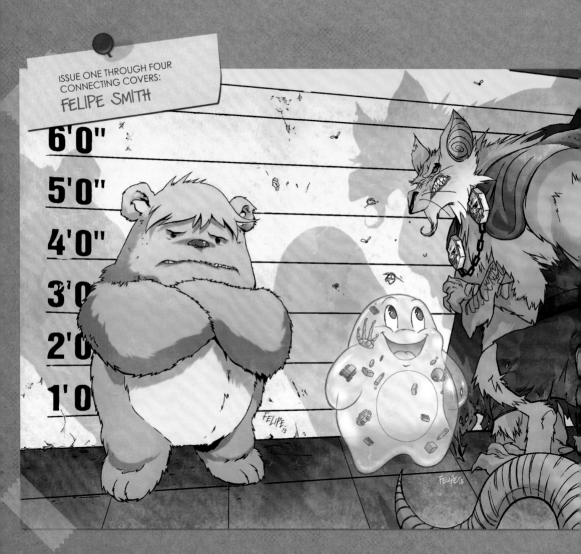

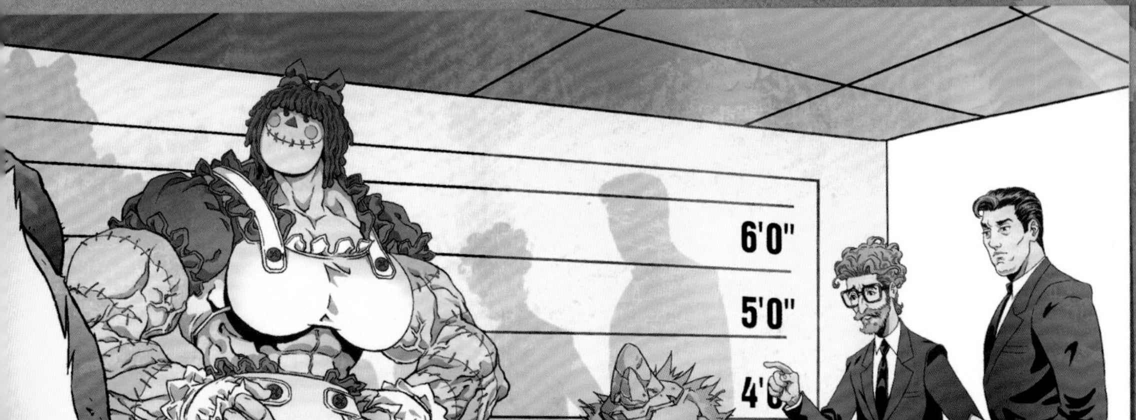
6'0"
5'0"
FELIPE '13
FELIPE '13

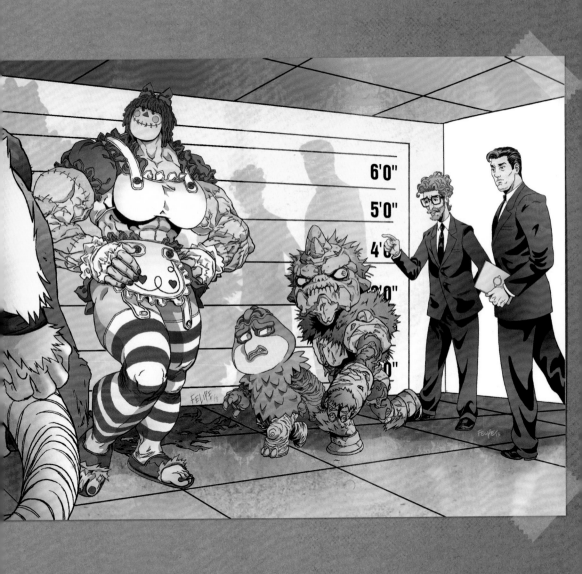

ISSUE ONE 2ND PRINT COVER:
BACHAN
WITH COLORS BY: MATTHEW WILSON

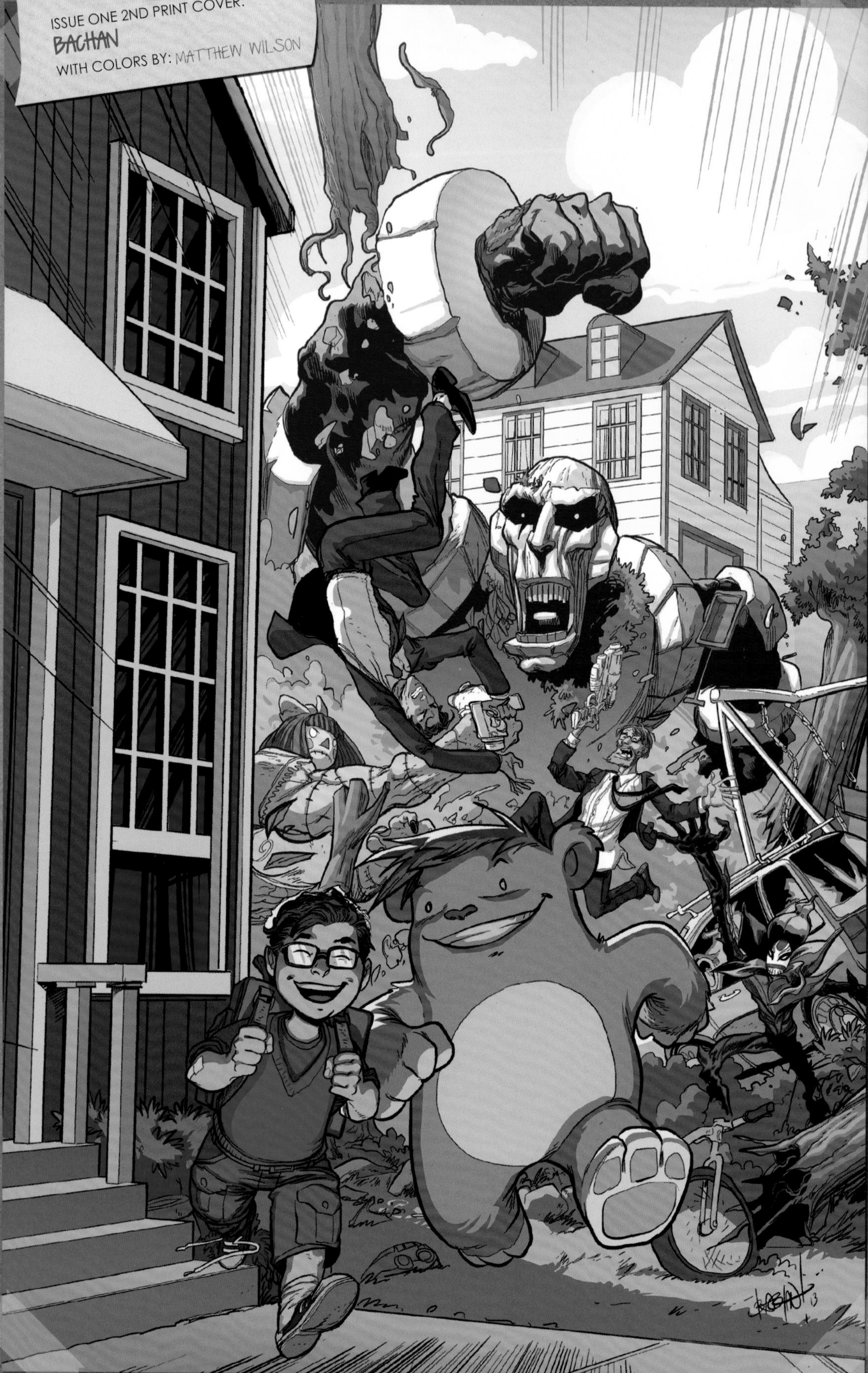

ISSUE TWO 2ND PRINT COVER:
BACHAN
WITH COLORS BY: MATTHEW WILSON

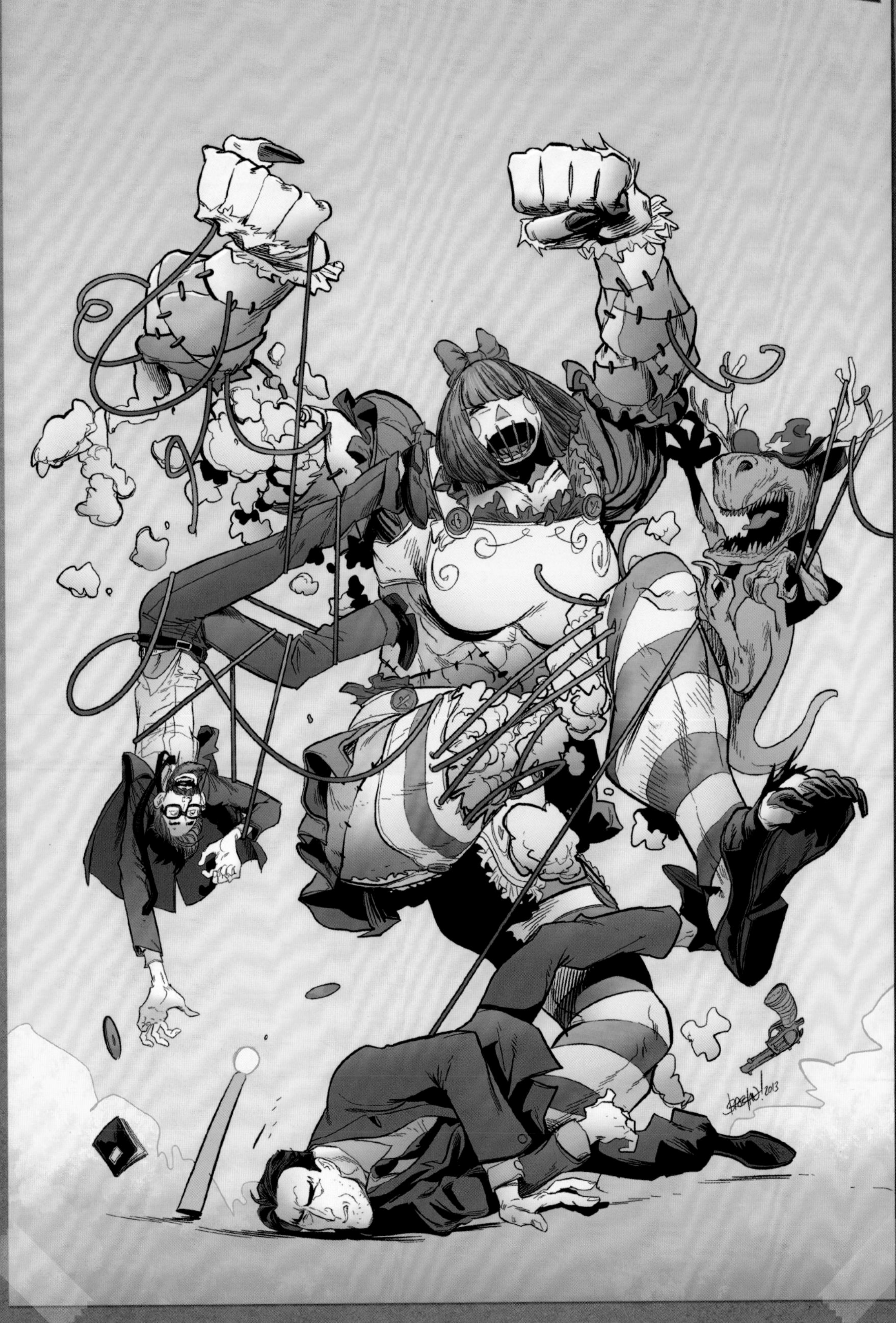

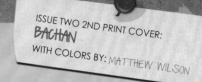

BEHIND THE SCENES OF IMAGINE AGENTS

BACHAN COVER PROCESS
ISSUE ONE 2ND PRINT

CONCEPTS

INKS

FINAL (WITH COLORS BY MATTHEW WILSON)

BACHAN COVER PROCESS
ISSUE TWO 2ND PRINT

CONCEPTS

INKS

FINAL (WITH COLORS BY MATTHEW WILSON)

FELIPE SMITH COVER PROCESS
ISSUE ONE THROUGH FOUR CONNECTING COVERS

CONCEPT

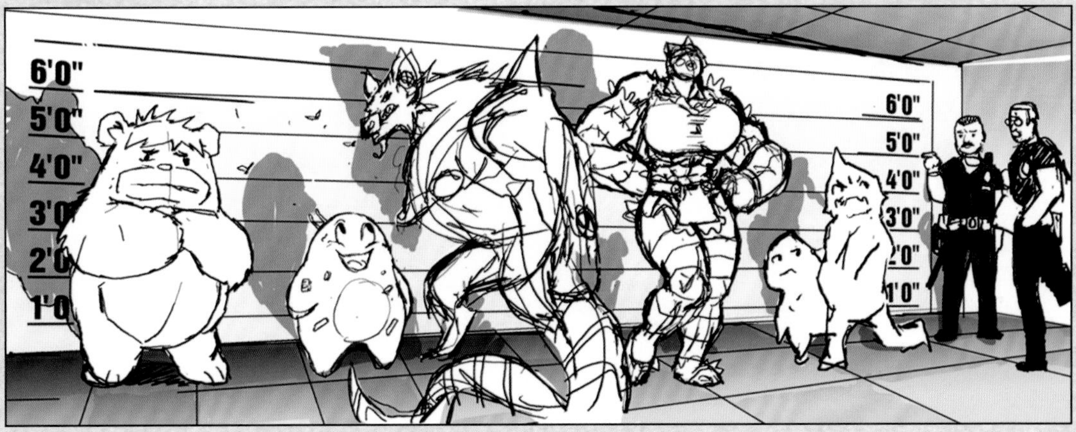
6'0"
5'0"
4'0"
6'0"
5'0"
4'0"
3'0"
1'0"

PROGRESS

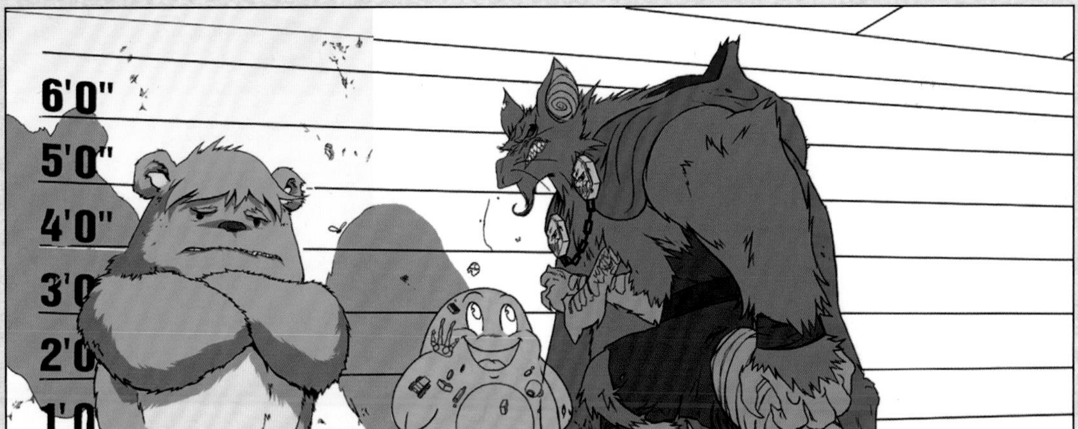
6'0"
5'0"
4'0"

FINAL

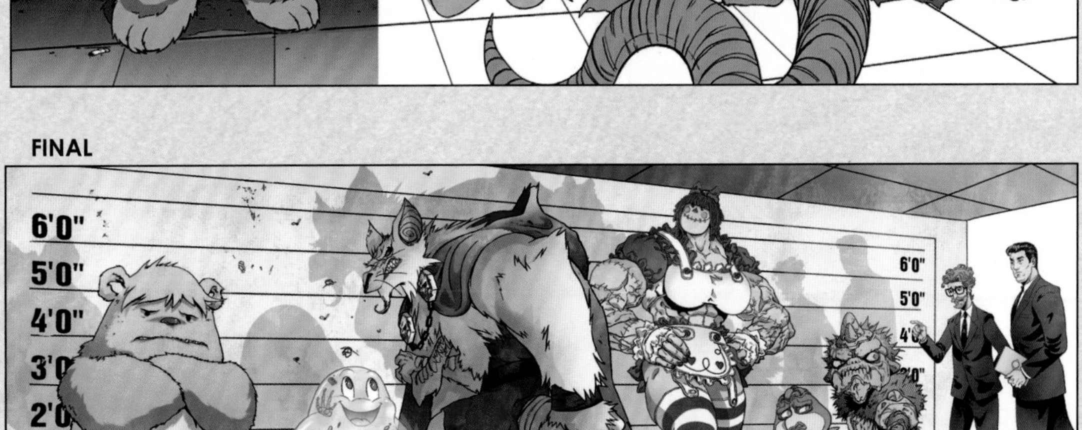
6'0"
5'0"
4'0"
6'0"
5'0"

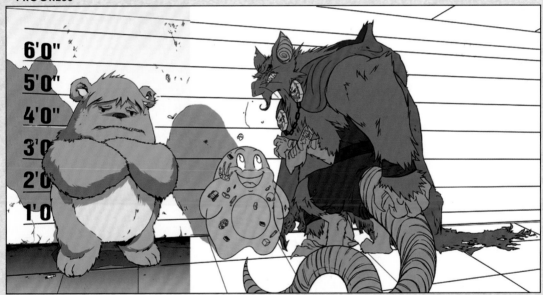

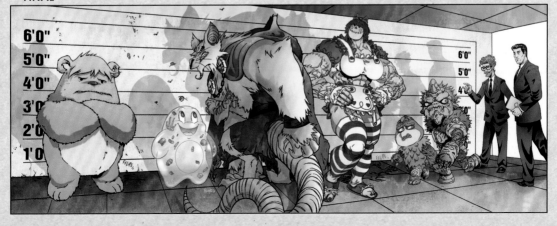

CHARACTER DESIGNS BY

KHARY RANDOLPH

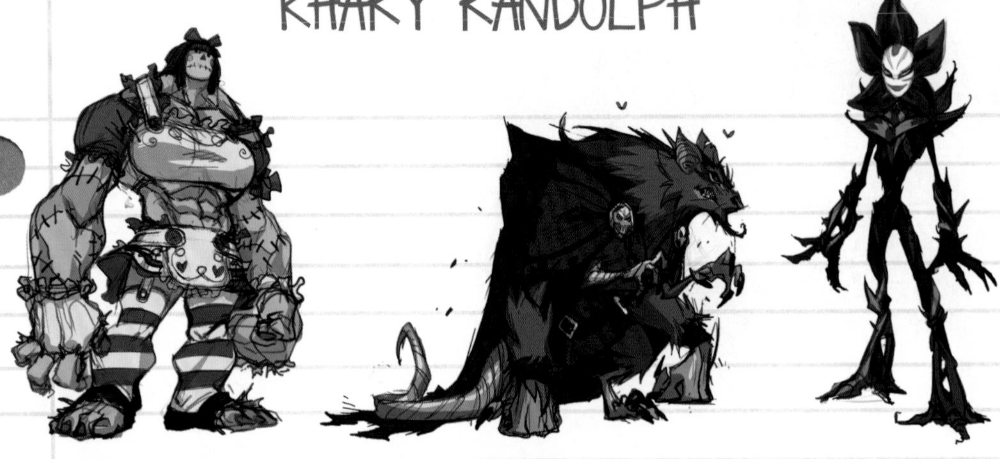

BIG DOLL DAPPLE PONO

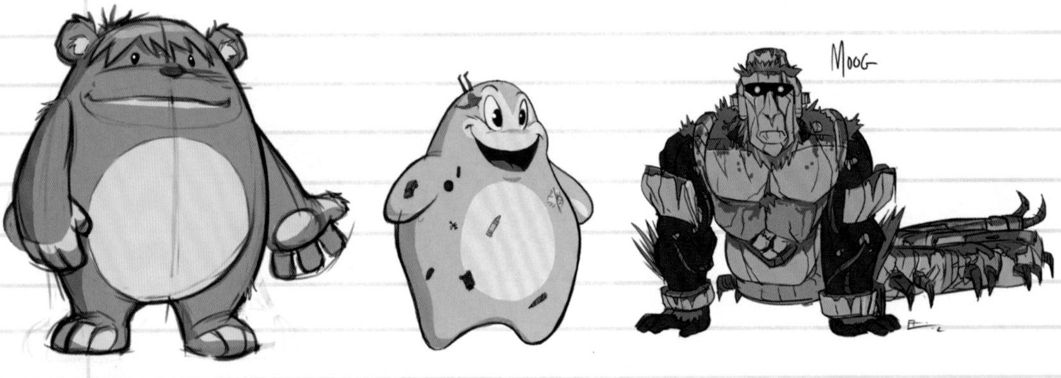
MOOG

FURDLEGURR BLOUNDER MOOG

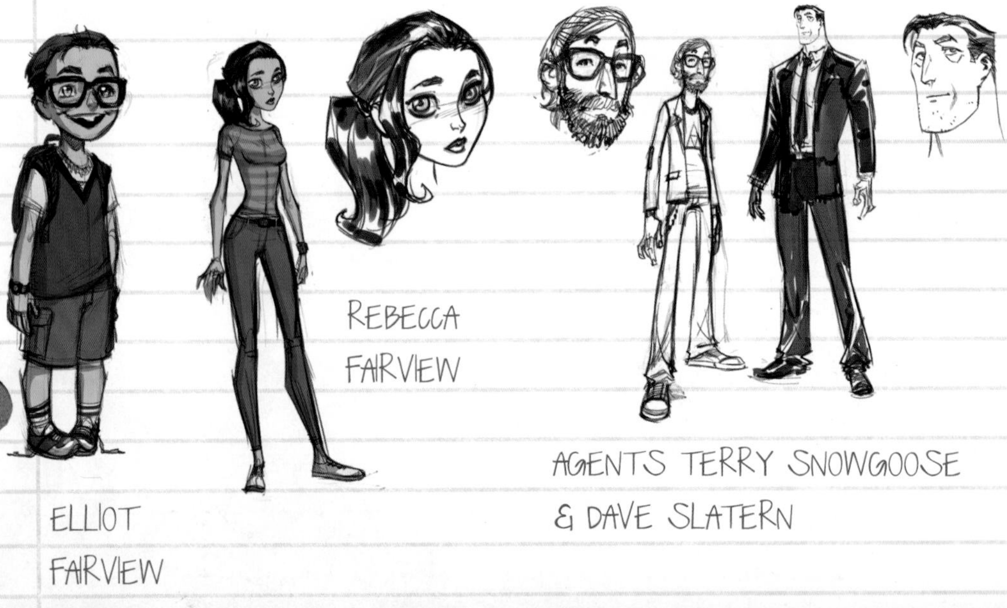

REBECCA FAIRVIEW

AGENTS TERRY SNOWGOOSE & DAVE SLATERN

ELLIOT FAIRVIEW

CHARACTER DESIGNS BY
BACHAN

BIG DOLL

DAPPLE

PONO

FURDLEGURR

BLOUNDER

MOOG

ELLIOT
FAIRVIEW

REBECCA
FAIRVIEW

AGENTS DAVE SLATERN
& TERRY SNOWGOOSE

ALTERNATE LOGO DESIGNS BY HANNAH NANCE PARTLOW

I.MAGINE AGENTS

I.M.A.G.I.N.E. AGENTS

i.m.a.g.i.n.e. AGENTS

FIGMENT CHARACTER DESIGNS BY

BACHAN

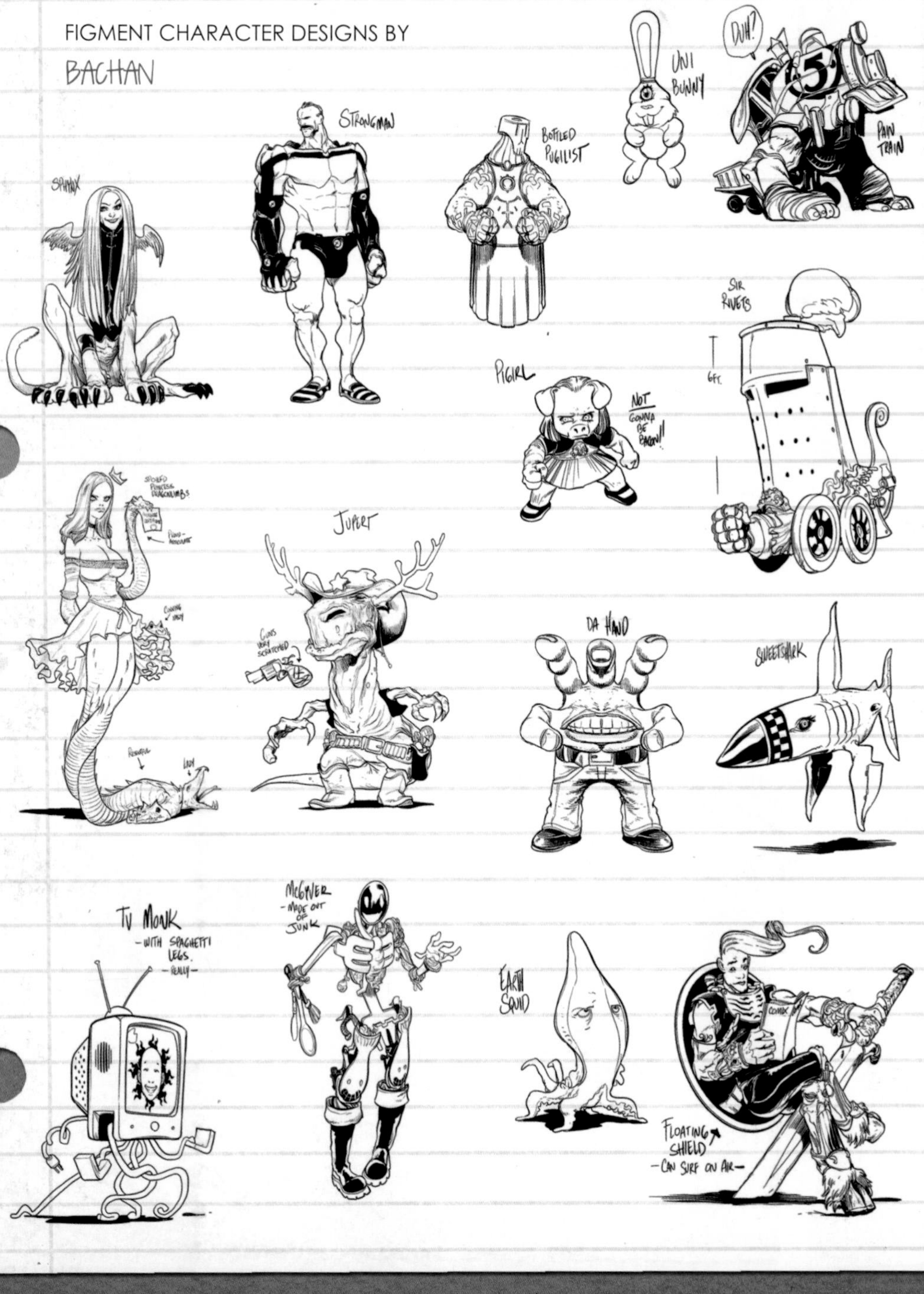

UNI BUNNY
DUH?
5
PAIN TRAIN
SPHINX
STRONGMAN
BOTTLED PUGILIST
SIR RIVETS
6FT.
PIGIRL
NOT GONNA BE BACON!!
JUPERT
DA HAND
SWEETSHARK
TV MONK
- WITH SPAGHETTI LEGS.
- REALLY -
MCGYVER
- MADE OUT OF JUNK
EARTH SQUID
FLOATING SHIELD
- CAN SURF ON AIR -

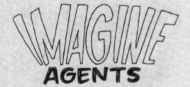